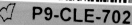

THE BORDER
Brownsville to El Paso

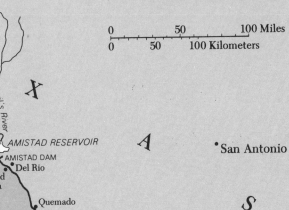

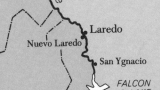

ON THE BORDER

By the same author

The Assassination Please Almanac

ON THE BORDER

*Portraits of
America's Southwestern Frontier*

TOM MILLER

HARPER & ROW, PUBLISHERS, New York
*Cambridge, Hagerstown, Philadelphia, San Francisco
London, Mexico City, São Paulo, Sydney*

1817

FIRST EDITION

Designer: Sidney Feinberg

Maps by Jean Paul Tremblay

Library of Congress Cataloging in Publication Data

Miller, Tom.
  On the border.
  Bibliography: p.
  Includes index.
  1. United States—Boundaries—Mexico.
  2. Mexico—Boundaries—United States. 3. Southwestern States—Description and travel. I. Title.
F787.M54 1981   979   79-2631
ISBN 0-06-013039-3

---

81 82 83 84 85 10 9 8 7 6 5 4 3 2 1

To my mother and the memory of my father

CONTENTS

MAPS

ACKNOWLEDGMENTS

Writing this book was a long venture. Many people made that venture easier by being unstinting in their counsel, friendship, and suggestions. Foremost among these were the people of the borderland. They allowed me to capture their lives and trusted me to record them faithfully.

The people listed below, some of whom live far from the border, were of particular help in gathering and preparing the information in this book: Ronaldo and Jane Cruz, Joe DeCola, Harvey Ginsberg, Margo Gutiérrez, Gerald Harwood, Robert Houston, Craig and Rocío Martin, Charles Miller, John Miller, Boyd Nicholl and Laurie Kintzele, Rodolfo Orihuela, Lionel Perez, Martha Sowerwine, John Stockley, Alison Whitehead, and Reed Wolcott; also the Border Patrolmen who showed me the lay of their land.

Two people stand apart from the rest for their contributions —Milton Jamail and Norah Booth. From the time when this book was in the conversation stage until the entire manuscript was complete, Milton shared with me his considerable expertise about the border, its personalities, and its problems. Norah Booth accompanied me on the trip, photographing places and faces from Brownsville to Tijuana. Her assistance with interviews and research was invaluable.

INTRODUCTION

Every year officials from the Cochise County, Arizona, towns nearest the border get together with their Sonora, Mexico, counterparts for sport and pleasure. They call the event "A Celebration Nation to Nation." In the spirit of international *amistad,* politicians on both sides proclaim their mutual and eternal goodwill. On other days they might take issue over the problems of migration, drugs, pollution, and smuggling, but on this day the *abrazo,* the embrace, is in order. As part of this annual observance, officials play volleyball against each other in a game advertised as "a symbol of solidarity and a hand of friendship extended."

Conventional volleyball rules are followed, and the court is regulation size. The only unusual feature is the net. Instead of the normal cloth mesh stretched between two poles, this net is the seven-foot chain link fence separating the United States from Mexico, topped by three strands of barbed wire which slant toward Mexico. On the barbs shreds of clothing are visible, left by Mexicans who have tried to scale the barrier.

As the ball is slapped back and forth, the barbed wire works to the Mexicans' advantage. When the game is over the Mexicans emerge victorious, and both teams approach the "net" for comradely handshakes. Alas, the fence turns the "hand of friendship extended" into a most delicate problem. How do you shake hands with a fence in the way? The mayors pause at the paradox of the situation, laughing nervously at their predicament. Finally they adjust to the crisis. The officials each extend three fingers through the fence, rubbing them against the fingers of their opponents. It is the best they can do.

Such ironies and contradictions thrive on the border between the United States and Mexico, a region that does not adhere to the economic, ethical, political, or cultural standards of either country. Since the 1850s, when the boundary was first established, it has earned a reputation as a place where every conceivable form of illicit activity is condoned.

The border has come to represent many things to many people, yet it remains the most misunderstood region of North America. Our southern frontier is not simply American on one side and Mexican on the other. It is a third country with its own identity. This third country is a strip two thousand miles long and no more than twenty miles wide. It obeys its own laws and has its own outlaws, its own police officers and its own policy makers. Its food, its language, its music are its own. Even its economic development is unique. It is a colony unto itself, long and narrow, ruled by two faraway powers. The symbiotic relationships shared by the many pairs of border towns, such as El Paso and Ciudad Juárez or Calexico and Mexicali, are born of necessity. The cities couple like reluctant lovers in the night, embracing for fear that letting go could only be worse.

The general impression of border towns is that they are sleazy and sleepy, dusty and desolate, places where the poor and the criminal mingle. In truth, many are like that. But the border is also sexy and hypnotic, mysterious and magical, self-reliant and remarkably resilient. It changes pesos into dollars, humans into illegals, innocence into hedonism. No other international boundary juxtaposes such a poor but developing nation with such a wealthy and industrialized one. The border must absorb the blows from both sides, learning when to jab and when to duck.

To write this book I set out to travel that borderland. I began at the Gulf of Mexico, and four months later I reached the

Pacific Ocean. In each border town I talked with the residents and shared their life-styles. Most were eager to discuss their rich history and current problems. What I found was more encouraging than disturbing, more enlightening than depressing. I stayed at motels called Frontier and La Siesta. I ate at every Bordertown Cafe I could find. In Tijuana and El Paso I got caught in downtown traffic jams; in the Chihuahuan and Sonoran deserts I drove down arroyos with no outlets.

Almost all the literature about the border stresses the illegal, the vile, and the violent. My purpose here is to show instead the wide range of activity and attitudes among its people, to illuminate their day-to-day struggles and pleasures. The recent increase in the northward migration of Mexican laborers is certainly part of that struggle. Because Mexican border towns have no room to absorb more people from the interior, newcomers establish nearby shantytowns of their own. On the American side, Mexican workers already fill all the jobs they can, so late arrivals must travel farther north searching for work. In Coyame, Chihuahua, a *pueblito* west of Presidio, Texas, I wanted to make a long-distance telephone call to another part of Mexico. A man in a highway cafe told me where to find the *larga distancia* office. As it turned out, the office was in somebody's house, so I asked a neighbor if the operator, a man known throughout the town, was home.

"Oh, no," he replied. "He is away."

"I should make the call fairly soon," I said, checking the time. "When do you think he will return?"

"I don't know," the neighbor shrugged. "He went to the United States to work. He'll probably be back in a couple of years."

TOM MILLER

Tucson, Arizona

1

ON THE BORDERFRONT

ARMANDO GONZÁLEZ is the first man on the border. His home, a shack held together by cord and nails, rests on the Mexican side of the Rio Grande where the river enters the Gulf of Mexico. There at the eastern tip of the two-thousand-mile frontier, sand dunes jut into the Gulf. Flocks of gulls and terns glide patiently overhead watching for shrimp boats to return with the day's catch. Fishermen on both sides of the river's mouth exercise equal patience waiting for trout and redfish to bite. From a distance the scene resembles a motel room painting. Up close it assumes a vitality of its own.

During the Civil War two towns stood next to where Armando lives. The Union town was Clarksville, Texas. The Confederate stronghold was Bagdad, Tamaulipas, Mexico, through which the South exported thousands of bales of cotton to Europe each month. Since it could not cross the border, the Union army at Clarksville was helpless to stop the cotton trade.

Both towns were destroyed by a hurricane shortly after the Civil War. Ever since, souvenir hunters have sifted through the sand along the Gulf looking for military buttons, coins, weapons —artifacts of any kind. Armando González's prize discovery is a well-preserved blue bottle that he thinks dates back to the Civil War.

Armando was raised by his grandfather, Lucas, who died in early 1978. Soon after his grandfather's death, while Armando

was away from home, the shack by the river's edge was ravaged
by storms and plundered by thieves. Armando has since rebuilt
it, salvaging what he could from the wreck of Lucas' place.
"Things were better when my grandfather was here," the
twenty-year-old explained. "It used to be that friends and relatives would come out on weekends from Matamoros," twenty
miles west. "I had more fun then."

In front of Armando's home the Rio Grande is a hundred feet
wide and travels at less than ten miles an hour. At times you can
walk across without getting the tops of your shoes wet; following a tropical storm it will be over your head. The river's depth
and speed are important to Armando, who, like Lucas before
him, goes out in a rowboat to fish and, on occasion, ferries
people to the American side.

"When I take people across, it is only as a favor. My cousin is
a foreman in the United States, and when he needs extra help
he'll cross the men here. Yesterday some people came all the
way from Puebla. They were Spanish, *güero,* blond, with blue
eyes. They didn't cross over to the American side, though. They
just wanted to look around. They'll be back." Armando smiled.

"I have crossed here myself. I went to Dallas once and also
to Florida. I was gone for two years. In Dallas I operated heavy
machinery, Caterpillar tractors and things like that. The immigration people never caught me. I made five and six dollars an
hour, but whenever I'd get my paycheck I knew I'd worked one
more hour than they paid me for. In Florida I worked in a
factory. One time I ran a red light at two in the morning, and
they picked me up for driving without a license. Nothing happened, though. They must have thought I was from Cuba."

Rain began to fall. The roof of Armando's shack leaked
in a dozen places and water sprayed in the window. The
dirt floor became muddy, and the couch—the front seat
from an old pickup truck—was getting wet too. Covers from
different issues of *Alarma!,* Mexico's pictorial journal of grisly violence, were tacked to the walls. Armando slept on an
old army cot. Next to it was a footlocker on which lay a Coleman lantern and a comic book *novela* about the FBI. In the

corner was a bottle of 6-12 insect repellent.

A tropical storm was passing through and mosquitos were out in force, whole armies of them attacking anything within striking distance, swarms of them bigger than your thumb. They sounded like a sawmill in high gear, and they could bite through two layers of clothing leaving bruises the size of quarters. Armando just flicked them away. I got into vicious fistfights with them.

"People come all the time and hide drugs over at the sand dunes," said Armando. "They come back later and float them across to the other side. Usually they bring rubber rafts and fill them with so many bags of marijuana they practically sink from the weight. A few weeks ago an American girl swam across, pulling her raft with her. She met someone on the other side and hid the raft in a marsh. When she came back a few days later, she couldn't find her load.

"Once when my brothers and uncle from Matamoros were here they found five hundred kilos of marijuana, all wet. They couldn't turn it in, of course—that might cause trouble for them —and they didn't know who it belonged to. So they just left it. A few days later some men came and picked it up.

"The Americans who come here usually want to fish or look for relics. Sometimes I help them. I've found all sorts of things —spoons, plates, cartridges, gold coins, silver coins, sabers— everything. One time we found the body of an American buried in the ground. One American couple—I forget where they were from—wanted to take me back to the United States as their houseboy, but I'd rather live here."

Not far from Armando's home, a couple of other fishing shacks are used by people from Matamoros. Armando doesn't know them. "They take people across to the American side, but they are informers, too. Sometimes they'll inform to the authorities on the other side and sometimes to the Mexican ones on this side. I don't like them very much. My grandfather would never have allowed them to live here. They aren't good for the area."

Armando González doesn't know Stanley J. Piotrowicz. The two have as little in common as any two men on the border, yet Stanley Piotrowicz is Armando's closest Texas neighbor to the north. Piotrowicz is one of fifty residents in Kopernik Shores, an unlikely settlement a mile from the mouth of the Rio Grande. Kopernik Shores is made up of first-generation Polish immigrants who were lured from the American Midwest to a desolate strip of Texas land by a promoter's advertisements in Polish newspapers and on Polish-language radio programs. "Come retire in South Texas," John Caputa invited his working-class audience. Some day this will be the Fort Lauderdale of the West. High-rises! Restaurants! A country club! Invest now.

More than two thousand people sent in their money to buy lots, sites unseen. Eventually thirty-two homes were built in the late 1960s and early 1970s. The settlement turned into a retirement village with no city services and an ill-begotten town government gratefully repudiated by state authorities and forgotten by everyone except its self-appointed mayor, Stanley J. Piotrowicz.

Kopernik Shores' flirtation with home rule is the stuff of which situation comedies are made. In 1975, residents were persuaded to sign incorporation petitions, thinking the forms were requests for a state-approved water system. (Kopernik Shores water was trucked in daily from Brownsville, twenty miles away.) When incorporation came, Stanley Piotrowicz, the octogenarian head of the local senior citizens council, was the lone candidate for mayor.

The high point of Stanley's term came when the Polish government issued a statement expressing pride that an American city had been named for the sixteenth-century astronomer Copernicus. The low point came shortly thereafter, when a Texas judge ruled that the town's government had been invalid from the beginning. During its brief life, the mayor ignored most laws regulating Kopernik Shores' administration. Mayoral promises of a water system went unfulfilled. The one city council meeting held during Kopernik Shores' short life took place in a room without electricity. The gathering disbanded at dusk, having accomplished nothing. Mayor Piotrowicz became the object of derision, and plots to overthrow his regime circulated. When the town government was dissolved by judicial decree, most residents were relieved. Piotrowicz, though, has not given up. Every week he walks the halls of the Cameron County courthouse in Brownsville lobbying for a rehearing so Kopernik Shores can re-establish its twenty-seven months' glory.

Today most of the settlement's thirty-two homes have FOR SALE signs gracing their front lawns. The one-story ramblers lie in two rows along the one paved road, inexplicably called Weems Street. At the end of Weems Street stands a gaudy *al fresco* shrine to the Virgin Mary. Overgrown weeds shroud the only business that once attracted outsiders, a country club restaurant. Kopernik Shores appears nearly abandoned, a modern American ghost town. The Boca Chica Homeowners Association, named for the beach a mile away, is the current civic umbrella.

Helen Dolega, who has lived in Kopernik Shores since 1971, enjoys her life there. "The air is very good for us," she says. "It's much nicer than wherever else we've all come from. When you get to be this old, it's refreshing. People say, 'Oh my goodness, you're way out there at the very end of the border, next to the Gulf.' And I say, 'Yes, it's where God left his shoes.' "

En Route

From Kopernik Shores to Brownsville is a straight shot down an old two-lane county road. The drive from Armando's hut to Matamoros, across the river from Brownsville, is more difficult, going south for five miles along the beach before reaching the nearest paved road. If a car drifts too far toward the water, it slowly sinks. If it strays too far off the damp sand, it loses all traction.

The beach's official name is Playa General Lauro Villar, although everyone calls it Washington Beach. Villar was a hero of the Mexican Revolution, one of the innumerable officers whose place in history is preserved by cartography. Boarded-up summer cottages line the beach, and the fishermen are easily outnumbered by the pelicans.

Before leaving the eastern tip of the border, I sought out a souvenir to commemorate the start of my journey, something to remind me of this spot where the border begins. I decided upon a handful of seashells and, after rinsing the sand out of them, stored them in the glove compartment of my car for safe-keeping.

In Matamoros I stopped at the Hotel Colonia where I met Luis Rendón, head of tourism for the town. To be head of tourism in a Mexican town is a plum that usually goes to a businessman who can afford the time to take part in ceremonial functions and who will work to boost the town's image. In Rendón's lifetime—he's in his forties—Matamoros' population has grown from 20,000 to 290,000. He took me to the Drive Inn, a restaurant for tourists and well-to-do Mexicans, where a tuxedoed maitre d' greeted us. Since one of Rendón's duties is establishing and enforcing drink and food prices at restaurants around town, he always gets first-class service. As we sat down, he described upcoming improvements to the city.

"Sixty percent of our streets are unpaved," he said. "We have a five-year plan to pave them all. There are parts of town which used to be ponds, but we have filled them in with dirt. A city park is on one of them. The Holiday Inn is on another. And we are contemplating a new bridge to cross the river from Brownsville."

Matamoros appeared to have many bad drivers, I noted. "Yes," Rendón admitted, "it is true. Many of them have come to the city for the first time and are so used to donkeys and pickups on dirt roads that they cannot adjust to city driving. To Americans I always offer these three rules for driving south of the border. One: Remember, you are no longer in the U.S. Two: Drive offensively. If you hesitate, it may cause problems. Three: Drive by your senses, not by the traffic signs. If you see a sign which says *alto,* it doesn't necessarily mean stop. If you think you should drive through it, then you should. Sometimes you should stop when there are no signs, because people like to tear them down or shoot at them until they're illegible."

As we discussed driving on the border, a *jalapeño*-eating contest was taking place in the adjoining room. Two men in their thirties—one from Shreveport, Louisiana, and the other from Austin, Texas—were competing to see who could swallow more of the hot peppers. Each had a plate of fifty *jalapeños* in front of him, and a crowd of American tourists had gathered around to cheer them on. One onlooker insisted on buying the contestants beer to wash down the peppers. A character wearing sunglasses approached the curly-haired man from Shreveport and whispered in his ear like a fight manager between rounds.

The man from Austin, swarthy with greased-back hair, popped another *jalapeño* in his mouth. A raven-haired lady approached him to rub his back, and waiters brought crackers to dull the contestants' taste buds. Word went around the room: a hundred dollars was riding on the contest!

Shreveport's face grew redder as he swallowed another pepper. He nudged the man with the shades next to him and winked at his opponent. Austin took a sip of Carta Blanca and downed another *jalapeño*. Two dishes of ice cream came from the kitchen as a post-contest antidote. The Shreveport plate held fifteen peppers; Austin was at sixteen and slowly bit into another. He exhaled the fiery afterbite, his mouth like an exhaust pipe.

Shreveport took his time, studying his plate as a chess master might contemplate a Sicilian defense. A sip of beer, half a cracker, and one more pepper. His face grew still redder, and a blonde with two pounds of jewelry on her arm came up and kissed him. "This is pukesville," Shreveport grimaced.

Austin stared at his remaining peppers. A hush fell over the crowd as his eyes watered and sweat rolled down his face. With a solemn nod which slowly broke into a grin, he pushed his plate away and conceded victory to Shreveport. A cheer went up from the crowd. "Drinks all around!" the shady character called out. The waiters looked at each other, rolling their eyes.

"*Americanos, están locos, ¿verdad?*" said one. Americans are crazy, no?

Back at his table, Rendón went on about the city's history. "My grandfather was mayor here. My father was mayor here. *I* should be mayor here by now," he sighed, "but there were problems. I like being *subdelegado de turismo*, though. I have made many friends through my job. Just last night I was in the restaurant of a friend where the drinks were overpriced. I could have sent an inspector there today, but I didn't. They could have been fined ten thousand pesos." I mentioned that his job offered many opportunities for *la mordida* (literally, the bite), for payoffs.

"Yes it does," he agreed. "That is why they give these jobs to people who already have good incomes. Besides, I am too moral for that. It runs against my grain." After a long pause he arched his eyebrows, a gesture I was to see often among Mexican politicians. "But I could be making a lot with *mordida*, no?"

Before leaving Matamoros I purchased a lottery ticket. Mexico's Lotería Nacional has three weekly drawings with tickets priced from fifteen pesos (approximately seventy-five cents) to twenty-five pesos (about a dollar and a quarter). The winning numbers are published in newspapers and posted in lottery outlets throughout the country the day after the evening drawing in Mexico City. Profits go to charitable causes such as hospitals, orphanages, and clinics. If your ticket matches a winning number, you can win hundreds of thousands of pesos. The chances of that are, of course, slim. But if the last digit on your lottery ticket matches one of the two or three numerals listed at the bottom of the winners sheet, you score *reintegro* and are reimbursed the purchase price of the ticket. The likelihood of that is far greater, but the practice is insidious. Most people simply apply *reintegro* money toward another ticket for the following week.

After Matamoros I bought a lottery ticket in each border town, and came to think of the tickets as one of the leitmotifs of my journey. I felt certain that the ticket I bought in Matamoros would be a winner, a sure sign that my venture was blessed from above. I stuck the ticket in my wallet and crossed the river.

"You're doing a book on the border?" the Anglo bank teller in Brownsville asked in hushed tones as she converted my dollars to pesos. "Another one of those exposés? There've been so many," she sighed, "and I'm afraid they're all true." Her eyes darted around the room at the bank's brown-skinned customers. "You know the border is the only place where if your name is Smith or Jones you're in a minority. That's right."

It was my first encounter with that type of anti-Mexican feeling on the border, a strain of racism which was to recur all the way to the Pacific Ocean. The manager at my motel was more blunt. At the drop of a peso he'd launch into a tirade about how all Mexicans are on welfare or drugs. "The ones I hire, I gotta show them how to do the work and when. They don't come to work when I ask them to—their bodies tell them when to come to work. If they want to take the day off, they just don't come. They don't speak our language and they come over here expecting jobs. Why doesn't Mexico educate its own?" he asked as a late-model Chrysler pulled up. "Why should we?"

A well-dressed Mexican walked into the motel office and inquired in English about a week's lodging for himself and his family. He and the manager talked briefly, and he went off to compare the motel price next door. As he left, the manager flashed a banker's grin. "That man who was just here?" he said, rubbing his palms. "I sure hope he stays with us. He works for the Bank of Mexico. I want to ask him about investing in Mexico. I understand you can make a killing there."

Nicarao Restaurant, downtown on East Thirteenth Street, was just the antidote for the motel manager's bigotry. It's the finest cafe in all of Brownsville, an inexpensive working-class diner where huge servings of standard Mexican fare are prepared to perfection. Soups, *huevos rancheros*, burritos, tamales, *carne asada*, exotic fruit juices, the works—all served in infinite combinations. The Spanish-language menu was scattered about on the wall between the posters of Woody Woodpecker, Porky

Pig, and their *compadres*. The jukebox's Mexican tunes competed with a Spanish-language radio station. The obligatory fluorescent lights and velvet paintings completed the setting.

"There was a time when I couldn't eat in cafes here." Carl Shults was talking about discrimination in Brownsville when he and other Border Patrol agents would try to rent houses and eat in certain diners. "They'd say, 'I'm sorry, but we don't serve Border Patrol agents,' or 'We don't rent to Border Patrol agents.' Back in those days," the chief of the Brownsville station recalled, "the public didn't take kindly to us. We were the only ones who thought the alien situation was a serious problem. Everyone else sort of laughed. Now they realize the gravity of the situation."

Shults drove me to the Port of Brownsville where hundreds of shrimpers go out every morning for the day's haul. "A couple of years ago I told my men I'd throw 'em a barbecue if we ever apprehended six hundred wetbacks—whoops! I can't say that word anymore or I'll get fired. It's hard to break a twenty-four-year habit. Anyway, I told 'em I'd throw 'em a barbecue if we picked up six hundred aliens in one month at the Brownsville station. Well, I threw that barbecue a while back and we've been at six hundred or more ever since. We're almost at a thousand a month now." We passed three Mexican youths walking toward town. "I hate to do it, but I'm going to have to pick them up on our way back." By the time we returned, they were gone.

"Wetback"—a Mexican citizen in the United States without proper papers. Since many swim the Rio Grande, they have wet backs. The word is simple and convenient. (It also applies in the western section of the border where there is no river.) Although used universally, "wetback" is roughly equivalent to "nigger." Part of the problem is that there is no acceptable substitute. Academicians and bureaucrats usually say "undocumented alien," a dehumanizing mouthful in its own right. Some people call them "illegals," but that carries the unwarranted stigma of a courtroom conviction.

"Wetback" is sometimes used with no ill intention. Newspapers still put it in headlines ("Sixteen Wetbacks Picked Up On Briscoe Ranch"). It may not be disparaging to many people, but it's no compliment, either. Angry at a Chicano, someone might mutter, "Go back to Mexico, you goddamn wetback." In Spanish, *mojado,* or wet, is used in slang, but it doesn't carry the underlying contempt of its English counterpart. Border Patrol agents use "wetback" all the time, except in public. A memo circulated in 1977 soon after Leonel Castillo became commissioner of the Immigration and Naturalization Service told Border Patrolmen to find another term. The directive, a continuing object of derision within the service, has brought on a new vocabulary. One Border Patrolman I met calls them "persons of Hispanic descent lacking proper credentials." He tells the story of a Mexican who boasted, "My daddy was a wetback. I'm an illegal alien. But my son is the pride of the family. He is an undocumented Mexican national!" "Wetback" will remain in everyday vocabulary for generations before its use diminishes.

Back in Brownsville, Shults showed me the railroad bridge from Matamoros over which many Mexicans cross into the United States. An agent is usually stationed by the bridge in a van during the night to watch for covert crossings. Embedded in the ground next to the bridge on the U.S. side is a two-foot-thick metal pole with a slanted top. "A few of my men greased that pole because the aliens were using it to jump from the bridge onto the ground. Well, some lady jumped on it and sure enough, she slipped off. Broke her leg, too. I guess the county hospital will have to pay."

Shults was concerned about inexperienced Border Patrolmen coming to the Lower Rio Grande Valley from the combat zone, the Border Patrol sector at Chula Vista, California, which intercepts migrants from Tijuana. It is a particularly tense area, where periodic violence erupts among smugglers, cops, migrants, and border guards. "Those rookies who start at Chula, they're almost shell-shocked from the experience. They tear out wires under car hoods and punch out windows over there

—the Border Patrolmen, not the aliens. These agents have to change their way of thinking when they get to peaceful areas of the border like here. I won't tolerate that kind of activity or mistreatment of detainees or any such nonsense like that."

2
RÍO RICO, U.S.A.

IN MEXICO, the river we know as the Rio Grande is called the Río Bravo. Under any name, it is given to sudden and impulsive changes. A heavy rain can wash out a bridge, flood a town, or alter the river's course. Officially, the international boundary is the deepest point in the river channel. But when the river shifts its flow, eroding land on one side can build up soil on the other. Farmers on both sides have lost—and gained—hundreds of acres this way.

Various measures have been taken to avoid the worst depredations of the Rio Grande. In 1906, the river between Brownsville and Reynosa formed the shape of a backwards S near Weslaco, Texas, which meant that a portion of Mexico hooked in between United States soil and a chunk of America did the same to Mexican land. You could go north from Texas into Mexico and travel south from Tamaulipas into the United States. The two top parallel sections of the Rio Grande in the backwards S were twisting closer and closer together, and it appeared that within a few years the area between would flood, changing the course of the river and destroying the irrigation system of the farmers downriver. To prevent flooding, the American Rio Grande Land and Irrigation Company constructed a cutoff diverting the river at the top bend in the S to the bottom leg of the S, and the danger of a suddenly changed boundary was averted. The newly established stretch of the Rio

Grande was in a safer channel, one with a hard clay floor and high banks.

When U.S. authorities learned of the artificial cutoff, they were irate. A private company cannot arbitrarily alter the course of a river, especially when an international boundary is involved. The government pressed charges, the company pleaded guilty, and the American judge assessed damages against the company of five thousand dollars for each rancher whose land was adversely affected by the river's realignment. As a footnote, there remained that little parcel of American land which previously had jutted into Mexican soil. It was called El Horcón, and it was now on the Mexican side of the Rio Grande. And that's how everyone treated it.

The area remained a backwater farming community until Prohibition came to the United States. For most American drinkers, Prohibition meant buying from bootleggers or making home brew. Near the border the options were greater. One could buy liquor in Mexico and smuggle it back home, or simply cross over for an evening and enjoy life there. America had the demand and Mexico was a willing supplier.

Prohibition was the midwife of many Mexican towns between Matamoros and Tijuana. One of these instant towns was Río Rico, which sprang up on the south bank of a bridge constructed at Thayer, Texas, in 1929. Río Rico was what America wanted. It had colorful barrooms, well-stocked liquor stores, a classy bordello, cabarets, souvenir shops, and a dog racing track. On a good weekend afternoon, more than a thousand fans would pack the track, then spill out for a night on the town. Within ten months the bridge paid for itself in tolls. Río Rico thrived.

The end of Prohibition in 1933 signaled the decline of Río Rico. Tourism dropped, unemployment rose, and people drifted away. The bridge, Río Rico's lifeline to the United States, was washed downstream in a flood in 1941. The flood also inundated Río Rico itself, forcing the entire town to move a bit farther south. A ferryboat replaced the bridge, operating for

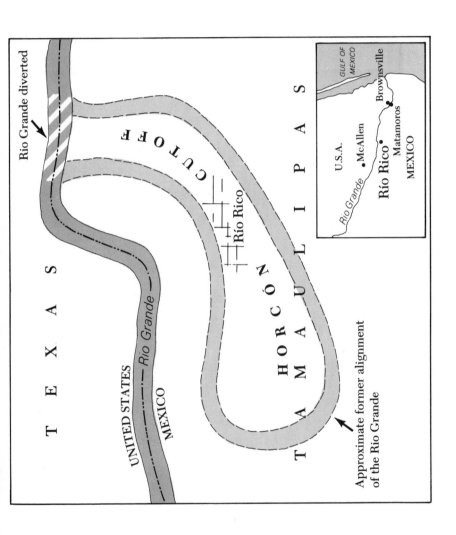

twelve years until it too was discontinued. The isolated community settled into obscurity.

Over the years the Rio Grande would occasionally overflow its banks, each time forcing the Río Ricans to move gradually south. Although no one was aware of it, two-thirds of the town had inched into the northern part of El Horcón, the tract of land which had been American until the irrigation company's arbitrary cutoff. The town's police station, church, school, town plaza, and a stretch of a public road all fell within the limits of El Horcón, as did many houses. The residents of the town went to the local Mexican school, served in the Mexican army, used the federal hospital, and paid their taxes to the Mexican government. If anyone knew the difference, he kept quiet. That is, until 1972, when Homero Cantú Treviño, a lifelong resident of Río Rico, claimed he was an American citizen born in El Horcón in 1935.

As a border resident, Cantú had been entitled to a border-crossing card from the U.S. Immigration and Naturalization Service. The card entitled Cantú to spend seventy-two hours in the United States no farther than twenty-five miles from the border, visiting friends and shopping. (No such card is required of Americans visiting Mexican border towns.) Like other able-bodied men from Río Rico, the thirty-seven-year-old wanted to stay and work.

There were two ways Cantú could accomplish this: legally and illegally. To remain illegally would have been easy—simply overstay the three-day permit and blend into the Mexican-American majority in the Lower Rio Grande Valley. To immigrate legally was much more difficult. Cantú was in none of the categories that would permit him to attain "resident alien" status. He had no immediate family in the United States, nor was he in the performing arts or a scientist, nor a worker with a job offer in a field where a shortage existed. Cantú explained all this to Laurier McDonald, an Edinburg, Texas, lawyer, and asked whether there was any way he could get papers to stay in the United States awhile.

"As far as I'm concerned, you're a United States citizen,"

McDonald told him. "At least according to law."

Cantú didn't understand. "You mean I don't have to go back to Mexico? I can stay?"

"Sure you can. I'll type up this letter for you. It'll say you're an American citizen as far as I'm concerned, but be sure and carry it with you wherever you go." Cantú carefully folded the letter and stuck it in his back pocket. He walked out of the lawyer's office a slightly bewildered but happy man.

Cantú's visit to the lawyer could not have been more fortuitous. McDonald, an immigration lawyer of some standing, had just been researching the confused status of Río Rico. Within a few weeks the attorney received a phone call. Cantú had been picked up by the Border Patrol and was about to be VR'd. (Rather than go through time-consuming deportation proceedings, in most cases a Mexican without papers can sign a waiver admitting he or she is not legally in the United States and agrees to a "Voluntary Return.") McDonald persuaded the immigration officer to let Cantú stay until his nationality could be resolved.

Many Mexicans followed Cantú's example. That same year over two hundred men from Río Rico emigrated to the United States legally and otherwise. Río Rico, population four hundred, was reduced to women, children, and old men. But when word spread that you could get a temporary visa by simply claiming Río Rico as your birthplace, immigration officers in the Lower Rio Grande Valley were flooded with Mexican applicants, all insisting they were born in that tiny forgotten town. Phony Río Rico birth certificates, some with the name of the town misspelled, were available on the black market. Suddenly Río Rico had a population of thousands. Most of the born-again Río Ricans gravitated to Laurier McDonald's office, and most of them were thrown off balance when he started asking for corroborative evidence—baptismal certificate, school records, brother's or sister's birth certificate, or military records.

In November 1976, a court ruled on Cantú's claim. The judge agreed with the Justice Department that Cantú should be de-ported. "Citizens of Mexico," he wrote, "pass as freely without documents between the cutoff and the Mexican part of that area as they do between any other parts of Mexico." Cantú's constitutional argument—that since he was born on United States soil he was an American citizen—was dismissed because the United States did not have jurisdiction in Río Rico at the time of his birth, nor was there American protection for the town. Cantú appealed the decision.

Some branches of the government had recognized that Río Rico was, at least technically, American. The year after the judge ruled against Cantú, the State Department officially gave El Horcón back to Mexico. To further acknowledge its prior American nationality, the U.S. government paid back taxes on that tract to Hidalgo County, Texas, for the years in question.

Finally Cantú's appeal was resolved. Neither the fact that the United States did not exercise authority in the Horcón tract nor that Mexico had illegally assumed jurisdiction there changed anyone's nationality, an appellate judge said. "When does nonaction lead to noncitizenship?" he wanted to know. Before the land was affected by the unauthorized cutoff in 1906, the people were without question American. "Why is there an issue as to their citizenship thereafter?"

Homero Cantú Treviño's six-year claim that he was an American citizen was at last recognized.

The road to Homero Cantú's birthplace begins in Nuevo Progreso, a town established in 1953 at the southern end of a new bridge spanning the Rio Grande from the United States. Together with Lionel Perez, a friend from Edinburg, I headed east on Calle Coahuila, a paved street which soon became a lumpy road atop the levee along the river. The farther we drove from town, the more scattered the little one-room shacks near the road became. After several miles there is nothing along the levee but the rusting bodies of a few long-deserted cars. To the left is the river; to the right, untilled farmland. The nearer one gets to Río Rico, the greater the number of abandoned cars.

José Paloma was the first Río Rican we encountered. He was

on the riverbank cutting hay for his animals. Waving his machete about, he pointed to where the old bridge had crossed the river in Río Rico's richer days. Later there had been a pontoon bridge, he added, but it was dismantled within a year. Lionel and I walked around mud puddles to the middle of Río Rico. When we finally reached the town plaza, it was empty and overgrown with weeds.

If this was the heart of Río Rico, it appeared to have suffered a coronary. Although the Roman Catholic church, which parishioners had abandoned for one in Nuevo Progreso, was receiving a new coat of paint, the painter seemed to have quit a month earlier, his job half finished. Next to the church was the police station: COMANDANCIA DE POLICÍA, RÍO RICO, TAMPS. The building was not much larger than a toll booth and looked as if it hadn't been used in decades. A few puddles beyond was the two-room schoolhouse, Escuela Amado Nervo. The couple who taught there had left for the weekend. We followed a series of puddles to Misión Bautista, the Baptist church, where a man was fattening up his pigs so he would have lots of *chicharrones*, fried pork skin, for the Christmas season.

The local constable, the one civil servant in Río Rico, lived across town. As we waded toward his house, Lionel told the story of Jacinto Treviño, a legendary local outlaw in the twenties and thirties. "Jacinto Treviño was a famous smuggler, and he was a pretty tough old dude. He had several wives and many kids. Some were born in the United States and some in Mexico. Several times authorities sent *los rinches* [the Texas Rangers] to bring him in, but nothing happened."

This is Jacinto Treviño's story, as summarized by Américo Paredes in his classic study of border culture, *"With His Pistol In His Hand"*: "Jacinto Treviño is in Matamoros when the news comes to him that an American on the north bank has beaten Jacinto's brother to death with a piece of an iron pipe. Jacinto crosses into Texas, kills the American and makes his way back to the river, carrying his brother's body and fighting off *los rinches* at the same time. Later he hears that the *rinches* have offered a reward for him; so he again goes across the river, engages them in a gun battle, kills several and returns to the south bank."

We passed under the town's only street lamp, which had no bulb in it, and Lionel reminisced about *corridos,* the romantic folk ballads so much a part of Mexican culture. "When I was growing up in Del Rio, we'd have neighborhood *corridos* that no one else in the city knew about. Then there were some that were well known all over town but no other Mexicans in the state had ever heard of them. And then there were the *corridos* which everyone in *la raza* knew about. 'El Corrido de Jacinto Treviño' was one of those. You can still hear it sung in cantinas along the border."

The *corrido* goes like this:

Ya con ésta van tres veces en que se ve lo bonito,
La primera fue en McAllen en Brownsville y San Benito.
This makes the third time that he has been seen,
First it was in McAllen then in Brownsville and San Benito.
En la Cantina de Beca se agarraron a balazos
Por donde quiera volaban botellas hechas pedazos.
All the shooting began in the Cantina de Beca
Broken bottles were flying all around.
Esa Cantina de Beca al momento quedó sola
No más Jacinto Treviño de carabina y pistola.
The Cantina de Beca was empty for a moment
Only Jacinto Treviño remained with his rifle and his pistol.
Entrenle rinches cobardes válidos de la ocasión. . . .
Come on you cowardly Rangers, you like to take easy chances. . . .

We finally arrived at the constable's place. A heavyset man came lumbering out of one of Río Rico's more prosperous homes. The three of us chatted awhile, trying to figure exactly where the Horcón tract line was. "I think it runs next to that pine tree," the constable said, pointing to the other side of the road. "The problem of who is a native and who isn't is complicated because this area used to be a very good cotton-growing center, and migrant workers from other parts of the country came and went. *La gente,*" the people, "they know who was born here."

Then he introduced himself. His name was Jacinto Treviño. His father was the legend. When his father died in 1934, Jacinto, Jr., was only two years old. "My father was born on the other side of the river, in Texas. It is true he killed a ranch foreman who had beaten up his brother, but he was just a good man who got bothered. He was no bandit. I was born not far from here, but I was raised on both sides of the river. It's like what happens to all of us, *¿verdad?*"

Treviño works in the United States part of the year and spends the rest of his time in Río Rico tending his tulips and roses. He wore a small badge, but what he did as town constable was never clear. As we talked, he plucked mulberries off a tree in front of his house, handed some to us, and ate the rest. His mouth had five teeth in it: two stalactites and three stalagmites.

"There was a Jacinto Treviño College across the river, you know," he said with matter-of-fact pride. "It was started by La Raza Unida party. They named it after my father." We talked a bit more, then bid him farewell. Jacinto Treviño, Jr., waved his straw hat at us as we walked off.

"This Río Rico case," Lionel explained, "it really had nothing to do with national allegiance or immigration law. It had to do with survival. Not simply just getting by—no, it's a matter of eating. Not eating more, but just eating, period. As U.S. citizens, they can eat."

En Route

Along with Norah Booth, a photographer friend accompanying me on my border travels, I started out from Nuevo Progreso for Rio Grande City, Texas, sixty miles upriver. Our trip took us through Reynosa, Tamaulipas, and McAllen, Texas, and to a ferryboat crossing linking Díaz Ordaz, Tamaulipas, with Los Ebanos, Texas.

Nuevo Progreso, which we had passed through on our way to

Río Rico, comes alive on weekends with American tourists who cross over for food, haircuts, and curios. Like other Mexican border towns, Nuevo Progreso boasts doctors and dentists who, because they charge considerably less than their American counterparts, have a substantial American clientele.

The town's red-light district is down some virtually impassable streets. Here, as elsewhere, the theory is that if you want to go whoring bad enough you'll tolerate the worst of conditions to get to the brothels. Bars with names like El Houston, La Paloma, and Las Coronelas (the name given to camp-followers during the Mexican Revolution) lined the two-block area. According to a Chicano friend, a lifelong border rat who has frequented red-light districts from Matamoros to Ciudad Acuña, Nuevo Progreso's Boys Town is the absolute worst. "Even horny Mexicans won't go there," he said. While church bells rang on a Sunday noon, the *zona roja* was deserted save for some abandoned cars and a fiftyish woman in a Leon Russell tee shirt. As we left the area, a girl dressed only in a towel appeared at a barroom door preparing to go to work on the day shift.

Before leaving for Reynosa I checked the previous day's list of winning lottery tickets. That mine wasn't among them didn't keep me from buying another ticket for the next day's drawing.

Reynosa itself is a comfortable drive from Nuevo Progreso along Mexico's Highway 2. On the way we had to awaken a snoozing *inmigración* official to let us by his checkpoint. When Norah asked to take his picture, he got up, quickly tucked in his shirt, brushed back his hair, and stood at his post smiling. By the time we pulled away, he had resumed his earlier position. As we drove on, the three driving rules Señor Rendón gave me in Matamoros came in handy. I added Rule Four: Do not go one-on-one with a Mexican bus, especially on a bridge.

Pemex, the country's nationalized petroleum industry, is Reynosa's main industry, but the city also caters to migrants from the interior looking for work on either side of the Rio Grande and to American tourists.

For those crossing illegally into the United States, the greatest anxiety is not caused by *la migra,* the Border Patrol, but by *coyotes.* A *coyote* is a guide who promises, for a fee, to get you safely into the United States. Depending on how one looks at it, they are either preying on the desperation of their brethren or offering a necessary and valuable service. They are paid what the traffic will bear. Many of them are honest, but some are apt to leave as soon as they sniff trouble. The worst simply take the money and run.

For a peasant from the interior to have sold all his worldly possessions to come to a border town such as Reynosa is not at all unusual. Near where migrants bide their time, a creek runs through the town. To the newly arrived and uninitiated, the creek could be the Río Bravo with the land of milk and money to the north. *Coyotes* with absolutely no scruples will get what they can—twenty dollars, forty dollars, fifty dollars—and take some unsuspecting countryman across the creek and abandon him, in reality having led him from one Reynosa street to another. His life savings depleted, the bilked *campesino* may be forced to play the trick on another sucker. *Bienvenido.* Welcome.

After another couple of days we headed for McAllen, Texas, opposite Reynosa. Before crossing the international bridge we stopped at the main plaza to check out my most recent lottery ticket.

Hot damn, I won!

Actually I didn't really win, but the last digit on my ticket matched one of the *reintegro* numbers. The lady in the Lotería Nacional booth handed me twenty pesos, to which I immediately added five pesos and bought a ticket for the next drawing. Nearby, a shoeshine man was selling some not-so-official lottery tickets which showed only three digits. This unsanctioned but tolerated lottery is run by the shoeshinemen's union and is geared to the winning numbers in the national lottery. The five-peso *quintana* tickets, as they are called, say *rifa entre amigos* on them, raffle among friends. In other words, it is a numbers game. I bought into it and we crossed over to McAllen.

In the early morning hours Willie Lopez broadcasts his radio program from an unpretentious house in a working-class section of McAllen. Lopez, a heavyset man with a triangular face rounded off at the corners, reels off advertisements for cafes, garages, lawyers, record stores, gas stations, and politicians for two hours every day. Periodically a record will interrupt the chatter. By means of a leased telephone line, Lopez's Spanish-language show is carried from his den to a radio transmitter in Reynosa and broadcast over a Mexican station's airwaves. His audience and advertisers, however, are primarily north of the border. Although Lopez lacks the requisite Federal Communications Commission permit to transmit a live show from the United States to Mexico and have it simultaneously broadcast back to the United States, he has been entertaining his South Texas audience in this manner for years. *"Ésta es radio X-E-O-R, trece y noventa; la estación de la gente contenta,"* he announces. "This is radio X-E-O-R, thirteen-ninety; the station of satisfied people."

Lopez, whose on-the-air name is Chula Frontera del Norte—"Beautiful Northern Border"—was featured in the film *Chulas Fronteras,* a moving documentary about Mexican-American life in the Rio Grande Valley. In it, he plays his *corrido* about the melon pickers' strike of 1967, "Rinches de Tejas," part of which goes like this:

> *En el Condado de Estrella en el mero Río Grande*
> *Junio de sesenta y siete sucedió un hecho de sangre . . .*
> It was in Starr County right on the Rio Grande
> In June of '67 that the bloody affair took place . . .
> *Esos rinches maldecidos los mandó el gobernador*
> *A proteger los melones de un rico conservador.*
> The governor sent those damn Rangers down
> To protect a rich packer's melons.
> *Mr. Connally, señores, es el mal gobernador*
> *Que aborrece al Mexicano y se burla del dolor . . .*
> Mr. Connally, *señores,* is that rotten governor

Who hates the Mexican and jokes about pain . . .
Me despido, mis hermanos, con dolor de corazón
Como buenos mexicanos pertenezcan a la unión.
Farewell my brothers, with pain in my heart
I bid you be good Mexicans and join the union.

Willie Lopez loves to dabble in politics. He showed me a letter from Senator Edward Kennedy. A picture of Willie Lopez and Hubert Humphrey. A picture of Willie Lopez and Leonel Castillo (then head of the Immigration and Naturalization Service). Pictures of Willie Lopez and a half-dozen more politicians. At Christmastime he sent out calendars with a picture of Willie Lopez and Walter Mondale. "I know these people," he boasted. "I can call Washington and get through to President Carter if I want. I can call Mexico City and get through to President José López Portillo if I want. I've got friends in both capitals."

Among Lopez's advertisers is Discoteca RYN, a McAllen record store. Its owner, Ramiro Cavasos, who records, writes, and performs his own music, became my best source on *música norteña*. His little shop is packed with 45s and LPs from both sides of the border, and he seems to know every song. For an introduction to borderland music, Cavasos recommended "Los Más Famosos Corridos de Rinches y Contrabandistas en la Frontera del Río Bravo," by Los Tremendos Gavilanes del Valle.

In 1848, U.S. General Zachary Taylor entered Mexico and captured the city of Monterrey. The invasion took place at Los Ebanos, today the site of the last hand-drawn ferryboat across the Rio Grande. The eighty-foot barge can accommodate two standard cars or three sports cars. The ferry is powered by four men who ride it pulling on a rope anchored between two trees, one on each side of the river. It operates eight hours daily when the river isn't too high, and costs seventy-five cents a car each way. According to a historical marker on the U.S. side, the first recorded river crossing there was in the 1740s. The marker fails to mention the time when the brakes on a car slipped and it rolled off the barge into the river, drowning four ladies on their way to a wedding.

Most of the passengers on the Los Ebanos ferry are tourists. During a good weekend the barge makes more than thirty fifteen-minute round trips a day. On the Mexican riverbank sits Florencio Barrientos, the *aduana*, or customs official, who spends slow days playing gin rummy with Irene Galavis, a neighbor, beneath a thatch-roofed ramada. Every morning they start with twenty pebbles each. When we arrived, Irene was three pebbles ahead. The customs house, if one could call it that, was a bare dilapidated building with broken windows and no doors. Nearby, five-year-old Alejandro, a friend of Irene's, was busy catching butterflies.

Gilberto Martínez Garza, the toll collector for the ferryboat on the Mexican side, told me that in 1968 the nearby town of San Miguel de Camargo renamed itself after the incumbent president, Gustavo Díaz Ordaz, to attract attention and federal funds. There was even a *corrido* written about the name change, he boasted, a couple verses of which he happily sang for us. But being called Gustavo Díaz Ordaz, Gilberto lamented, did little to alleviate the town's poverty, and most of its residents still call the place by its previous name.

When we left, Florencio had just won back four pebbles from Irene.

3

STARR TREK

THE PRESS is giving Starr County a bum rap. Look at the clippings: "Eight officials convicted for stealing votes from the uneducated, the ill, and the elderly"—Associated Press. "The marijuana capital of the United States"—the Washington *Post*. "One of the three poorest counties in the nation"—the Houston *Post*. *Texas Monthly* profiled the drug trade in Rio Grande City, the unincorporated county seat. The San Antonio *Express-News* reported the Rio Grande City junior high school principal as saying, "If this were a city, the motto would be 'the city of eternal apathy.'" Rio Grande City, according to *U.S. News and World Report*, is where "smuggling is a way of life."

When federal officials estimated that fully 30 percent of Starr County's eighteen thousand residents made their living from contraband, newspapers throughout the country ran the item. Next to the article would be a little map of Texas, with an arrow pointing toward a black splotch in the Lower Rio Grande Valley. Starr County was that black splotch upon Texas. Why can't the press say something nice for a change? Living in a place known for its poverty and smuggling is no fun.

Geographically and culturally, Starr County is ideal for smuggling. Much of the property along the county's fifty-mile boundary with Mexico is owned by families having extensive ties on both sides of the river. Floating contraband from one relative's front yard to another's back yard is a sure way to combat poverty in a county where almost 50 percent of the population receives welfare benefits. What bothered authorities more than the smuggling itself, though, was that the drug traffickers flaunted their success. Smugglers were both ostentatious and cool about it. Construction workers earning minimum-wage paychecks cruised Main Street in customized Mark IVs. Palaces rose out of nowhere, owned by truck drivers whose only visible means of support was hauling auto parts to nearby Roma. Dodge Ramchargers with all the options were paid for in cash. There was also cash on the line for real estate. The smugglers and traffickers had broken away from generations of Starr County poverty. Local business prospered.

All of this bothered the federal Drug Enforcement Administration—so much that they poured one million dollars into a major clean-up campaign. An eight-man DEA team spent four months trying to bust some of the most solidly organized crime rings in the country. They called their effort "Operation Wishbone."

Terry Bowen, a DEA undercover agent who took part in Wishbone, ran into problems right away. "The trouble with investigating Mexicans is that these people live in such a closed society," he explained one morning at his McAllen office. "It's hard to get someone to turn a relative in. In a Mexican family on the border, blood is thicker than water. They scout for each other." Bowen shrugged. "It's been that way as long as anyone can remember." Indeed, during the mid-1800s when a U.S. official paused at Rio Grande City, then called Davis Landing, he noted that smuggling "is identified with the best part of the population."

Bowen continued, "If the smugglers see any strange face in town and there's a deal going down, they'll call it off. A gringo face in Rio Grande City means a narcotics agent. Period. On our first day the traffickers knew who we were and why we were there."

Bowen's slight lisp disappeared when he talked about undercover work. He hunched forward, eyes narrowed slightly. "We made buys. We learned where their stashes were. We traveled the back roads. We built conspiracy cases—that's just about the only kind you can build in situations like that. There were times when twenty tons of marijuana a week would pass through Starr County.

"Here's how the Starr County smugglers operated: Someone goes down to the staging area at San Luis Potosí and picks up marijuana at three or four dollars a pound. He'll bring it back up to the Camargo area across from Rio Grande City.

"Take a ton. The man in Camargo has paid eight thousand dollars for it. His runners swim it across the river to whomever he's dealing with—a close friend or a relative. The man in Rio Grande City pays about thirty dollars a pound for it—that comes to sixty thousand dollars a ton. The ton gets broken down into four-hundred pound lots and sent in five different vehicles to, let's say, Houston. The guy who is sending it expects some of it to get caught. If two loads are lost and three make it, he's still made good money. In Houston he'll get at least a hundred dollars a pound for it. If nothing goes wrong, the guy in Rio Grande City has netted about one hundred forty thousand dollars. Of course if you only want a quarter ton you'll have to fly down and pick it up yourself. Right now grass is going for fifty-five dollars a pound on the U.S. side if you buy on the border. San Antonio, one hundred dollars. Dallas, one hundred fifteen. That's only if you're connected to these families, though."

The DEA insists Operation Wishbone, which climaxed in April 1977, was enormously successful because of the many indictments handed down and all the dope confiscated. But the DEA has strange criteria for success. Eighteen months after the big roundup, both Bowen and his boss, Larry Orten, estimated that the flow of marijuana through Starr County was as great as it had been before Wishbone began. Orten lamented, "They know how we work now."

"It's true," Bowen admitted, "for every one that goes to jail, more of them come up. There are a hundred daddies from Starr County in jail, and they have five hundred sons who took over the business. We could send twenty-five people to Starr full time and we'd still continue to be beat."

"Let's face it," added a dejected Orten. "We've got a wide open border between the U.S. and Mexico."

Orten wanted to demonstrate how community support rallied 'round the cops. "I wasn't here during Wishbone, but I heard a story that when we were taking prisoners in for processing, a crowd gathered and they were cheering. Is that right?"

Bowen paused. "Yeah, well, that was the friends of the defendants."

"But they were cheering?" Orten seemed confused.

"Yeah. For the defendants. It was a big joke to them." Bowen exhaled a dry chuckle. "We processed them all at the Border Patrol station. The prisoners would smile and wave at the TV news cameras. Their friends were driving new cars and pickups in circles around the station. It was a big party for 'em. They didn't take it very serious at all."

"Look, ten years ago people were picking on Starr County because of its machine politics. Now it's drugs. There's not one person of power from the county who's in state or national politics, so it's easy to pick on this county." Ricardo Hinojosa, a graduate of Rio Grande High School and Harvard Law School, was explaining why his native Starr County was constantly under attack from law enforcement agencies and the press. "You can make a name for yourself attacking Starr County and no one will fight back," the McAllen lawyer complained. "The DEA did just that. They know there's more drugs going through Hidalgo County in a month than Starr County in a year, but if you bust in Starr, you look good.

"There are people on welfare here, and you have some very wealthy folks here, too—but you also have a lot of people who just get by on the minimum wage. The people are really quite good in Rio Grande City. When I became Republican party chairman in Hidalgo County, the newspapers said I was the first Spanish-speaking political chairman ever in McAllen. My sister couldn't understand why they'd mention that. She still lived in Starr County, which is ninety-seven percent Mexican-American. She didn't know what discrimination was because everyone in Starr is Mexican, while Hidalgo County is only eighty percent Mexican-American."

Over the next few days I sought out more natives to explain the good qualities of Rio Grande City and its fifty-seven hundred citizens. The Chamber of Commerce, unfortunately, had closed a few months earlier. At the office of the weekly Rio Grande *Herald* ("the largest paid circulation in Starr County") I asked to see some back copies. "Are you going to write about us?" the receptionist inquired. "There are so many good things to say about Rio Grande City."

"Such as?"

She stopped.

"Well, we have a lot of history."

Estela Perez Contreras was behind the counter at Rely Office and School Supplies on Mirasoles Street. She spotted me for an out-of-town journalist right away. "Writers always say bad things about Starr County. Never good things."

"And they are?"

There was a silence while she gathered her thoughts.

"Well, I don't have to go searching for my roots. They are right here and I can prove it." She was emphatic. "I can trace my family tree back eleven generations." Which she proceeded to do.

"My father was the U.S. Deputy Marshal for many years here, and chief scout for the U.S. government during the last revolution in Mexico. He loaned his ranch on the river to U.S. troops. During World War I he was the county food administrator. He was a staunch Republican. He resigned when FDR was elected. . . .

"And so, when we hear the Mexican national anthem, we are proud. When we hear the American national anthem, we are proud. We're unique! We have the best of both. We can change our name, but not our blood." She threw up her hands in futility. "Ah, *pobre México. Tan lejos de Dios y tan cerca de los Estados Unidos.*" Poor Mexico. So far from God and so near to the United States.

I stayed at the Ringgold, a hotel years past decaying splendor.

George Boyle, an elderly fixture on the Rio Grande City scene and an enthusiastic historian, is the Ringgold's manager. There are many nights when he and his wife are the only people in the eighty-five-year-old building.

"Here's your room key," Boyle muttered after I registered. "It won't do you any good, of course. Everyone in town's got a set of keys to the place. The doors are so weak anyone could break in." The only other guests at the Ringgold, two oil-field workers from Corpus Christi, reported that their room had been broken into a few nights earlier. They awoke in time to thwart a burglary. The intruder excused himself, saying he must have had the wrong room. I slept with a chair propped against the door.

Rio Grande City was spooky, a feeling which came not from rude treatment but from nontreatment. In every other border town I had no trouble meeting engaging people from all walks of life. In Rio Grande City I was a ghost. Friendly hellos were acknowledged with suspicious stares and perfunctory nods.

One Saturday morning I breakfasted at the O.S.T. Cafe. At nine o'clock, movement on the streets was just beginning when suddenly at the cafe's screen door two men wielding knives angrily yelled at each other. A blur of activity followed; one of them jumped sideways as the other sliced through the air. The taller of the two hopped in his pickup and sped off, his assailant in pursuit. These weren't spasms of emotion left over from Friday night anger. This was the first fight of a brand-new day.

A few weeks later a new controversy arose in Starr County. *Oui*, the magazine of kink and kitsch, had listed Rio Grande City as one of America's meanest towns. Readers learned it is "the home of snakes, spiders, and the Mexican Mafia." *Oui* noted that Rio Grande City consists mainly of shacks and run-down adobes and that organized crime killings are not infrequent. "Gringos are as popular as Klansmen would be in Watts," the author observed. "It is not a nice place to visit and even more gruesome to live there."

The people of Starr County did not take kindly to this portrayal of their county seat.

One woman suggested the writer visit San Benito, near Brownsville, "where they find dead bodies in the orchards."

Texas Monthly, which previously had noted Starr County's extensive drug trade, rose to the town's defense. Addressing itself to Hank Nuwer, the article's author, the *Monthly* proclaimed, *"Tú no sabes si es caca o si es Shinola."* You don't know shit from Shinola.

Estela Contreras at the stationery store was indignant. "We may be a unique kind of people, but not freaks just because we hold onto our culture. I for one just wish and pray to God to leave us alone."

Marcelo Silvas, editor of the Rio Grande *Herald,* said the *Oui* article was "quite a verbal slap. Perhaps we should say, 'Thanks, we needed that.' "

Outraged at this latest attack on their home, the townspeople met at the American Legion Hall to defend themselves. Basilio Villareal, a local tire and butane dealer who chaired the meeting, boasted that the best thing about Rio Grande City was peace of mind. "You can leave your cars wide open with guns on the gun rack and no one takes them."

Estela Contreras attended, complaining about the press. "The ones from outside—we welcome them and they get rich," she told the faithful assembled. "The way they write—they've been doing it for years and no one here seems to care. Let's forget about politics and everything. Let's get together and do something for ourselves."

And so was born the Concerned Citizens of Starr County. One by one the natives stood to bear witness to all that is good about the area. The *Herald* and the *South Texas Reporter*—the weekly from nearby Roma—contributed to the list.

Here are the things they found good about Rio Grande City: We are friendly; game and rock hunting thrive in the area; local farming and ranching are prosperous; we have oil deposits; we are proud of our religious accomplishments; most of us are law-abiding; we have two banks; the high school faculty has bachelor's and master's degrees in education; the owner of the second most profitable Hispanic business in the country, Pete

Diaz, Jr., lives here; our baseball, basketball, and football teams excel; our civic organizations work hard to help the needy; our Boy Scouts and Girl Scouts are among the proudest in the area; and Richard Nixon campaigned here in 1972. As for the drug traffic, well, that is not in Rio Grande City anyway, noted the *Reporter*, but in the rural areas along the river.

The embattled Rio Grande citizens started talking about raising money to buy advertisements in *Time* and *Newsweek* so they could tell their side of the story.

En Route

A big Winnebago pulled up in front of the Hotel Ringgold the day Norah and I planned to leave town. On the outside a streamer read MCDONALD FOR CONGRESS. Inside the mobile home were Lendy McDonald, a retired veterinarian from Bayview, Texas, near Port Isabel, and his wife. A McDonald rally was scheduled for the courtyard of the Ringgold, and a campaign volunteer was setting out refreshments. The 15th Congressional District, which McDonald hoped to represent, covers fifteen thousand square miles, and includes fifteen counties and parts of two more. Close to 80 percent of the district is Mexican-American, and McDonald spoke no Spanish. His bilingual opponent, Kika de la Garza, from Mission, near McAllen, has represented the area since 1964, and had served in the state legislature for twelve years prior to that.

De la Garza is an old-style South Texas pol, a traditional Democrat who has worked tirelessly on behalf of the district's best interests: banking, oil, and agribusiness. Through the years he has risen to the number-three ranking position on the House Agriculture Committee. Since his first election to Washington, de la Garza has seldom encountered opposition at the polls; McDonald, who had faced de la Garza in the previous election, was ready to try again. This was to be his one Starr County appearance.

The rally attracted a dozen people, lured by a notice in the

Rio Grande *Herald.* The candidate's birthday was that week-end, and all twelve supporters sang "Happy Birthday" to him. When Congressman de la Garza celebrated his birthday a few weeks earlier, his campaign staff gave Mrs. de la Garza a brand-new station wagon. In keeping with the relative strength of the two candidates, at McDonald's birthday party a campaign aide gave Mrs. McDonald a toy car bought at a five and dime.

The crowd chatted until McDonald was ready to deliver his speech. "Everything's going to the migrants or the immigrants or whatever you call them," complained a matronly Mexican-American lady. "There's no money left over for the regular schools."

"Yes," agreed a man next to her. "It's getting so we can't even support ourselves with our own tax money."

A McDonald volunteer asked if I were a voter in the district. He looked glum when I replied negatively, and went on to one of the others.

George Boyle confided that he was a de la Garza supporter —had been for years—but this was a nice opportunity to have people over to the hotel. Certainly the ancient courtyard with its overhanging semitropical plants and cracked-clay fountain was just the spot for a doomed political rally.

McDonald's campaign flier told us he won a Bronze Star and a Purple Heart in World War II, had been married thirty-three years, and was a "well-informed businessman candidate." A 32nd-degree Mason, McDonald believed: "Government can't promise or give you anything that it first doesn't deny or take away from another," and "A government big enough to give you all you want is big enough to take all you have!" He was against abortion. His prior political experience was one term as an alderman for the city of Bayview.

Folding chairs were set up and McDonald addressed the crowd. Even the overhanging plants paused to listen. "Mr. de la Garza didn't let his chair get warm his first term in Congress in 1965 before he voted to take the silver out of our coins," he told us. "Now I'll make you an offer today—I will sell you all of the regular-grade gasoline you want to buy from me at thirty cents a gallon. All I require is that you pay me in pre-1965 dimes, quarters, and half-dollars." The perplexed crowd was not quite sure how this would help the people of Starr County.

"You see," McDonald went on, "those coins are ninety percent silver, and I could take a dollar's worth and turn it around and get *three* dollars at the present rate."

McDonald also didn't like Congress voting itself a cost-of-living pay increase. The candidate announced that his lawyer had drawn up a statement saying that, if he is elected, he will not accept retirement benefits or cost-of-living raises. The money would go instead to charitable organizations in the 15th Congressional District. "And I challenge Mr. de la Garza to match this!"

There are some counties in the 15th District, a McDonald aide admitted, where voters don't even know a Republican is running for office until they read the ballot. Since 1906, when the 15th District started sending Congressmen to Washington, not one Republican has represented it. Old-timers still tell about the election night when precinct workers were busy counting ballots and ran across a Republican vote. This had never happened before in Starr County. They were confused and didn't know what to do. A few minutes later another Republican vote showed up and everyone was relieved. Someone must have voted twice, they figured, and both votes were promptly thrown in the trash.

On Election Day, when Starr County chose between Lendy McDonald and Kika de la Garza, 4,075 votes were cast. McDonald polled 360 of them.

Highway 83 west from Rio Grande City is filled with potholes and lined with mini-marts. Most drivers seemed to use it for demolition-derby practice. We finally bounced into Roma and stopped for a bite to eat to settle our stomachs. Soon after we were seated a man came over and struck up a one-sided conversation, spewing out his feelings about his Mexican neighbors a half-mile away across the bridge. "We're living next to a nation of criminals," he complained. "When we go over there, they take our money. It's a country of, well, bums. I'm trying to be polite." He nodded at Norah. "But when they come over here, why, they expect to be treated like visiting royalty." He forced a bitter laugh and rose to tote up a Mexican customer's bill. He was the cafe's proprietor.

"I had one Mexican woman send her steak back to the kitchen three times. First she wanted it medium-rare. Then she wanted it well-done. Then she wanted it rare. I tell you they're lazy and indolent. A Mexican customs man at the border makes as much as an army major in the interior. If they think you've got money on you, you've had it. I tell you, it's a nation of gangsters."

The classic film *Viva Zapata!*, with Marlon Brando, had been shot in Roma in the early 1950s, and we left the cafe in search of Zapata's ghost. Much of Roma remains as it was when the movie was filmed. We spent an afternoon walking about the town of three thousand, and eventually met Virgilio Guerra, a rancher. Now in his fifties, Guerra had been the stand-in for Marlon Brando. His skin was parched with a crisp burn lining his mouth. His smile looked like the desert floor cracking.

Guerra remembered the filming well. "Elia Kazan, the director, was a hard worker and helpful to everyone. So was Anthony Quinn. But Brando"—Guerra chose his words carefully—"I'll just say he was very dedicated. He would stand over to the side rehearsing his lines, walking back and forth. He was—not unfriendly."

The next morning we left Roma and crossed the bridge to Ciudad Miguel Alemán, which, like San Miguel de Camargo at the Los Ebanos ferry crossing, had changed its name to that of an incumbent president to attract notoriety and federal funds. Prior to 1950, Ciudad Miguel Alemán was known as San Pedro de Roma. Despite the name change, the town of fifteen thousand showed no exceptional signs of prosperity.

In the local schoolyard a man with a pushcart peddled a strange concoction called a *raspa loca,* a crazy sno-cone. This is how to make one: Put some shaved ice in a paper cup. Pour a small spoonful of lemon juice on top and sprinkle chile powder over it. Top it with two dashes of salt. Then repeat: shaved ice, lemon juice, chile powder, and salt. Drink your *raspa loca* through a straw. Five pesos, please.

4

LIFE IN THE PITS

AT THE OPENING weekend of Ciudad Miguel Alemán's annual *feria,* or "fair," the *torneo de gallos* was drawing cockfight fans from both sides of the border. Fully a third of the *torneo* spectators were *norteamericanos* who crossed over to watch roosters do battle where the fights are sanctioned and open. A Mexican cockfight is a welcome respite from the clandestine matches staged north of the border, where all but a handful of states have outlawed the sport.

By ten-thirty in the evening, a half-hour after the cocks from Aldama, Tamaulipas, and San Antonio, Texas, were scheduled to start fighting, the contestant from Tamaulipas was anxious to begin. His Texan opponent was still three miles away, delayed at the Mexican port-of-entry. The Tamaulipas man tugged at his cowboy hat. "The trouble with fighting against roosters from the United States is that you never know if they'll make it to the *palenque.*" He smiled and clucked. "Obviously someone didn't pay somebody off."

At last, officials announced, the man from San Antonio was on his way. The crowd, some three hundred strong, increased its bets on the fight. A prefight raffle was in progress, and my neighbor signaled the nearest *corredor* over to buy a ticket. A white-haired man with baggy pants and dark glasses approached, an elephantine arm reaching out for her hundred pesos. He wore red plastic badge "no. 17." Like the other runners, no. 17 kept busy trotting around the grandstands collecting money from bettors. Within minutes all twelve tickets for this raffle were sold. The chief *corredor* picked up a plastic Clorox jug, shook up the dozen dice inside it, and asked a young señorita at ringside to take one of them out. She handed him die number seven which he held aloft. *"¡Siete! ¡Numero Siete!"* Two rows back a quiet fellow with a glint in his eyes and a Fiesta in his mouth raised his hand slightly. He was a thousand pesos richer. My neighbor held ticket number four. Another hundred pesos down the drain.

The man from San Antonio arrived at last. He and his handler, Roberto Ochoa, quickly picked out their strongest and prettiest bird for the first match. José García, a youthful handler working for the man from Tamaulipas, studied his opponent's *gallo,* a red one with pretty yellow feathers toward the tail. At weigh-in, San Antonio's cock was a few grams heavier than the maximum allowed weight. Tamaulipas had an option: he could accept the overweight American bird as his opponent or insist on a trimmer rooster. "Hah, in the United States the cockfighters fatten the roosters up for the matches," he laughed. "Not here. We keep ours in trim fighting condition." He refused to fight the fat one.

Each finally had his bird selected and outfitted with *navajas,* sharp spurlike gaffs which fit onto the left leg. García cradled his bird affectionately as though it were a baby, whispering in its ear while eyeing its opponent. The crowd placed final bets on the match—winning bettors collect double their money less 20 percent split between the *corredor* and the house—and an eight-piece *mariachi* band sitting in the grandstand honked its last notes.

The two cocks were anxious to flex their wings as they were placed on opposite sides of a white square painted in the middle of the dirt ring. The bird from San Antonio, a healthy-looking rooster with green plumage, jumped first, flaring five feet in the air, its left leg swinging. The crowd erupted with an appreciative roar, and the Tamaulipas bird leaped up, its red feathers spreading full span. Ochoa was nearby coaxing his bird. García stood off to the side watching intently. San Antonio's bird sliced its left leg to Tamaulipas' midriff. A cheer went up as a few red feathers floated to the floor. Tamaulipas returned with a left to San Antonio's side, barely missing. Both birds fluttered back to the ground. Tamaulipas bowed his head slightly, giving San Antonio an opening. San Antonio took advantage of this, pecking away at Tamaulipas' skull with a dull *rat-a-tat-tat* sound. The injured bird slowly lifted its beak to retaliate, but his attacker sidestepped him. Tamaulipas sat motionless, a red feather in his mouth. San Antonio resumed pecking around the neck. Tamaulipas lay on the ground, stunned and helpless, his beak pointed down. San Antonio sensed victory and strutted about, pausing every few steps to peck at his defenseless opponent. Gamblers who had bet on San Antonio also sensed victory and shouted for the referee to stop the match. Tamaulipas lay still. San Antonio won by a knockout.

José García, his eyes slightly moist, stooped to pick up his bird. He held it by the tail, and as he walked away a few drops of blood fell from the dying loser. A respectful moment of silence followed in which all movement subsided, as if the scene were slow-motion frames from a movie. The *ritard* ended abruptly as the *mariachi* band cranked up and *corredores* ran through the aisles paying off winning bets.

As in many Mexican towns, Ciudad Miguel Alemán's *torneo de gallos* comes only once a year. To gain the cooperation of law enforcement agencies, a sum of money is passed from the promoters to various officials—local and federal. At a recent *torneo de gallos* in Cuernavaca, fifty-five miles from Mexico City, someone did not get his *mordida*. Halfway through the second fight *federales* raided the *palenque* with drawn guns. The Cuernavaca police, who outnumbered the *federales*, pulled out their weapons to drive off the raiders, when suddenly the doors swung open and federal reinforcements rushed in and overpowered the local cops. In the end the *federales* seized the birds from the *galleros* and the night's bets from the *corredores*.

The *torneo* continued the next night with protection by the *federales.*

Manuel Ramírez, the tournament judge at Ciudad Miguel Alemán, waits until all such arrangements are complete before starting his own work. Ramírez drives from *torneo* to *torneo* in his '68 Chevy, hauling the public address system and the scales and weights. As the judge, he is the final authority on each fight, six nights a week, ten months a year. A well-respected man on the borderland cockfighting circuit, Ramírez enforces rules regulating the size of lethal *navajas,* when to take time-outs, and when to end a fight.

"The rules are easy," the Matamoros native explained. "If one bird is in bad shape and keeps running from the other, he loses; if one bird doesn't peck back after being attacked, he loses; if one rests his beak on the ground and doesn't budge, he loses. But the main rule is the simplest—if one *gallo* dies, the fight is over.

"Tonight we are seeing some very spirited roosters, but they aren't the best. In two weeks we go to Reynosa. They have one of the biggest *palenques* on the border and always get the best cocks from both sides of the Rio Grande. This season I've already been to Monterrey, Río Bravo, Piedras Negras, Ciudad Acuña, Durango, and Ciudad Juárez." Ramírez looked up and smiled. "By now my car is a real *jonke.*"

While Ramírez weighed in the birds for the second match, I mentioned that I was planning to lay a hundred pesos on San Antonio's second bird. The judge nodded his head and smiled. "That would be a good bet."

The fight started slowly as the brightly colored rooster from Tamaulipas smothered the dark cock from San Antonio with its wing. They embraced for two minutes, seemingly falling asleep. Ramírez called for a time-out. When the *gallos* took up again, the dark cock leaped up in a spurt of activity pecking at the bright bird's neck. He kept at it, sitting prey over Tamaulipas until both birds, exhausted, lay in the middle of the pit breathing heavily. Their beady eyes peered around at the audience. "You're betting on *us?*" they seemed to say. "You're crazier than we are!" Ramírez called for another time-out.

When the birds squared off again, the *presidente,* or mayor, of Nuevo Laredo weaved around in his front-row seat cheering on first one bird, then the other. Tamaulipas got distracted by a beetle crawling by and paused to play with it. When *gallos* are face to face, they slice, claw, and peck at each other ferociously. Out of each other's eyesight, however, they walk around like the dumb chickens they are. The dark bird finally spotted Tamaulipas and fluttered back to the fray, vigorously pecking at his weaker opponent's shoulder. The bright bird tried to fight back, but his efforts were blocked by San Antonio's wing. Tamaulipas slowly lifted his head. Blood was oozing out of an opening in his neck. One more peck from San Antonio and he slowly lowered his beak for the last time. The judge announced the winner, and the requisite respectful silence was punctured by a blare of horns. Raúl, the pit-sweeper, came in to brush away the feathers. His broom turned the small puddles of blood into long red streaks. As my *corredor* handed me 180 pesos, Judge Ramírez winked.

Back where the weigh-ins took place a camp-follower who traveled the *torneo* circuit selling *navajas* and other cockfighting paraphernalia wandered about with a jewelry display case exhibiting his wares. The young man from Mexico City carried hundreds of sharp spurs with him, selling some to Roberto Ochoa, San Antonio's handler, and other cockfighters who came to the match looking for tools of the trade. During the break between fights, the queen of the *feria* entered the *palenque* in a silk gown, her glittering crown slightly askew. She strolled down to the center of the pit, with its cigarette butts, ripped-up betting tickets, scattered feathers, and streaks of chicken blood. In true beauty-queen fashion, she smiled and waved lightly to the crowd and took her seat at ringside.

The third match was over at two in the morning. The *torneo* had assumed a rhythm of its own, with gamblers, *corredores,* cockfighters, and cocks alternately active and sedate. Raúl swept the floor once more, missing a few feathers here and a

few puddles of blood there. And that was when Reynaldo Martínez strolled on stage. Martínez, who was wearing a *charro*
outfit of ceremonial cowboy clothes, is a popular Mexican singer
best known for his ballads about cockfighting. He is called "El
Gallero." As he started his most popular song, "El Hijo del
Palenque," the crowd cheered madly. Martínez followed his hit
with a *corrido* about a man who was in a gunfight in Mexico, fled
injured to the United States, and eventually returned home
healthy. The subject of the *corrido* happened to be attending
the *torneo* that night, and as Martínez excitedly introduced
him, the man stood and waved to the cheering crowd much as
a retired champion might at a boxing match. Not every day
does the hero of a *corrido* hear his praises sung. After a couple
more songs, Martínez left the pit, but the crowd yelled out for
more. "*¡Otro! ¡Otro!*" El Gallero returned to sing one last number.

The entertainment continued with Olivia Campos, another
popular singer on the Mexican cockfight circuit. With her red
lace, floor-length chiffon gown dragging through the rubble,
Olivia teased the boisterous crowd *coochi-coo*ing her way
around the pit. One man leaped over the railing and ran up to
kiss her, much to the delight of the drunken spectators.

The finale was Danny, a comedian who specializes in *torneos*.
Sporting a wide-brimmed sombrero and a foot-long paste-on
mustache, Danny lip-synched a song about a *gallero* while a
scratchy record played over the public address system. He held
a cotton doll of a chicken, first pummeling it, then dancing with
it, and finally singing to it. Danny's closing number was a female
impersonation. Donning a wig and makeup, he swished about
the pit lip-synching another song while the audience howled its
appreciation. What else was there to do at a border-town
cockfight at three in the morning?

As dawn came to Ciudad Miguel Alemán, the *torneo* drew to
a close. Final score: San Antonio, four; Tamaulipas, two. Twelve
more cocks would repeat the ceremony that night, and every
night that week. El Gallero, Olivia Campos, and Danny would

entertain again, and another houseful of rambunctious fans would wager thousands more pesos. Before leaving the arena, I stopped to ask José García, the cock handler for Tamaulipas, what happens to the *gallos* who lose. José, who had been tender and loving toward his birds, looked up with a crooked smile. "Tomorrow we will sell them to restaurants for thirty pesos each. They make good enchiladas."

En Route

We took the highway west from Roma, stopping briefly to cross over Falcon Dam. Built in the early 1950s as a hydroelectric plant and flood control device, the dam creates a huge reservoir used for boating, fishing, smuggling, and other recreational activities. To run such an enormous operation requires technicians, engineers, and bureaucrats on both sides of the border. The workers at Falcon Dam live in two colonies: the community on the U.S. side is Falcon Heights, and on the Mexican side, Nuevo Guerrero. Nuevo Guerrero was founded in 1950 when its antecedent, Guerrero, was slated to be flooded by the Falcon Reservoir. With none of the history and architecture characterizing other Mexican border towns, Nuevo Guerrero was a dull place indeed. A lottery outlet? There was none. Red-light district? They use Ciudad Miguel Alemán's. Even the activity in the streets was suspicious: workmen were actually repairing potholes. Nuevo Guerrero was obviously not a genuine border town. Norah and I left without further investigation.

As we headed north, highway signs for Laredo punctuated Route 83, prompting a dozen original verses to "The Streets of Laredo"—verses which Norah did not find nearly as amusing as I did. The main nuisance on the road, however, was not my singing, or crazed drivers or itchy cops. It was butterflies: tens of thousands of big, beautiful, gently gliding butterflies. Colorful suicidal butterflies, dive-bombing into the windshield and radiator by the droves. From out of nowhere, countless creatures of splendor and grace splattered before my eyes. I looked for

Mauricio Babilonia, the handsome mechanic in García Márquez's *One Hundred Years of Solitude*, whose presence was always preceded by swarms of yellow butterflies, but he was nowhere to be seen. Within a few minutes the butterflies became so thick that I had to stop and peel them by their delicate dead little wings off the windshield and out of the grille.

In the mid-nineteenth century two U.S. surveying teams passed through the area in an effort to chart the newly established boundary. The first came shortly after the American invasion of Mexico and the subsequent Treaty of Guadalupe Hidalgo in 1848. John Russell Bartlett, an adventuresome Rhode Island scholar, was in charge of the survey commission. While his crew trudged through the lowlands and deserts on foot, donkey, and horse, Bartlett traveled by carriage with a retinue of valets, cooks, and other servants, alienating both his own staff and many Mexicans with his aristocratic manner. He often strayed far from his assigned duty, taking off for months at a time visiting cities as distant as Acapulco to the south and San Francisco to the north, and abandoning his crew to suffer on the frontier, often without salary. A few of his men contracted yellow fever. One drowned in the Rio Grande.

During his border journey Bartlett refused to accept cultural differences. His description of a chance encounter was typical of his attitude:

"We met some Mexicans, from whom we inquired the distance. Wishing also to obtain some information relative to the products and population of the country, we asked, 'How many people are there in Chinapi?' The reply was *'Bastante.'* Enough.

" 'How many are enough?'

" *'Quién sabe?'* Who knows?

"In my intercourse and journeying with the lower classes of Mexicans, these same replies have been given to me a hundred times. Had I asked if the place contained five hundred people, the answer probably would have been, *'Quizás.'* Perhaps. But when they don't know what to answer, the universal reply is

'*Quién sabe?*' The proper expression, '*No sé,*' I don't know, is rarely heard."

By the time Bartlett had spent all his allotted money, he had not only failed to complete the boundary marking but had misplaced the border in the area just west of present-day El Paso, inadvertently ceding valuable land to Mexico. He was not a popular man.

The Gadsden Purchase of 1853, in which Mexico sold the strip of land along southern New Mexico, Arizona, and California to the United States, again changed the boundary. This time an experienced surveyor, William H. Emory, was dispatched to mark the line. Emory, a West Point graduate, had served as Bartlett's assistant and was already familiar with the borderland. His own work traveling the frontier was completed in Franklin Pierce's administration. Far more than Bartlett, Emory appreciated that the border served as a cultural membrane as well as a political delineation. "The boundary between the United States and Mexico is here only an imaginary line running down the center of the river," he observed, "and an offence can be committed on either side with impunity. A few minutes served to place the offender over the line, when the jealousies of the law on either side step in to protect him; and where national prejudices are involved, the criminal is not infrequently extolled for his exploits."

Emory and his staff maintained impressive diaries of their journey which even today give valuable insight into the land, the people, and the natural wildlife. And Bartlett? For a surveyor, he was an excellent writer. His New England sensibilities contrasted so sharply with the frontier environment that his published recollection of the borderland remains a classic in travel literature.

5

DISCREETS OF LAREDO

"I WORK in a small retail store. Someone comes in and buys twenty television sets. He pays cash, he gets a sales receipt, everything is clean. But he wants the TVs smuggled into Mexico, so he brings them to a man in town who seals them in a boxcar headed for Mexico City. I know the man smuggles because I deliver the goods to him. That's what I do for a living —I help Mexican shoppers get their purchases into Mexico."

The short man with the skin problem was explaining the facts of life, Laredo style. He had lived there since birth, seen generations of stagnant poverty among the townfolk, seen the wealth grow among the nouveau merchant class. Like so many others in this town of ninety-two thousand, he recognizes that shipping consumer goods into Mexico, in violation of that country's laws, can be a lucrative enterprise, condoned and even encouraged by pillars of the community. Mexicans spend so much money in Laredo that the city, whose residents earn among the lowest wages in the United States, ranks among the very highest in per capita retail sales. Mexican shoppers generally prefer U.S. products—televisions, clothing, stereos, appliances, blenders, furniture, cameras—to homemade ones. Superior American technology usually means a longer product life span. Many consumer goods are simply not manufactured in Mexico at all. Additionally, Mexican consumers often attach status to American products even if a similar item is available in-country. As the American town most accessible to the greatest number of Mexicans, Laredo, Texas, has become Mexico's shopping center.

Smuggling goods into Mexico is commonplace because of the prohibitively high import duties imposed by that country's government. The complex and well-established pipeline of Mexican smugglers imports items not only by freight train but over major highways as well. *Aduana*—customs—officials throughout the Republic receive systematic payoffs in the process. For Laredo merchants to sell goods to Mexican customers is perfectly legal. The merchandise becomes contraband only when it enters Mexico untaxed. Smuggled goods are called *fayuca*.

J. C. Penney, 80 percent of whose business is from Mexico, is located in River Drive Mall, a downtown shopping center virtually on the banks of the Rio Grande. *Chiveras*, or smugglers (literally, goatherds), come to town with shopping lists for a dozen or so families and fill the Penney's parking lot in the afternoons. They take their purchases out of the store wrappings and rip out any tags indicating they are new. Often clothes are worn immediately, two and sometimes three layers at a time. More clothes are crammed into suitcases—also just purchased for the return trip. The rest is concealed from the *aduana* in door panels, under seat covers, beneath trunk liners, and elsewhere. At La Posada, the city's best hotel, high-volume *chiveras* convert their rooms to warehouses, storing clothes for the return trip to the interior. Paper bags from shops all over town litter the hotel's hallways.

When the bridge is "tight"—that is, when high customs officials from Mexico are in town to monitor their underlings— Laredo department stores such as Montgomery Ward will keep purchased appliances destined for the interior until the situation returns to normal. Sales clerks and *chiveras* throughout the city maintain a cozy relationship, each profiting from the other. In Laredo, clandestine activity is business as usual. The town has become an American Andorra.

To spot the *chiveras,* simply cross the International Bridge to Nuevo Laredo and watch Mexicans pass their own customs.

Shoppers on foot carrying paper bags of new purchases often leave a ten- or twenty-peso note on top as *mordida*, which is considered nothing more than a gift to speed things along. The *aduana* pocket the money, nod slightly, and move on to the next person.

Enrico, a friend from Monterrey, 150 miles south of Laredo, explained how the game is played when driving home. "You have to pull around to the rear of the port building where the *aduana* go through your luggage pretending they're looking for *fayuca*. Actually they are looking for their money. It's best to leave the *mordida* on top so they don't mess up your suitcase. For a little two hundred dollar television set, the *aduana* may get fifty dollars, but the total expense is still cheaper than buying a similar set in Mexico. Another *aduana* checkpoint is at twenty-six kilometers out, and another one as you drive into Monterrey. If Mexico City is the destination, there may be ten or twelve *aduana* payoffs along the way. The government is very lenient about this. These customs men retire very well."

Enrico's observations had historical precedent. John Russell Bartlett, the U.S. survey commissioner who traveled the border in the mid-nineteenth century, noted that "the duty . . . imposed by Mexico on many items of merchandise amounts to a prohibition. Yet owing to the laxity of customhouse officials, the law has been evaded, and goods regularly admitted at a nominal rate. Each collector knows that if he exacts the legal duty, either the merchandise will be smuggled in or some brother-collector, less conscientious and anxious to pocket the fees, will be ready to compound for a smaller sum. It accordingly became the practice . . . to admit merchandise for the interior of Mexico by paying five hundred dollars on each wagon load."

In one major appliance store a twenty-four–inch color console television was tagged at $1,125. The store manager said he could deliver the set to Monterrey for another $315. "The bridge is still tight," he lamented. "When it loosens up, here's how we'll do it: You pay for the set here and we give you the receipt. When our *chivera* gets ready to deliver in Monterrey, he'll call you and you pay him the delivery cost. If the television is confiscated, we'll send out another one. We guarantee delivery."

In an office supply shop the story was similar. A new office-model electric typewriter cost $825. "Oh, you want it sent to Mexico? That will be an extra one hundred fifty dollars. Delivery guaranteed."

The pattern repeated itself in store after store. Each had its own *chivera*, each guaranteed delivery, and each undercut the legal Mexican price. At one store a salesman apologized that he had to delay smuggling because a new customs man was being broken in at the *aduana* station and the *chivera* had to negotiate his contract.

"A friend of mine works in a discount store," recounted John Speer, part-owner of an electronics store. "A Mexican wholesaler put in an order for Polaroid film—a quarter of a million dollars' worth. An order that size in any type of business here is not unusual, because Mexican storeowners treat our shops like showrooms, ordering in bulk from demonstrator models on the shelves. A Mexican businessman may go into one store and ask what the price is on a nineteen-inch Sony color television. Let's say it's four hundred fifty dollars. He'll say, 'OK, what's *my* price?' The merchant will say three hundred seventy-five dollars. Then the businessman says, 'How about if I buy ten of them?' And the salesman will lower his price another fifty dollars. So the man from Mexico says, 'Fine. I'll take two at three hundred twenty-five dollars.' Then it's up to the merchant to decide if he'll let it go at that. The way things are on the border these days, he will. It's a *chivera*'s market."

The "illegal permit" method is another way to smuggle goods into Mexico. The permits are available only through very special connections in the upper echelons of the *aduana* and cost a great deal, but they guarantee the *chivera* complete passage for his goods from border to destination, rather like prepaying a year's worth of bribes in one lump sum. The *chivera* is no longer smuggling. He has, in effect, legal contraband. One merchant whose *chivera* had just secured an illegal permit estimated that his sales would increase by $1 million annually as a result.

Storefronts on Convent Street, a narrow, seedy-looking thoroughfare running north from the International Bridge, give the impression that the shops have seen better days. The looks are deceiving. Convent Street real estate is among the most valuable in Texas. Business in the ten-block area adjacent to the bridge is so phenomenal that local realtors can't even recall the last land transaction there. Time and again, community boosters brag, "There's nothing you can buy in Paris or New York that you can't find in Laredo." A few stores stock only perfume and do very well. Even Gucci has a Laredo outlet. The city's leading haberdashery, Joe Brand, chauffeurs its well-heeled Mexican customers around in a Rolls-Royce.

Mexicans come to Laredo thinking they are getting top quality, unaware that most of the large chain department stores use the border area as a dumping ground for irregular items. In-country advertising creates consumer demand, then shoppers come to the United States and buy. "A good example is Yashica cameras," explained John Speer. "You can't *give* them away in Dallas or Houston, but because they're so well promoted in Mexico, Yashica does an incredible business in Laredo."

Speer's method of shipping new televisions into Mexico is foolproof. Instead of being paid off to allow his goods past the checkpoints, *aduana* officers come into his store and drive the merchandise back into Mexico themselves. When the purchaser tells Speer the goods have arrived at the destination, he pays the customs men their delivery fee. "Because the *aduana* is involved from the point of origin, no intermediary payoffs are necessary. I deal only with the *jefes,* the chiefs. Some very high officials are involved in this."

Of the $4 million worth of television sets that were exported from Laredo to Mexico in 1978, approximately $2.8 million was from smuggled sales. More than half of the contraband television sets went overland; the rest went by air. Flying contraband into Mexico from Laredo necessitates only a willing pilot and a safe landing strip. Because the goods are flying over all the payoff points, smuggling by air is actually cheaper than by land. One businessman who lives near the airport boasted that he can gauge Laredo's economy by how many Beech-18s and DC-3s he hears taking off.

Another merchant shed light on the air-smuggling operations. "There's a pilots' association, sort of like a club," she explained. "They'll fly goods anywhere you pay them to. The fellow I use makes the rounds of all his shops and then drives out to the airport for shipping, sort of like UPS delivery service."

At the airport a youthful pilot offered a guided tour. "This smuggling business can be dangerous unless everyone is square with each other," he confided as we drove down the tarmac. "The merchants tend to overload the planes because that's where the money is. See that one?" Before us was a grounded Twin Beech with both engines burned out. "One of the downtown merchants packed that sonuvabitch so tight that when it got about fifty feet in the air it stalled and came down—fortunately no one was hurt. But there's such a profit margin on these flights that businessmen can afford to lose a load now and then."

We drove past another plane which had had trouble, too. The right side of a Lockheed Lodestar—an old World War II bomber—was buckled under and the wheel caved in. The propeller was damaged and the right wing tip was dented. By the time investigators reached the plane shortly after the crash, all the merchandise had been removed.

"These pilots establish their own landing strips in deserts, on mountaintops, in the jungle, and on the plains. You can usually tell where the planes have been by the type of soil they pick up. For instance, if there's good red dirt on the wheels and belly, I'd guess that plane touched down north by northeast of Guadalajara. You get to learn these things after a while."

A pilot flying a single-engine plane can clear $800 for a ninety-minute trip. Twin-engine pilots earn more, and sometimes make two trips a day. The Beech-18 is the best plane to use, my guide related, because of its agility and capacity. The biggest aircraft in the smuggling service is a DC-3 cargo plane.

My guide seemed just the type to fly cargo into Mexico at a moment's notice. "No way. No way! You couldn't get me to do that in a million years." He was emphatic. "These guys—their lives are on the line virtually from the moment they start their engines. The plane may not be in good condition. Going into Mexico they could get caught. The plane could crash and they'd have nowhere to go. So many people are involved in each trip a pilot never knows if someone's going to betray him. They're either crazy or without brains. I've been approached more than once—a guy puts five hundred dollars in front of me for a thirty-minute hop. It's awful hard to say no, but I've never gotten involved. I don't have fuzzy enough nuts to do it."

A Mexican newspaper story told about one who did:

AMERICAN PLANE LOADED WITH CONTRABAND SHOT DOWN
OVER JALISCO—ONE DEAD

A small private American plane coming from Laredo, Texas, loaded with contraband televisions, tape recorders, and other electronic goods, was shot down in Jalisco last week, and the pilot died, authorities said. The U.S. Consulate in Guadalajara, the capital of Jalisco, refused to identify the dead man. Captain Carlos Fierro, Military Commander of the Guadalajara airport, said the twin-engine Beechcraft crash-landed completely in flames forty meters from a small country airstrip called Pacama. Nothing was left except the tail. The pilot burned to death. . . .

The man U.S. authorities refused to identify was retired Air Force Colonel Phil Willer, a pilot who first learned the smuggling business while stationed at Laredo Air Force Base, which closed in 1973. The man most knowledgeable about Willer's activities was a Treasury agent who had been monitoring smuggling out of the Lower Rio Grande Valley. When I visited his office he pulled out a thick stack of classified files on Willer and every other big-time smuggler. "There's a merchant in downtown Laredo who deals in volume televisions," he said, reaching for a photograph. "That's his brother-in-law there unloading a plane full of contraband in Mexico. He runs a store in San Luis Potosí.

"A lot of these pilots are ex-mercenaries who've flown for the CIA and Air America. When there's no war going on they smuggle goods south of the border. We did learn one new thing about Willer after his crash: the lab analysis on his plane showed traces of marijuana. Evidently he was carrying freight both ways."

The official Mexican position against contraband is that if smuggling were reduced, more Mexicans would buy in-country products. The result would be more money in the economy, more manufacturing, more retail sales outlets, and less unemployment. With more people working, fewer would be tempted to migrate to the United States in search of work.

To reduce flagrant violations of its laws, the *aduana* service is ridding itself of a few obvious smugglers within its own ranks. To investigate its own men, the *aduana* service uses *volantes,* customs inspectors who travel in unmarked vehicles, as mobile checkpoints on Mexican highways. "The *volantes,* they are more honest—that is to say, they are more difficult to bribe," one middle-class Mexican smiled. "It is ironic that smuggling helps individual Mexicans but hurts the country's economy as a whole. But we don't doubt that in the future, our technology will be as good as America's, and smuggling will no longer be necessary."

Emilio Reyes Flores is the number two man at the Zona Aduana Fiscal de Nuevo Laredo. The *subjefe,* whose office is next to the railroad tracks on the west side of town, was dressed in the height of fashion with a well-cut three-piece suit and alligator-skin boots. Hundreds of truck drivers and others needing his approval on import-export documents formed a line winding from his desk through his office, out the door, and down the hall. Before approaching Reyes' desk, each person left a few pesos with a man seated to the side, apparently a prerequisite to a fleeting audience with the *subjefe.* As Reyes initialed each form with a flourish, an aide would dramatically present him with the next.

"It is the uneducated who buy products in America," Reyes

offered between pen strokes. "They are under the impression that American products are superior. They go to Penney's or Joe Brand or Frost Brothers and the American merchants give them credit. They can put a few dollars down on almost everything."

The line grew longer and longer. A haggard old lady inched her way to the front and begged Reyes to grant her a permit to bring American goods into the Republic. A phone call interrupted her plea, and the *subjefe* engaged in animated conversation while his assistant proffered more forms for his initials. He slowed down once when a man in an officer's uniform came in to whisper in his ear. Reyes arched his eyebrows and nodded sagely. The man smiled and departed. The old lady stood patiently to the side, ignored.

"We have two aircraft at San Luis Potosí which we use to combat this aerial smuggling," Reyes went on. "Our men are getting better training now than they used to, and we have internal investigations going on constantly. We fire the men who are getting *mordida.*"

Before leaving, I complimented Reyes on his suit and asked where he bought it. Flattered, he pulled back the lapel to show me the label. The inside right pocket said:

JOE BRAND
Laredo, Texas

Everywhere I went they talked of the Silver-haired Fox, one of the pioneer air smugglers in the 1940s. Over the years he piloted every type of craft under the worst of conditions. He could take off on a dime and land on a peso. Was a stunt flier in Hollywood years ago. Started the cargo-smuggling business in the sixties. Been locked up in a Mexican jail for his troubles and lived to tell about it. There's never been anyone like him, all right. Retired Christmas 1977, but he still comes around. Full of piss and vinegar. A legend in his own time.

I wanted to meet him.

Our plane had just crossed the Rio Grande and was gaining altitude. Behind us lay the United States. Spread out on all sides was Mexico. The Silver-haired Fox, George Gibson, now in his fifties, was flying me to some of his old landing strips. "We're now officially wetbacks!" he called back from the cockpit. A lively character who looks something like Kris Kringle, Gibson was in a mood to reminisce about his years as a *contrabandista.* The southwestern outskirts of Nuevo Laredo passed below as he began.

"I learned to fly in World War II. When I went back to southern California after the war there was an opportunity to bring lobsters out of Baja California. The fishermen always had lots more lobsters than they could sell through their regular channels, so I started buying some and flying them into California where lobster fishing wasn't allowed certain times of the year. I had my own connections, and my fishermen would supply only me. They were always so amazed that this gringo would come out of the sky and land near their village. 'Long about 1950 the California Fish and Game people busted me for bringing in lobster out of season! I told them that the season only applied to *their* coast, not Mexico's, but they wouldn't go along with that. So I moved to Las Vegas and continued. Word got around, and by 1954 there were too many lobster smugglers and they began to take the business far too seriously. There were shoot-'em-ups. I didn't want any part of it."

We were at five thousand feet and rising. The inside of the plane had a deafening rattle. The exterior paint job was vintage Korean War—natural camouflage, Gibson called it. He spoke with confidence.

"The world mercury market was going good, so through some contacts I got into the mercury business in the state of Zacatecas. I moved more black-market mercury than anyone." Gibson brought seventy-four pound flasks from his mines and sold them to New York mercury brokers at enormous profits. "I even had U.S. government pilots moonlighting for me.

"Every time I went back for more mercury, the miners would give me money and ask me to bring back little things like clothes or a camera. Their shopping list got so long I finally had to pay someone to take care of it for me. Later I learned that the guys in Zacatecas would turn around and resell the stuff I'd be bringing them and they'd be making a profit on it!

"Well, mercury was a good racket while it lasted. Then the goddamn Mexican government came in and took over.

"By the 1960s I had developed landing strips everywhere in Mexico, and merchants in Brownsville, McAllen, and all over the Rio Grande Valley started calling. They'd say, 'Oh, Mr. Gibson, we'd sure like to meet you. We have some merchandise we must move into Mexico.' So I got started in the cargo business—at the time I was the only one. My first few runs were clothing and Persian rugs. For a while I was carrying hardware items—drill bits, diesel parts, that type of stuff. Now the only cargo which carries enough of a margin of profit to make the flights worthwhile is electronics."

We were halfway to the first site cruising at ten thousand feet. "The key to the whole thing is your landing strips," Gibson went on. "You need good, secure, isolated landing strips that are technically adequate to handle whatever type of craft you want to put on them. I figure I've established more than thirty strips in Mexico.

"The first thing I do is go down and tap the ground with the landing gear to test the firmness and buzz it a few times to see if I can get in real tight. If the strip is all right, I land and walk around to test it. Sometimes I have to move some brush. The next step is to find the nearest paved highway and see if any *aduana* checkpoints are close. The people who live near the strips pretty much mind their own business. They don't like officialdom any more than I do. Most of them are pure Indian."

We cleared the last mountain range and began our descent. "Each one of my flights was prearranged by telephone, but once I was in the air my receiver and I would have a signal in case anything went wrong at the last minute. If the hood of his truck was up, I'd go back. The one time I didn't pay attention was the one time I got busted.

"I was flying in Christmas tree lights. For some reason stores in Mexico don't stock them and every fall we fly down thousands of boxes of the darned things. Anyway, I was set up by a man in Laredo because I refused to haul his freight. As soon as I landed I was surrounded by Mexican authorities with machine guns. But the plane was stuffed to the gills and I couldn't get out of the cockpit—as a result *I* had to fly it out so *they* could put *me* in custody. They had me for seven months and eight days. I was released in May, 1973."

The first strip of the day finally came into view. A finger of land jutted out next to a ranch house. Gibson turned in for a final approach.

"See those trees over there?" Two mesquite grew side by side. "The taller one is my target. The strip runs diagonal to it. I usually taxi over to those bushes and land right there."

We skimmed the ground at three feet going 130 miles an hour. "The strip looks a little damp today, we might get stuck in the mud." Instead of landing we S-looped around and turned south.

"I had a deal with some officials in Guadalajara, some years ago," Gibson continued as we gained altitude. One fellow was the *aduana comandante* of the zone and his partner was the *jefe* of the judicial federal police in the area. The head of the *aduana* would meet me at the airport in uniform, have one of his aides park me, and the federal police would unload the contraband. The *jefe* at the airport would drive me to the Fenix Hotel where I had my own suite and the run of the bar. I liked dealing with officials that way."

The second strip we visited was a dry lake bed. Once when George was about to land there he discovered wider tire tracks on the ground than those from his plane. Empty ammunition boxes lay next to nearby bushes. Someone had discovered the strip and was using it for himself. George stopped landing there for a month. When he came back the hull of a burned-out DC-3 rested at the far end of the strip. "I could tell someone had come in all wrong and couldn't get out. Well, if the plane had been seized by the Mexican government, the owners never would have collected insurance money. So they torched it." We circled again to catch a glimpse of the hull and returned to cruising altitude. We were north of Torreón where George had more landing strips, but darkness was approaching. We headed back.

"I don't know why you keep calling me a smuggler," the Fox said after a silence. "I'm an exporter. I'm not a smuggler until I cross the border. On the U.S. side I'm a law-abiding citizen. The general image of a smuggler is a dope runner. I'm very down on drugs.

"I got out of the cargo business a while back, but I understand last year at McAllen there was practically open warfare. A new breed of cat has gotten into the business and I don't particularly care to associate with them. They have no sense of honor. They don't have the expertise to fly some of these planes and they're strictly in it for the bucks. There's no *esprit de corps* left. Greed and avariciousness have taken over."

The Fox's face beamed with pride. "To me it was more than money. I liked walking a tightrope. I figure I've flown over three thousand cargo runs and I earned a good living doing it. I called my own shots. By now there're probably fifty pilots from San Diego to Brownsville in this line of work."

We touched down at Laredo International Airport a short time later. On the way back to town a twinkle flashed in his eyes. "I still might move a little freight if the conditions are right. I admit it. I miss it. I like being up in the air looking around. To me, that's the biggest kick of this whole business."

En Route

"Oh, life," wrote Graham Greene about Laredo in "Across the Bridge." "That begins on the other side." And so I crossed over to find life. My guide was Joe Harmes, a local reporter. Our first mission in Nuevo Laredo was to find Carlos, who, by day, was an instructor at Laredo Junior College and who, by night, was a crazed and serious barhopper. Carlos was the embodiment of borderland brilliance, a backsliding philosophic *sabelotodo*, a know-it-all, who reduced the world to a belch while pontificating on its problems. "Just meet me in Nuevo

Laredo," he exclaimed when we tried to make arrangements.

"Where?" we asked.

"You'll find me. Ask around."

We drove up Guerrero Street stopping at different bars until we got to La Cava. Carlos was sitting at a booth on the far wall waving his arms about, making an existential point about dope-dealing. His companions were two Anglos from Laredo and a Nuevo Laredo friend. In the space of twenty minutes Carlos managed to conquer all of South America, dissolve the Catholic church, and corner the black market on every conceivable herb.

Soon the party spilled into the street where we split up into two cars. A friend was attending a wedding reception at the Club Leones and we agreed to meet there. As we were about to pull away, Carlos walked over. "Listen you fuckin' *chingados,*" he whispered furtively. "I can't bring these guys with me. I don't know how much more of them I can take. The line isn't drawn at Mexican versus American anymore"—he glanced across the street at his passengers—"it's Christian versus pagan, and these guys have no idea what it's like to be a pagan. Let me dump these Christians at the bridge. I'll meet you at the reception."

Carlos aimed his car toward the border while we drove off to the Club Leones. The club was filled with some five hundred drinking and dancing celebrants in elegant evening gowns and tuxedos. We found our friend just as the bride was tossing her flowers to the women clustered about her. The upper crust of Nuevo Laredo and Laredo society was in attendance.

Earlier in the day Gary Payne, manager of the Laredo Chamber of Commerce, had explained the social levels. "It's like fifteenth-century England, the way people are aware of their class on the border," he said. "In Laredo the high class doesn't recognize the low class. A middle class is developing, but it is still very small."

Laredo, like many other South Texas communities, was for generations run under the *patrón* system in which elections, salaries, employment, law, and order are controlled by one family. Laredo's mayor and *patrón* had been Pepe Martin, who in 1978 was convicted on federal mail fraud charges. As the Martin dynasty crumbled, the Sanchez family, which had been in the typewriter repair business, struck oil on leased land. Once the Sanchezes were millionaires, they became a force to rival the Martins, investing their newfound wealth in banks and a daily newspaper.

"The Sanchez family is one of the very few which has gone from one class to the other," Gary Payne went on. "Years ago Tony Sanchez, Jr., wanted to marry one of the Martin girls, and that just couldn't happen because of the class system. That's one of the reasons they set up the Laredo *News*—so they could get back at the Martins."

At the wedding reception another custom was taking place —the groom was stripped of his jacket, shoes, and socks, hoisted upon the shoulders of spirited friends, and carried around the room. On stage a nine-piece band in matching blue leisure suits blared out enough of a melody to satisfy every taste from disco to waltz. "At Mexican weddings," Joe shouted over the din, "the number of people doesn't indicate the number of friends the bride and groom have as much as the number of relatives. The father of the bride is somber because of his investment in the reception. The mother is concerned about the old man's drunkenness. The groom's parents are usually the only ones at the head table having a good time. It's not like small village weddings where the in-laws get to eat the goat while the rest of the guests settle for the leftovers. Here, everything is on the bride's father."

The wedding *fiesta* would go well into the night, and Joe insisted we had more important things to do than wait for Carlos. "We're off to Boys Town," he proudly announced, "the best whorehouses on the border." Joe hadn't been to Boys Town in weeks and was anxious to return. He wasn't after sexual favors, he insisted—he simply loved the ambience.

Nuevo Laredo's *zona de tolerancia* was on the outskirts of town down some treacherous dirt roads. The district is a walled-in compound with twenty-five bars lining five streets beneath ballpark lights. Each bar has its own prostitutes licensed by the government, and each prostitute receives a regular dose of penicillin at a clinic—also located in Boys Town.

Joe's favorite spot was the Marabú, one of the classier establishments in the *zona*. Outside were parked Cadillacs, pickups, Winnebagos, Volkswagens, and a horse. Inside the Marabú was a Formica wonderland of plastic plants and speckled walls. An elevated dance floor was circled by tables and booths, with a bar next to the door. The jukebox played "Macho Man" relentlessly but no one ever danced. Waiters scurried about serving drinks as prostitutes eyed prospective customers. The hookers were decked out in every conceivable fashion to appeal to the widest variety of tastes—little-girl clothes, high-fashion apparel, peek-a-boo dresses, leather, see-through nighties, glitter bras, miniskirts, slit slacks. Their ages ranged from seventeen to forty-five, their makeup increasing with the years. Most had come to the border to make money and this was the quickest and most convenient way.

Over the years Nuevo Laredo's *zona roja* has earned a reputation as a playpen for University of Texas fraternity boys and state legislators. The evening I visited, oil hands, truckers, salesmen, ranchers, cops, and students filled the Marabú, attracted by prostitutes who were alternately hostile and shy, aggressive and submissive. Some *putas* slowly paraded around the room waiting for the wink of an eye or the flick of a hand to signal interest. Others would approach prospective customers making fucky-fucky small talk. Their hands would go to work immediately. "Hey, honey," a drugstore cowboy from Houston blurted out to an aging hooker. "Whaddaya do for a living?" She stuck out her tongue and wiggled her ass.

The Marabú took on the air of a fantasy island where men could afford to ignore come-ons. Crossing from Laredo meant checking your inhibitions at the bridge. As William Burroughs observed in *Naked Lunch*, "Something falls off you when you cross the border into Mexico." You may be a faithfully married, church-going man in the United States but over here you can grope and paw and make a fool of yourself and no one says a word about it. If you want a temporary liaison, your whore takes you by the arm and parades you to the bar where you pay twenty-three dollars—twenty for the sex and three for a bed. You head out back to a courtyard lined by a promenade of rooms. A half-hour later you emerge. Indeed, the biggest attraction at the red-light district is not sexual at all. It is psychological. No man is ever rejected in Boys Town.

Or that's what I assumed until I met a fellow from Los Angeles. A good-looking man, he had no trouble talking with the hookers, but every time he suggested going out back, they demurely refused. After each turn-down he returned to the table confused and frustrated.

"What do you have to do to get laid in this place? Maybe it's my approach."

"*Approach??* In Boys Town?" a veteran hooted. "The only approach they understand is heybabyletsfuck."

One sympathetic prostitute finally told him the truth: The management didn't approve of the girls taking on black customers. Sorry, she said, she'd like to, but this was a class joint and if they started catering to blacks they could lose their Anglo clients. He should try one of the "lesser" clubs down the street.

"Jesus Fucking Christ," he pounded the table. "This is the last place in the world I expected discrimination!" He sat stunned, then slowly walked out the door.

A short while later he returned with renewed determination. He had faced racism before and conquered it, why should this time be any different? He downed his drink, cruised the floor, found the *puta* of his dreams, and convinced her he was Puerto Rican but his parents forgot to teach him Spanish. Flushed with pride he paid his money and strolled out back with her, arm in arm.

6

KICKAPOO ON THE TRAIL

LONESOME POLECAT was the Kickapoo Indian's name. He was short, he went barefoot, and his only clothing was a loincloth at the waist. He spoke in broken English and had no function except as a recurring subplot in "Li'l Abner." On top of his head Lonesome Polecat balanced a barrel of Kickapoo Joy Juice.

Lonesome Polecat sprang from Al Capp's imagination. The real Kickapoo Indians were an Algonquin Woodland tribe from the Great Lakes region which migrated south in the mid-nineteenth century. Some stopped in Oklahoma and Kansas while others abandoned the United States altogether and settled in the Mexican state of Coahuila. These became known as the Traditional Kickapoo. Part of the year this small band makes its home directly beneath the International Bridge connecting Eagle Pass, Texas, and Piedras Negras, Coahuila. The riverside settlement is a way station between their ancestral home at Nacimiento, Coahuila, 150 miles to the south, and the migrant farm labor circuit they travel in the United States during harvest season. The Kickapoo have camped out alongside the river every year for more than a century, their presence a constant source of annoyance to Eagle Pass officials, within whose city limits they reside.

Kickapoo homes are built of cardboard, cane, deerskin, and wood. They are shaped like geodesic domes, thirty feet wide and nine feet tall in the center. Metal wrapping straps hold them together. Some of the huts are braced by cement pillars holding up their sky, the International Bridge. Each wickiup is home for an extended family of two and sometimes three generations. In late spring, when the settlement is most populated, scores of Kickapoo crowd into the tinder-box huts, with many more living in pickups parked next to the village.

When the Rio Grande overflows its banks, the Kickapoo village is flooded. Every now and then the Kickapoo hear a dull *thunk!* overhead. They glance at each other and wince—another accident on the bridge. At least once a year a cigarette carelessly flicked from a car passing overhead burns down a house. Empty beer bottles and other garbage descend daily. The Kickapoo still chuckle about the three pounds of hashish which landed in the lap of a tribe member sitting in front of his hut. They were not surprised when, later that day, two men came by beating the bushes looking for their stash.

Next to the cluster of Kickapoo huts is the nine-hole Eagle Pass golf course, which serves as a playground for Kickapoo children. Traps on the fourth and sixth holes make ideal sandboxes. The greens are perfect for shooting marbles. The par-five fourth hole makes a smooth skateboard area. Diapers and other refuse blow out onto the fairway, much to the annoyance of golfers and the groundskeeper. Lost golf balls and abandoned clubs are part of every Kickapoo child's toy collection.

The Kickapoo buy most of their food at Moncada & Sons Grocery Store up the hill from their village. The Moncadas offer a line of credit to the impoverished Indians, and serve as their local mailing address. Some Kickapoo rent camper space for their homes in the grocery store's parking lot. Across the street from Moncada's is Lily Mae's, the closest bar to the Kickapoo settlement. Occasionally, Eagle Pass police will pick up Indians wandering home from Lily Mae's and arrest them for public drunkenness. Since Kickapoo homes are out in the open, there is no private place for them to drink. The irony is often lost on law enforcement officers.

Only since the late 1970s has the city of Eagle Pass acted to help its annual visitors with rudimentary city services such as garbage pickup. The Texas Indian Commission officially recognized the tribe in 1977, a prelude to state assistance. The federal government recognized the Kickapoo during Andrew Jackson's presidency when the Indians were issued a pass allowing them to come and go as they pleased:

> Fort Dearborn [Illinois]
> September 28, 1832
>
> This is to certify that the families of the Kickapoo Indians, thirty-seven in number, are to be protected by all persons from any injury whatsoever, as they are under the protection of the United States and any person violating shall be punished accordingly.
>
> Wm. Whittles
> Mj 2nd Reg. Inft.

Some Kickapoo still carry wrinkled photocopies of Major Whittles's safe-conduct pass, flashing them at immigration officers when they enter the United States. Mexicans hoping to gain admittance to the United States by claiming to be Kickapoo are invariably denied entry. Eagle Pass immigration inspectors know that the binational Kickapoo usually travel together, come only during certain seasons, and have distinguishing physical characteristics—wide, high cheekbones; rich chocolate-brown skin; and deep facial features. A few Kickapoo still wear their hair in the traditional braided ponytail.

From its resting spot beneath the bridge, every able-bodied Kickapoo family goes out to earn its annual subsistence in the fields of Texas, the Midwest, and the Northwest. Before leaving each year, the Kickapoo families are blessed by Pancho Valdez, the tribe's religious leader who was born in the last century. Groups of *campesinos* travel together, stopping at the same farms year after year. In nearby Carrizo Springs, Texas, they top onions. In Lubbock they pick cotton. They work the sugar-beet fields in Utah, Montana, Idaho, and Oregon. A few travel to Florida for the citrus season. Some visit the Yakima Valley in Washington for the apple harvest. Others pick cherries and cucumbers in the Great Lakes states.

By mid-autumn the Kickapoo's five months of wage-earning are over, and their aging cars and pickups rattle back to the village on the border. Migrant farm work is not a particularly profitable life, but it is the one the Kickapoo know best. Efforts to ease the Indians into other forms of work always fail because the Kickapoo are afraid they'll lose their contracts with farmers on the migrant circuit if they miss a year. Traveling that circuit is part of their life cycle. During harvest season fewer than five families—usually women and children only—remain at Nacimiento, Coahuila, and not many more stay at the Eagle Pass settlement.

Neither the city of Eagle Pass nor the Kickapoo Tribe is satisfied with the current riverside settlement. Both would prefer that the tribe have a place of its own. To this end, the Texas Indian Commission, on behalf of the tribe, asked the U.S. Department of Housing and Urban Development to underwrite a new Kickapoo village. The funding application went smoothly, and now Walt Broemer, the state Indian Commission's top administrator, has called a meeting at the San Luis Community Center in Eagle Pass to give the tribe and its ruling council a progress report. The Kickapoo at Nacimiento traveled by horse and bus to the border to join their brethren for the assembly.

When word spread that the Kickapoo would likely be shopping for Eagle Pass land with government money, the price of property downriver—the desired location—suddenly rose. A local architect came to the meeting hoping his tentative design for the new Kickapoo community would be accepted. The proposal included space for homes, a recreation center, school, and acreage for crops. "Looks good," Broemer nodded as the Kickapoo started entering the meeting hall.

In all, thirty Kickapoo came to the meeting. Women and children stood in the rear, while the men leaned against the wall to the side. Broemer was joined up front by George Whitewater, a Kickapoo fluent in both English and the tribal tongue. "I'm their attorney, their counselor, taxi driver, accountant, advisor, and interpreter," the retired civilian Air Force employee said later. "I'm everything. I'm the one who gets things done. I'm the only one who's working."

Broemer's opening remarks about the HUD application were repeated by Whitewater in Kickapoo, a guttural language with varied pitches and an economy of words.

In the first year of the three-year grant, Broemer said, the tribe could select the site, build their homes, and install utilities. The following year community services such as a health clinic, school, and parks would be developed. Job training would begin in the final year of the grant. To please everyone in the tribe, the new village would allow for both traditional housing, similar to the thatched-roof homes in Nacimiento, and more conventional homes.

A young member of the tribal council seemed unimpressed and approached the front to question Broemer. "What about these forms you want us to fill out?"

Broemer explained that to complete the federal housing grant application, he had to list how many Kickapoo families there are and the number of tribal members in each.

A murmur of concern spread among the Kickapoo. Within the tribe there is no delineation where one family ends and another begins. The government paperwork was obviously not prepared with them in mind. "Unless we can satisfy HUD that we will abide by their rules and regulations," Broemer told the gathering, "they won't give us the money."

Whether or not to fulfill the HUD requirements would be a crucial decision in the tribe's history, and they sensed it. Filling out that type of form would mean the beginning of a new presence in their lives. The gap between Broemer and the tribal council seemed vast. The Kickapoo told him they would think it over.

George Whitewater sat at his desk in the San Luis Community Center the next day. His dark face was freckled, and he wore his hair in a braided ponytail. A paper American flag was tacked on the wall behind his head. Because he has a telephone and is in tune with the white man's ways, Whitewater assumes the role of tribal spokesman whenever press inquiries come in. In newspapers he is referred to as the "war chief," "a prophet," or simply "Chief Whitewater." In reality, the Traditional Kickapoo have no war chief and Whitewater is not a leader of their tribe. He is not even a Traditional Kickapoo. George Whitewater, born Mah Teck Que Net Nee fifty-nine years ago, is a member of the Kansas Kickapoo tribe, whose history and life-style contrast sharply with their migratory cousins in Eagle Pass. Nonetheless, Whitewater was eager to explain the Traditional Kickapoo culture and problems.

Yes, he admitted, there is dissension within the tribe between the more orthodox elders and the younger ones who seek change, but the tribe has a unity seldom found elsewhere. It has, for example, managed to resist Christianity. In fact, Whitewater continued, the tribal culture avoids as much outside influence as possible. They have adopted Mexican names to conform to their immediate environment, but within the tribe they still use traditional names. (Most Kickapoo are fluent in Spanish and their tribal tongue. Along the migrant trail in the United States they speak enough English to get by.)

There is a story in Kickapoo lore that tells of Mexican President Lázaro Cárdenas' visit to the Kickapoo in Coahuila in the 1930s. He was warned by tribal leader Papaqueño: "I am the head of my people and you are the head of yours. I don't interfere with you; you don't interfere with me." For its part, the U.S. Border Patrol heeds Papaqueño's advice toward the Kickapoo and all tribes along the border. Unofficial policy dictates: Don't mess with the Indians.

In Eagle Pass, Whitewater complained, Mexican-Americans discriminate against the Kickapoo. He withdrew his own children from the local public schools because the other kids kept calling them *cochinos,* pigs. Earlier this century the Mexican government built a school for the Kickapoo near their land at Nacimiento. Mysteriously, it burned down. Some years later the government built another school for the Kickapoo. Mystery repeated itself.

George Whitewater frowned on my request for a visit to the Kickapoo beneath the bridge. "They are very sensitive to outsiders," he said. "They get nervous."

Fifteen minutes later, chatting with four Kickapoo who had just returned from the fields of Montana, I found a scene different from the one Whitewater had painted. They were sensitive, but at the same time enjoyed the opportunity to speak with outsiders. Nearby, a barefoot five-year-old in a Kawasaki tee shirt played soccer with a golf ball in the dust beneath a willow tree. Women in jeans and colorful blouses talked among themselves, chain-smoking the afternoon away. The young man who had spoken the previous evening offered beers to me and to John Stockley, a food-stamp caseworker who has helped the Indians document their claims for state benefits. "What do you think about the new village plans?" the Kickapoo asked Stockley.

"You're not going to get me to influence your decisions," Stockley laughed. "It's up to you."

The schism between the aged traditionalists and the younger Indians which Whitewater had mentioned earlier was not apparent. As for Whitewater, well, they grinned, he is helpful. But perhaps there is more to the new plan than what he has told them? As we talked, a pickup bearing Idaho plates rumbled into camp. By looking at the license plates in the campground parking lot, one can trace the tribe's migrant journeys. When we left, the Kickapoo were still discussing their impending decision.

Shortly thereafter the tribe decided to go ahead with the HUD application. Although federal funds were approved and land was purchased, the entire transaction was voided by a state Attorney General's ruling. And most of the Kickapoo have moved their homes slighty west, out from under the bridge, to avoid damage from falling debris and cigarette butts.

The Kickapoo will continue to travel the migrant trail through the Midwest and to the Pacific Northwest, always returning to their settlement at Eagle Pass and their ancestral home at Nacimiento. Even their new ties with the federal bureaucracy can't disrupt the yearly pattern they've followed for generations.

At least that's what they say.

En Route

Jack Stockley, father of the Kickapoo's friend John Stockley, was a crotchety old man of seventy-six, yet something in his countenance suggested honor and integrity. When we met him at his son's house in Quemado, Texas, he still had a weekend job feeding quarantined livestock at the stockyards in Eagle Pass. A cowboy all his life, Jack Stockley was alert and sharp, full of the prejudice and tales which come with being a lifelong border rat.

Quemado, a town along the river between Eagle Pass and Del Rio, produces melons, onions, and pecans—some of which we munched straight off backyard trees. This afternoon Jack was relating his experiences as a tick rider—someone who rides along the river looking for stray livestock.

Cattle which tick riders find in the area between a posted quarantine line paralleling the river and the Rio Grande itself must be dipped in a solution to rid them of any deadly fever ticks they may have picked up. Cows who venture too close to the river from the north or cross it from the south are fair game for the tick riders. If an animal bearing a fever tick is discovered in a farmer's pasture, all the livestock in that field must be dipped every two weeks for nine months. The tick line, which stretches from Brownsville to Del Rio, is administered by the Animal and Plant Health Inspection Service of the U.S. Department of Agriculture. One hundred twenty tick riders police the area. Mexico has no similar program.

"I used to ride the twenty-mile stretch up from Eagle Pass with another fellow," Jack told us. "Now they have more riders in the same area but there are fewer cattle to pick up. And we didn't use trucks; we were strictly on horseback. We'd have up to a hundred cattle at a time at the stockyards. If they have just seven or eight these days that's pretty good."

The animals that wander over from the Mexican side of the

Rio Grande are called "wetstock"—a variation of "wetback."
"The tick riders who are out now," Jack complained, "they
haven't caught any wetstock in weeks."

"That's because the cattle don't usually come over to the
parking lots of restaurants," John chimed in.

"Well, they caught only one last month," Jack continued. "It
couldn'ta been on a Saturday because those guys take Saturdays
off. No matter how few they find, though, the job still has to be
done. A fever tick will kill a cow within two weeks sure."

Jack Stockley is among the last of that rare breed of Anglo
who used to cross into Mexico seeking work. "They paid us
more in Mexico than we could earn here. Cowboys were getting thirty dollars a month in the U.S. We got a hundred pesos
a month in Mexico, and the work wasn't as hard, either. That
was just after the First World War when the peso was worth
about fifty cents."

Across the Rio Grande from Quemado are some *ejidos,* land
which *campesinos* till collectively. Most *ejidos* were created by
government land appropriations resulting from agrarian land
reform after the Revolution of 1910. A few have been formed
by landless peasants banding together to seize a section of a
large landowner's property. Sometimes this has been done with
weapons, although usually not. The government often sanctions
—and sometimes encourages—this process. The new *ejidatarios* establish their own skeleton form of government and
align with neighboring *ejidos* to market their produce coopera-
tively. The *ejido* system has never realized its goal of egalitarian
land distribution and increased production. By its cooperation,
however, the government creates a safety valve for the landless
and deflects a potential class struggle between impoverished
campesinos and the landed aristocracy.

Jack took us across to visit some neighboring communities.
"The *ejido* system is shameful," he declared as we drove north
from Piedras Negras on Mexico's Highway 2. "There's a big
ranch and it'll work a lot of people, but the *'jidos* will whittle
it down to where there's nothin'."

We approached a highway checkpoint where an *inmigración* official leaned into the pickup and inquired our destination. *"Queremos ir a Jiménez,"* Jack replied handing the man a dollar bill. The official nodded as he pocketed the money and withdrew.

"Once the *'jidatarios* get some property they become lazy," Jack lamented. "They don't work the land right like the landowner does. Each *'jidatario* 'round here gets twenty goats to start with. Sometimes the government will supply them, but usually the man who forfeited his land has to provide them."

We passed a sign announcing Ejido de Navajada, a new settlement where surveyors were marking off plots of land alongside workmen hammering stakes into the ground. A few thatch-roofed houses of adobe, hay, and branches were already completed. A Pepsi-Cola sign hung on the side of one.

El Moral, another *ejido* a few kilometers farther, consisted of a general store, a few decrepit houses, and a boarded-up cantina which Jack told us used to be the site of many killings. "Bandits run out of the United States settled in this area. There are still some half-breeds back here with American names."

We drove on to Jiménez, a *pueblito* the Stockley family used to visit on horseback by fording the Rio Grande. John recalled a dance in Jiménez he attended in the 1940s at which a Mexican army lieutenant had ordered a subordinate to stop dancing with his girlfriend. "When the soldier kept dancing with her, the lieutenant ordered another soldier to shoot the first one—which he did. Did they punish the soldier? No. He was just following orders. Was the lieutenant reprimanded? No, because he didn't do the shooting."

Jack nodded. "They don't take to authority too well over here. Each year when the Mexican government would send in a tax collector he'd never come out. Finally, they just stopped sending them in to Jiménez and some of the other border communities."

A horse-drawn carriage clopping down La Popular, Jiménez's main street, was the only other vehicle in the road. Next to a small grocery store a man was busy making adobe bricks. Nearby a big hand-painted sign declared:

EL DERECHO A TRABAJAR ES EL DERECHO A COMER

The right to work is the right to eat. At noontime on a crisp autumn workday, most of Jiménez's fifteen hundred residents were out in the fields earning their right to eat.

7

THE BORDERBLASTERS

JOHN R. BRINKLEY was not a popular man with America's medical establishment. In the late 1920s, Brinkley diagnosed medical problems over his radio station, KFKB, in Milford, Kansas, often prescribing remedies available at one of his own drugstores. His most ambitious medical activity was a "rejuvenation operation" for men. Feeling tired and run-down? he asked listeners. Not as active as you once were? Come to my clinic.

The minor surgery "Doctor" Brinkley sold on the radio consisted of opening a man's scrotum and implanting goat glands in the center of the testicles. Brinkley claimed the results would make patients more active and healthier, lower their blood pressure, and, not incidentally, make them better lovers. "We make old men execute young ideas," Brinkley crowed.

Brinkley earned the ire of the Kansas City *Star*, which vilified him from its front page. The American Medical Association—which he called the Amateur Meatcutters Association—brought him to court, alleging his credentials false and his operations useless.

Some of Brinkley's former patients were his best defense witnesses. From hill-country farmers to Texas oil millionaires, they journeyed to Kansas proclaiming the wonders of goat-gland surgery. Other former patients were among the best prosecution witnesses, charging that they had been duped. By the trial's end, Brinkley was professionally discredited.

Brinkley used his one asset, KFKB ("Kansas First, Kansas Best"), for revenge against the state's establishment. A gubernatorial race was scheduled soon, and Brinkley campaigned over the airwaves as a write-in candidate. Despite his lack of political experience and late entry into the race, one-third of the electorate wrote in his name. Shortly after Brinkley's defeat the Kansas State Medical Board revoked his license to practice, and the Federal Radio Commission, forerunner of the Federal Communications Commission, shut down his station. Brinkley decided to relocate his business.

Communities throughout the United States wrote the ersatz doctor, each urging that he move his enterprise to their town. A letter from the Del Rio, Texas, Chamber of Commerce was especially intriguing: Why not make Del Rio your headquarters, but broadcast from across the Rio Grande in Villa Acuña, Coahuila?

The idea appealed to the forty-six-year-old goat-gland doctor, and in 1931, John R. Brinkley—who listed himself as M.D., Ph.D., M.C., LL.D., Sc.D., and Lieut. U.S.N.R.—founded Mexican radio station XER with a power of seventy-five thousand watts. As Brinkley said, "Radio waves pay no attention to lines on a map." An era of broadcasting history had begun.

"This is X-E-R," Brinkley's friendly voice told listeners throughout North America, "the sunshine station between the nations." Brinkley solicited listeners' letters, which started arriving from all forty-eight states and fifteen foreign countries. One week in January 1932 more than twenty-seven thousand pieces of mail came in.

Brinkley's goat-gland clinic took over the top floor of the Roswell Hotel in Del Rio. Between Brinkley's three hundred employees and the many townspeople who catered to the steady stream of patients arriving daily by train, Del Rio thrived during the depths of the Depression. Brinkley's Del Rio estate became a shrine to which listeners made pilgrimages. Electric lights spelled out his name in front of his mansion. Flamingos, tortoises, and penguins graced the elaborate grounds. Sunday mornings he would play organ music over the air from his living room. John-Boy, his son, became a national celebrity sitting on his pappy's knee.

Brinkley's folksy delivery was the source of his appeal. He'd tell the gang back in Mule Gulch, Tennessee, that Charlie from down at the general store had arrived safely, was at the clinic that day, sends his love, and will be home by next weekend.

Business was brisk until the Mexican government threatened to close down XER in 1933. Brinkley dispatched Charles Curtis, vice-president under Herbert Hoover, to intercede, but the final Mexican demand—350,000 pesos (about $175,000)—was too exorbitant. *Federales* shut down the station.

Brinkley rebounded quickly by advertising his Del Rio clinic on U.S. stations and by taking over station XEAW in Reynosa. And he established a second clinic at nearby San Juan, Texas— this one to treat problems of the rectum. "Remember," Brinkley cheerfully advertised, "San Juan for rectal troubles, and Del Rio for the old prostate!"

The election of Lázaro Cárdenas as president of Mexico in 1934 gave Brinkley a new opportunity to re-establish a station at Villa Acuña. Using a Mexican *prestanombre,* or front man, Brinkley was soon back on the air with XERA, pitching his potency operations with renewed fervor. Prices ranged from "The Poor Man's Special" at $125—good for one examination and a prostate treatment—to the $1,000 "Businessman's Treatment," which came with a lifetime guarantee. Those complaining about high prices were reminded that "Doctor Brinkley will use the money for the betterment of mankind." In fact, only a fraction of his income was spent in the interest of others—new uniforms for the Villa Acuña police and a library for Del Rio. The rest of his wealth was spent on ranches, farms, mines, a plane, three yachts, and countless automobiles.

Brinkley's success inspired other entrepreneurs to start borderblasters. The nearest was XEPN at Piedras Negras, with one hundred thousand watts, opposite Eagle Pass about fifty miles downriver. XEPN listeners were invited to write in questions —accompanied by a dollar per query—to astrologers and psychics who replied to them on the air. A lady would write that her ring was lost, and "the spooks" would tell her that a plumber would find it while working on her sink.

Aside from goat glands and spooks, the biggest influence early border stations had on American culture was in the field of country music. Reaching parts of rural America that city stations could not, the borderblasters provided for many the only nighttime entertainment available. Hillbilly singers performed on the air, then plugged their records and songbooks. Best-known of the hillbilly groups on XERA was the Carter Family from Appalachia, who made Del Rio their home from 1938 until 1941, when they relocated in San Antonio to prepare weekly shows for another Mexican station in Monterrey. The Carters—A. P., Sara, Maybelle, Janette, Anita, Helen, and June —would crowd into a studio, a Pentecostal preacher named Brother Bill Guild would introduce them, and they'd light into their theme song, "Keep on the Sunny Side." Between songs Brother Bill promoted Carter Family records and products such as Colorback ("Just comb it through your hair and you'll get your color back!"). Each week tapes of the sessions were shipped from San Antonio to Monterrey.

In 1941 the new administration of President Avila Camacho shut down XERA. Devastated by the loss, outquacked by rival stations, sued by dissatisfied patients, and harassed by authorities in two countries, Brinkley quickly went bankrupt. He died a broken man the following year.

A few years later a third station was started in Villa Acuña— XERF, whose main office, like its predecessors, was in Del Rio. While the Mexican ownership of XERF has remained a mystery, control of the station has always rested with who-ever maintained the U.S. advertising accounts. The key to border stations was always American business acumen and technology. The announcing was in English; the audience was almost entirely American; the programs and commercials were usually recorded on the U.S. side; advertising time was sold in the United States to American companies; and the station's mailing address was invariably north of the border. Mexico supplied land for the studios and broadcast towers, some technicians, and the call letters.

On-the-air entertainment at XERF was provided by cowboy singers and evangelists, both of whom found the X-stations ideal for their purposes. One of the first preachers to take advantage of the border stations was the Reverend J. C. Bishop who paid $100,000 for forty years of fifteen minutes of air time nightly. During his peak years—1956 to 1962—Bishop, who operates out of Dallas, received four hundred letters a day.

The most colorful of the preachers, Dallas Turner, started on the air in the 1940s and has been there ever since. Turner is filled with tales of the X-stations, a subject he dearly loves.

"When I got to my first border station I learned very fast that they didn't hire you to sing, they hired you to sell, sell, *sell*. I was a pitch man. A pitch man's success depended entirely on his ability to pull mail. The greatest announcers in the country would come to the border and they wouldn't last overnight. The best radio pitch men came off the carnival circuit or from the vaudeville halls. The first and greatest of them was Don Baxter, who called himself Major Kord. He specialized in selling piano lessons by mail, but he did most of the other ads, too. He was a pioneer—a guy who could stand up and fight the microphone. He'd wave his arms and go through all sorts of calisthenics.

"We had one fellow, Billy Truehart, who sold tap-dancing lessons over the air. He'd bring a board to the studio, put a microphone down by his feet, and tap dance and pitch at the same time. He sold thousands of courses that way. We also had Don Howard doing 'Frank the Diamond Man,' or 'Bill the Diamond Man'—he'd change his name on each station. 'Friends,' he'd say, 'I wish there was television at this time because I hold in my hand the most *beau*tiful diamond. . . .' He had a deep melodic voice.

"Every morning I'd just take a jug of cough syrup and start recording. I might record for X-E-R-B at Rosarito, south of Tijuana, in the morning, for X-E-G in the afternoon, and at night for X-E-N-T at Reynosa. All my shows were basically the same, but I had to keep track of which name I used on which station. I'd do one as Nevada Slim the Yodelin' Cowboy, another as Cowboy Dallas Turner, and a third as Yodelin' Slim Dallas. I also pitched my songbooks over the air for a dollar; the station would keep half the take. On a good day I'd get a hundred fifty orders."

In 1950, when Acuña was growing from a *villa* to a *ciudad*, Turner sold advertising time to the preachers for some of the borderblasters.

"One of them, Gerald L. K. Smith, always had two bodyguards with him. I signed him to a twenty-five-thousand-dollar contract. He was a very anti-Semitic individual, and because of this they had to throw him off the air at X-E-L-O. He promised me he wouldn't say anything against the Jews but we ended up giving him his money back."

By this time Turner had become a heavy drinker. One day in a run-down Kansas City hotel he was about to shoot himself. As fate would have it his radio was playing "God Put a Rainbow in the Cloud." Hearing the song, he laid down his gun, picked up a Gideon bible, and Jesus walked in. Turner went into on-the-air evangelism where he has stayed since.

This is your good buddy, America's cowboy evangelist, Dr. Dallas Turner, his nightly spiel begins, *speaking to you from the studios of X-E-R-F at beautiful Ciudad Acuña on the banks of the silvery Rio Grande in romantic old Mexico.* Actually Turner is speaking to you from the den in his house in Reno, Nevada. Station XERF simply plays tapes he ships to Del Rio. "On a border station you never admit you're pre-recorded," Turner explained. "On American stations you have to say if you are. I wouldn't be half as effective if listeners knew I was really in Nevada."

Paul Kallinger has been on XERF since 1949. Billed as "your good neighbor along the way," he booms the station ID with the slightest encouragement: *"Coast to coast, border to border, wherever you are, wherever you may be, we're right here at fifteen-seventy on your dial at X-E-R-F in Ciudad Acuña, Coahuila, Mexico. Our mailing address is Del Rio, Texas. . . ."* In the mid-fifties, when country and western music dominated XERF, Kallinger was among the most popular disc jockeys on American radio. Most of the developing country-music stars of the day—Johnny Cash, Faron Young, Porter Waggoner, and others—dropped in to sing on the air. "Getting exposure on my show was essential for breaking a national hit. One time Elvis Presley came down here while he was still on the Sun label. I told him, 'I'm sorry Elvis. I don't allow any rock 'n' roll on my show.' He said, 'Well, thank you anyway. I was just passing through Del Rio and I thought perhaps you'd put me on your program.'

"I pitched 'Sunshine Chicks': *'one hundred number-one, first-grade baby chicks for two-ninety-eight!'* We sold double-edged, surgical-steel razor blades, rosebushes, fruit trees, d-Con rat poison—we introduced that. Most of our ads were on a P. I.—per inquiry—basis. The advertiser didn't pay for air time, but he did split the money with the station once the mail orders came in. So it was in the station's interest to draw the biggest response. I've even been accused of selling autographed pictures of Jesus Christ! We'd never do that on X-E-R-F. I think they did it on X-E-G."

The legendary $2.98 autographed pictures of Jesus Christ are part of borderland mythology. Whomever I spoke with at one station insisted the ad was on another. Although no one has actually seen one, everyone readily concedes the autographed pictures do exist. (Would you settle for a Lord's Last Supper tablecloth?)

Bob Smith had just finished a stint as "Big Smith with the Records!" on a Shreveport, Louisiana, station in the late 1950s when he and a friend figured that big money was waiting for them in border radio. Smith thought XERF was the greatest stage in the world and he wanted to be front and center on that stage. After driving the 550 miles to Del Rio, Smith walked into the middle of a management-labor dispute. Station employees were disenchanted with their bosses and were willing to go with the highest bidder. In effect, the station was up for grabs. Bob Smith was the first to flash some cash.

Within a day the station was under his control. Smith altered the programming, took over the advertising accounts, changed his name, and started a genuine underground cult throughout teenage America. At the center of the cult lay rhythm and blues and gritty rock 'n' roll. The cult's mysterious guru was Bob Smith's better-known alter ego, Wolfman Jack.

Smith captured teenage imaginations with his crazed style as Wolfman Jack. His on-the-air growl, his manic chatter, and his savvy record selection combined to make the most of XERF's powerful range, then at 250,000 watts. *"Dis is de WOLFMAN talkin' atcha!"* he'd bark. He urged listeners to get naked, vote for him for president, "blow the evil weed," wiggle their toes, kiss their teachers. The mystique of the border enhanced his image. His was an unknown quantity with a most bizarre quality. To hear him tell the XERF story is alternately illuminating and frustrating. He is the master of shuck and jive.

"The ole Wolfman come on from midnight till four in the morning pitching all kinds of mail-order deals: gain weight, lose weight, buy records, roach clips, songbooks, everything. I tried selling something called Florex which we advertised as sex pills. The Federal Trade Commission made me stop. They got a sample and discovered we were selling sugar pills.

"X-E-R-F had thirty employees along with facilities for them to eat and sleep. We grew our own food—we had sheep and ugly goats and the works. Twice a month we threw a big party for the *federales,* the cops, who came on horseback. We'd hire either a country band or some *mariachis*. The women from town would all show up and we'd cook the goats and drink wine and get totally blitzed while the Reverend J. Charles Jessup was on the air screaming about God. We were the hot item in Acuña. You'd go down to Boys Town, to the red-light district, and you'd hear the station in all the bars, especially when I was on. They were very proud that the station was in their town.

"People who came to Acuña looking for the studio would

have to pay a cabdriver fifty bucks to get him to take them out there. A few of the preachers wanted to visit the facilities but I always told them their lives would be in danger if they came. It was tough enough to keep the bad dudes—the ones who wanted to gain control of the station—away from the door. We had to stay armed all the time and keep sandbags around the station. I always traveled with bodyguards. We tried to act as bad as we looked."

The greatest controversy about XERF during Wolfman's tenure revolves around a shoot-out over control of the station. Early one morning while Wolfman was at home in Del Rio listening to some preacher on the station, a kid's voice interrupted: *"¡Pistoleros! ¡Pistoleros!"*

Wolfman headed out across the river to the station.

"A rival faction had come back and tried to scare us out of there. They were like Indians circling the fort. They rode on bicycles, motor scooters, motorcycles, horseback—all those rinky-dink Mexican things. It was comical to see them trying to shoot at us. The scene was like an amusement-park shooting gallery: you'd watch a guy riding, someone shoots at him, and *kchiiing!*, he falls off his bicycle. We finally chased them all away. Nobody got hurt bad on our team, just a couple of wounded. Two guys on their team got killed.

"We kept the peace by giving them money and kisses at the same time we showed them force. We paid *mordida* to the *federales, mordida* to the union bosses, and *mordida* to the troublemakers. If we didn't come up with the green, nothing would get done." Bob Smith, a.k.a. Wolfman Jack, became a pirate king. Station XERF was his kingdom.

"We kept the business operation very hush-hush because there was *so* much money. To pitch 'The Lucky Forty,' an oldies album package, I'd cut one seven-minute spot where you play a little bitty portion of each song, and run it on Monday night. Wednesday when the mail came in, I'd get four to five thousand orders for that one record. The major broadcast executives in America were trying to get their hands on that station because they knew what a gold mine it was. We had the most powerful signal in North America. Birds dropped dead when they flew too close to the tower. A car driving from New York to L.A. would never lose the station. I had listeners in New Zealand! I made funny remarks about Khrushchev and they jammed X-E-R-F in Moscow!

"Hundreds of people tried to reach me with payola but I never talked with any of them. I knew the one time I'd step out of line I'd have the U.S. boys on my rear end. Record companies would send me tons of new releases without me even soliciting. I threw half the stuff away—gave it to the kids in Acuña."

Stories about American children who sneaked their transistor radios under the sheets at night to listen to the Wolfman's deranged babble are legion. He brought an outlaw spirit to the airwaves, turning on an entire generation of white youngsters to greasy rhythm and blues. In the last years of the Eisenhower administration when Percy Faith, Connie Francis, and Paul Anka were topping the charts, XERF played Wilbert Harrison, Joe Turner, Jerry Butler, and Lloyd Price nightly.

"All my listeners assumed I was black. Most of my orders came from the white population though, 'cause they wanted to be hip, to get into what's happening. I didn't realize I was influencing people that much until many years later when songs were written about me. At the time, I was more into, 'How many pieces of mail did we pull for the record package we pitched last Tuesday?' That's all I was concerned with."

The hellfire and brimstone preachers remained on the air, despite the new direction in which Smith took the station. "The station was their life's blood—they'd bring the Lord down Himself to stay on the air. X-E-R-F made millionaires out of a number of preachers."

After a few years Bob Smith left Del Rio. The station—or rather the advertising accounts—reverted to Arturo Gonzales, the local lawyer who had handled XERF's U.S. dealings prior to Smith's arrival. Wolfman moved to another border station on the West Coast. Listening to XERF, however, you'd have thought the Wolfman was still in the studio screaming away. Every night for another two years he continued to growl his way through more mail-order madness and rhythm and blues. Station XERF was simply playing tapes he sent every week. Wolfman Jack's new West Coast home was the setting for his scenes in *American Graffiti,* the 1973 movie in which he portrayed a frenzied and compassionate border-station deejay— the way he likes to be remembered on the X-stations.

Another borderblaster, XELO in Ciudad Juárez, developed a successful formula mixing country music, preachers, and per-inquiry ads. The station, which previously had been located in Nogales and Tijuana, received P. I. orders at a post office box in Clint, a small town just east of El Paso. In 1973, P. I.'s were phased out, the station changed its name to XEROK, and rock 'n' roll took over.

Mexican union demands made live broadcasts from its Juárez studio too expensive for XEROK, and a 1934 U.S. law forbade transmitting live broadcasts from the United States to a foreign station for simultaneous transmission back to the United States. (The statute was dubbed "the Brinkley law.") As a result, all 168 hours of XEROK's week were pre-recorded on the U.S. side and delivered to the facilities in Juárez. For example, a show broadcast between one and four o'clock on a Thursday afternoon would be recorded from eleven to two the previous day. To resolve the problem of phone-in requests and contests, XEROK devised a scheme in which a disc jockey would record a contest at, let us say, twelve-twenty on a Wednesday for broadcast at two-twenty the following afternoon. The disc jockey taping in the studio Thursday afternoon would be alerted to pick up the contest line at two-twenty, record the call, and splice it into the contest portion of his show to air on Friday.

In 1979, XEROK reverted to a country-music format and, like its predecessor XELO in its glory days, rented a post office box at Clint for P. I. ads. Typical of the new wave of P. I. ads was this come-on: *"If you've ever wondered how a truck driver can stay on the go for nineteen hours at a stretch, here's your answer: They've got a red and white capsule called Fast-Track. . . . One capsule helps lift you out of that tired, washed-out feeling in just twenty clicks of the clock. . . . But you don't have to drive a truck to need Fast-Track! . . ."*

A year later XEROK switched to a new format identified as *radio cañón—¡boom! ¡boom!*

Back in Acuña, XERF's offices are today in a quiet residential neighborhood not far from the main plaza. Daytime Spanish-language shows, now a requirement for all border stations, are programmed here. A rooster crows in the yard across the street. A dog lazily stretches on the sidewalk out front. The main studio, the transmitter, and the broadcast tower are behind locked gates in the countryside on Highway 2 west of town. The only acknowledgment afforded the landmark station is a small roadside sign which says

---

ESTACION RADIO

XERF

The preachers still come on at night.

En Route

San Felipe Creek, which winds through Del Rio, divides the South Texas Mexican from the West Texas Anglo. Old neighborhoods near Brown Plaza and the other Mexican barrios are inviting and comfortable, while housing developments and shopping centers in the west-side Anglo sections testify to a steadily growing economy.

Two miles of countryside separate Del Rio from the Rio Grande. This buffer zone is like a no-man's-land in which the traveler leaves behind American ways in anticipation of the *ambiente* of Mexico. Curiosity and anticipation well up within the first-time border crosser. The only certainty is that you must surrender fully to the other side. "Over there everything is going to be different," Graham Greene advised when he experienced this phenomenon. "Life is never going to be quite the same again after your passport has been stamped and you find yourself speechless among the money-changers. The man seeking scenery imagines strange woods and unheard of mountains; the romantic believes that the women over the border will be more beautiful and complaisant than those at home; the unhappy man imagines at least a different hell; the suicidal traveller expects the death he never finds. The atmosphere of the border—it is like starting over again; there is something about it like a good confession; poised for a few happy moments between sin and sin. When people die on the border they call it 'a happy death.' "

Norah and I must have crossed the bridge at Del Rio–Ciudad Acuña four times daily, each time needing approval from U.S. or Mexican immigration officers. Passing Mexican *inmigración* was simple: slow the car to a half-mile an hour, establish eye contact with the man on duty, wave slightly—an open-palm, forty-five-degree turn works best—and nod. Invariably, the officer would return our signal with a perfunctory nod of his own and wave us by. (This technique worked at every crossing into Mexico except Matamoros where *inmigración* officials always asked to inspect the trunk.)

Entering Del Rio from Mexico was entirely different. For the first few days we encountered increasingly inquisitive U.S. immigration officers. By law we were required to tell them only our citizenship, place of residence, how far into Mexico we'd gone and for how long, and what goods, if any, we were bringing back.

Our out-of-state license plates aroused their suspicion, however, and they'd ask, "Whatcha doin' in these parts?"

"Oh, just drivin' around," we'd reply.

Of course no one is "just drivin' around" across international frontiers, so they'd get more curious. A couple of times I mentioned I was researching a book about the border. Snickering, the men on duty would glance at each other. "It's the old 'I'm-writing-a-book' routine. Wonder what they're really up to?"

And they'd pull us over and search the car. After three days of this all the officers knew my '68 Valiant and left us alone. Four days later we routinely approached the U.S. border station one last time. The friendly officials who had been waving us through the previous few days all leaped out at us. "This'll give you something to put in your book," one customs man chuckled as Wesley, his purebred black Labrador, hopped into my car. Wesley romped through the front sniffing for drugs, paused at the seashells we'd been carrying from the eastern tip of the border, then jumped over to check the back. Finally, he pranced around the trunk sniffing its contents too. The entire station watched, disappointed that these two mysterious travelers carried no trace of contraband.

In Ciudad Acuña we stayed at Mrs. Crosby's, a gracious hotel with the best dining room in town. We must have tried every course on the menu, foremost among them steak *tampiqueña,* chicken *portuguese,* chicken *mole poblano,* and *chicharandías* —tortillas with breast of chicken. Another advantage of staying at Mrs. Crosby's was that we were just down the street from the Lotería Nacional storefront, where I learned that my last three numbers had all lost. What this meant, I assured myself, was that my odds of winning the next time were increased threefold. I bought another ticket.

Eleven thousand foreigners were expelled from the United States for being here illegally in the first decade of this century. Currently, the U.S. Border Patrol, whose Del Rio office is ten minutes from the bridge, picks up that many in four days. The Border Patrol has become both victim and villain in America's shifting attitudes toward Mexican immigration, caught between the problem's causes and its solutions. The agency insists that with more personnel—1,800 agents now work the southern frontier—the flow of migrants from Mexico could be reduced considerably. But even if enough border guards were hired to link arms from the Gulf of Mexico to the Pacific Ocean —2,551,560 by my calculations—the problem would still not be resolved.

How many migrants escape detection is of course not known,

but an educated guess might be that one in every four or five is apprehended. Of those who elude capture, well over half will return to Mexico within a year. As a result, the number of Mexicans in the United States without proper papers may be high at any given time, but there is constant turnover, which makes the number seem higher still.

Bringing Latin Americans into the United States illegally and shipping them around the country is a well-developed industry. To combat this practice the Immigration and Naturalization Service has developed "anti-smuggling units" to break up smuggling rings and track down the money behind them. Hugh Williams, chief of the Del Rio Border Patrol sector—the INS divides the U.S.–Mexican border into eight sectors—explained a case his men had worked on in which the central figure was a junkyard owner in Waco, Texas. The Waco man told his recruiter that he would pay thirty dollars a head on delivery for ten able-bodied Mexicans. The recruiter went to the section of Ciudad Acuña where migrants from the interior gather and announced that he wanted to pick up ten of them the next day on the other side and deliver them to jobs. The recruiter had no trouble collecting his three-hundred-dollar bounty.

The Waco man maintained a list of farmers throughout the South who "bought" Mexicans from him at $250 apiece. If, for example, a cotton farmer in South Carolina needed five field hands, the Waco man would ship them out and collect $1,250. The South Carolina farmer would then deduct $250 from the wages of each of his new field hands. After the Mexicans had worked off their cost, the farmer would sell them on to another farmer for $250 apiece and the deductions would begin again.

"In effect," Williams said, "each farmer is getting $250 worth of free labor plus the resale price on the Mexicans. There have been cases where we've found Mexicans who were at their fourth or fifth farm and hadn't made a penny the whole time they were in the U.S. It is indentured servitude. These smuggling rings have been operating for years. We're looking at peonage. That's really what it is—peonage."

We left the area on the Mexican highway and headed west toward Amistad Dam, which, like Falcon Dam downriver, is a joint U.S.–Mexican project in flood control and conservation. Behind the dam is Lake Amistad, an eighty-five-thousand-acre reservoir fed by the Devil's River and the Rio Grande. With each mile we traveled, the carrizo cane beside the river grew thinner and the riverbank rose higher. We were entering another phase of the Rio Grande, one which promised massive bluffs and spectacular vistas.

A statue of the Aztec rain god Tlaloc watched over Lake Amistad from the Mexican side of the bridge atop the binational dam. Tlaloc's view was overwhelming and we pulled over to take it all in. The morning was quiet with a gentle breeze and no traffic. The loudest noise was a faint hum from the dam's generators. We stood at midpoint, half in Mexico, half in the United States, marveling at the river and what it means to different people. It was a good day to be traveling the border, we told ourselves, and we felt lucky to be doing so.

8

CONFESSIONS OF A PARROT TROOPER

"HEY, YOU WANT to buy some birds? Very pretty. Very cheap. They make good pets." Humberto was selling yellowhead parrots by the cageful in Ciudad Acuña. Rafael wanted to sell me some in Tijuana. In Nogales, Enrique made an offer. On street corners in Mexican border towns from Matamoros to Tijuana, buying birds has become a temptation to American tourists. Except under the most stringent conditions, however, bringing them back into the United States is clearly illegal.

Humberto shrugged when I mentioned that. "Just put them in a paper bag and stuff them under the seat. Maybe give them a little pill before crossing to make sure they're drowsy. They always make it. No problem."

"So you want to know about parrot smuggling?" The district director of customs for Laredo leaned back in his swivel chair and smiled. "This is the way I heard it got started: Years ago there was a senator whose daughter brought in a parrot from Mexico. The girl caught psittacosis—parrot fever—from it and died. Consequently the senator made sure a law was passed which made the importation of psittacine—hookbilled—birds very difficult. That's when the parrot-smuggling industry began and it's been growing ever since."

Currently, pet parrots brought in from Mexico must be quarantined for at least thirty days at one of five government facilities on the border. Before your parrots are accepted—only two per family are permitted—you must get a Mexican government veterinarian to certify that your birds are healthy, and make reservations for quarantine space with the Department of Agriculture. The isolation service costs approximately eighty dollars for one bird, and a hundred dollars for two.

While the birds are in quarantine, veterinarians check them for traces of a contagious illness called Exotic Newcastle Disease, a sickness which kills nine of every ten birds exposed to it. Any poultry near a bird plagued with Exotic Newcastle Disease is killed to prevent germs from spreading still further. In 1972, for example, seven million birds—mainly chickens—had to be killed in southern California because of an outbreak of Exotic Newcastle Disease. The Department of Agriculture spent fifty-six million dollars eliminating that one epidemic.

Diagnosing the disease is not difficult. One day your bird will start sneezing and show signs of breathing problems. It stops eating, its eyes and nose discharge a peculiar mucus, it starts shivering, and it becomes dizzy. Within a day or two your bird is dead.

Exotic Newcastle Disease, however, is extremely rare. Smuggling birds across the border is not. At retail pet shops, the price of a parrot starts around three hundred dollars. The greater your distance from Mexico, the higher the price. Fashionable pet shops in the Midwest charge seven hundred dollars and more for healthy parrots. "The profit margin on smuggled birds is phenomenal," a West Coast customs official remarked. "The demand has increased because of Baretta's pet cockatoo, 'Fred.' Pound for pound, there's more money in parrot smuggling than there is in marijuana. Making seizures on smuggled parrots is more difficult than any other type of contraband. No one takes it seriously—not even customs agents. With marijuana we can catch up with smugglers five hundred miles north of the border. But parrots? Once they're across you can't prove a damn thing."

Most of the birds sold on the border are trapped by Indians in the south of Mexico and sold to a middleman who brings them north by second-class bus. The birds are passed on to a street vendor who peddles them amidst the trinkets, pottery, clothing, and lottery-ticket hawkers who line the main tourist avenues of major border towns.

In the sixties and early seventies, government agents used a composite profile to ferret out drug smugglers: white, male, shaggy hair, between eighteen and thirty-five, slightly nervous. But a typical parrot smuggler? No such thing. They are couples in Winnebagos. Grandmas in new Buicks. Teenagers in Volkswagens. Businessmen in Fords. Anyone in anything. The birds are hidden in cloth sacks and shopping bags, in hollow furniture and door panels, under the carburetor and around the engine. Even under women's skirts. A favorite ploy is to feed birds liquor-soaked bread to keep them tipsy and quiet for the crossing. Every parrot smuggler has a method.

Each year about two thousand parrots are intercepted at the border by customs agents, and the smugglers are warned not to try again. On rare occasions a bird-smuggling case will come before a federal judge. Except in the most extreme cases the defendant will get probation. The largest seizure in recent years occurred in 1978, when a California man was discovered with 562 birds in his station wagon. He received a sixty-day jail sentence and his birds got the death penalty.

The California man wasn't as wise as a fellow I met at a bar in Laredo frequented by local officials and other criminals. "I was at a birthday party for my brother a few years ago," he told me, "and a history professor from my college was feeling sad because one of his double yellowhead parrots had died. He was complaining that the laws were stupid—you could buy birds for fifteen or twenty dollars in Mexico, but by the time you find them in pet shops north of the border the price had multiplied twentyfold or more. I was just amazed. I wanted to learn the whole parrot smuggling scam from beginning to end."

Today that student is the ringleader of a parrot-smuggling operation with branch offices throughout Texas, with possibilities of franchises all over the United States. He is working his way through college supplying all the birds he can to pet shops.

"I didn't know what to look for on my first trip shopping for parrots, or how to tell if the birds were healthy or not. At the time I spoke only a little Spanish. With a friend who became my partner, I found a man in Ciudad Acuña who had parrots. We bought ten from him at twenty-five dollars a bird—although I found out later we could have bought them cheaper.

"I knew the area around Lake Amistad—my family used to go there on vacations when I was a kid. There is one place where the Rio Grande is about thirty-five yards across and fairly shallow. The current isn't very swift at that point and I knew I could swim the birds across there. We figured out what time the dam would close and when the customs men would leave.

"We put ten birds in one cage, and put the cage on a small, one-man rubber raft—the kind you play with in a backyard pool. The birds were pretty cramped and the weather was cold. We didn't know it was the wrong season for smuggling. Anyway, we put a cover on the cage and I shoved off. My partner drove around to the U.S. side to meet me at a rendezvous point.

"Crossing was no trouble. I was on the raft and the cage was between my legs. I paddled the backstroke over to the U.S. side. As soon as I beached I deflated the raft and started off along the three miles to my pick-up point. The first road I had to walk had thirty-foot-high fences lining it—I figured if someone comes down this road I'm a goner—so I started walking very fast. When I was almost in the clear I heard a noise like a jeep was coming. I thought, 'Oh shit, I must have tripped a sensor'—I'm very familiar with all the devices the Border Patrol uses and I got scared. I threw the cage in a ravine and ran to a grassy area and put my head down and thought, 'I'm not gonna move until somebody pulls me up.' I lay there five minutes and the noise kept getting louder. It turned out to be a train.

"Finally, I got to the highway with my cage. I was lying behind a bush waiting for my partner when a Border Patrol car slowly cruised down the same road I had just been on. Just after the Border Patrol left my partner arrived. I flagged him down, threw the birds into the back seat, hopped in the front, and we took off for San Antonio."

Three of the ten birds in the smuggler's first load died. The rest he took to a bird doctor. "He wanted to know what I was doing with a cageful of parrots. That seemed pretty suspicious to him since he didn't usually see thousands of dollars' worth of birds at once. I told him, 'A friend of mine has an aviary in Dallas, and he gave me the birds to sell in San Antonio. I've never seen my friend's aviary, and I don't want to sell any bad birds. That's why I want you to check them out.' He was a little wary, but he gave me some medicine to feed them. Since then I've read all sorts of books on how to feed the parrots, their health, and how to take care of them."

That first batch didn't sell very fast. "I had been after double yellowheads, but as it turned out these were a different breed. Pet-store owners freaked out—they had never seen parrots like these in their lives. They said, 'Are these painted?' I said, 'You tell me. You run a pet shop, not me.' After a while I managed to sell all seven. One store owner looked at me like he was in a trance and said, 'Get me double yellowheads—I'll buy all you can get.' By the way he said that, I knew I was on to something big.

"The man in Acuña never did have what I was after, but a contact I had farther downriver led me to a house full of birds in Nuevo Laredo. By this time I knew what I was looking for. The birds in Nuevo Laredo were the real McCoys—and they were young. Younger yellowheads are worth more because they are easier to train. If you get an older one, he's going to be wilder than the rest.

"My customers always wanted to know whether they were buying male or female parrots. With a lot of birds the female is duller in color, but that's not always the case with parrots. The only way to find out is to feel the undercarriage of the bird— the diaphragm is shaped different in the two sexes. The only scientific way to sex parrots, though, is to have a vet insert a tiny periscope into the parrot and look for certain identifying structures."

I asked the smuggler why parrots are so popular. "They're

the only bird that will accept a human," he explained. "People raise doves but you can't get a dove to crawl on your finger or hop on your head. The parrot alone will tolerate human companionship. People are infatuated with them because they take on human characteristics. You can teach them what to say if you get them young enough. I sold one bird to a woman who had a vocabulary of two hundred words—the bird, not the woman —and it could sing three songs: two operatic arias, plus 'La Cucaracha.' It had perfect pitch.

"I feed my birds twice daily. At first I only fed them masa harina, but as I smuggled more and more of them I learned they needed a more nutritionally balanced diet. Now I dice up carrots and apples and lettuce and throw it all in a blender with a big scoop of peanut butter. I make a batter out of it and feed them straight from a cup.

"In the beginning, I bought parrots in groups of ten. Business became so good a friend of mine started selling them for me. At the time I was paying twenty dollars apiece for them, and he paid me a hundred thirty dollars for each one. Anything he could sell them for over that was his to keep. I know he made a killing on them, and some months, well, I was making a thousand dollars a week bringing them in.

"Crossing the birds at Laredo was different from crossing them at Amistad," the birdman related. "We developed a good working relationship with our supplier in Nuevo Laredo. As soon as we'd pick up the birds at his house we'd go to a Pemex gas station and my partner would inflate our inner tube. Then we'd drive over to the east end of town and walk down to the river with the tube and a full cage. We'd lay the cage on top of the tube and my sneakers on top of the cage. I'm not sure how deep the river was there, but I could walk across a quarter of the way. When the water level got up to my chest the undercurrent was so great that it'd throw my feet out from under me, so I'd swim the rest of the way holding the tube in front of me. The first time we crossed I ended up a hundred twenty yards downriver from where I expected to. We solved that problem, and I've used the same spot dozens of times since."

Soon the smuggler was selling his birds through franchise outlets. "I had a Houston salesman. He'd buy some birds from me, go back home, sell them, and come back for more. Then I had a guy work San Antonio. Our deal was that he'd pay me a hundred forty dollars for each bird and sell them for a hundred seventy-five dollars. He made more money on a weekend working for me than all week at construction. I had a third guy take Austin and another fellow cover Dallas for me. I ended up taking orders from my salesmen. They'd tell me how many they could unload and I'd pick them up in Mexico and bring them back north.

"Running parrots has been good money. I earned a vacation in San Francisco and I went to Cozumel, too. I bought a whole new wardrobe and made all the payments on my car.

"Last year I got a new partner. He's the type who doesn't like to fool around. He said, 'Look, we need to design a cage that will hold *fifty* birds. If you're going to smuggle, why risk only ten at a time? The more times you cross the river, the more chance there is of getting caught. Just make fewer trips but bring fifty at a time.'

"That made sense to me. So we came up with a cage which wasn't very high but it was almost five feet long. My partner drove the car and I did the crossing. We started using walkie-talkies. He was Parrot Trooper II and I was Parrot Trooper I.

"I persuaded my banker to loan me the money to help finance the first big load—I told him the money was for a vacation, which in a way it was. I paid him back the first week. Word got around about all the available birds and people were buying like crazy. Some guy offered to take them east to sell. I could make even more money doing that, except parrots are very temperamental. If the birds get in a draft they'll catch pneumonia. If an air conditioner or heater is blowing they'll catch cold and die faster 'n hell. There's also a slim chance of parrot fever, but they can only get that from the filthiest food, the dirtiest water, and the most intolerable living conditions. Still, I always medicate my birds with streptomycin and tetracycline to make sure. I may send some east yet.

"I've got another year left of college and I'm starting to think —with the size of my operation, if I get caught I'd probably get a felony rap. But it'd be a first offense so I'd likely get five years probation. Also, my parents have been giving me a lot of flak. They know what I'm doing and they don't like it at all. I tell them, 'Look, when I worked for an oil company I was making three dollars an hour. I'd get my paycheck, go out one night, blow fifteen to twenty dollars and just sit figuring it took me seven hours working my butt off to go out at night. That just wasn't worth it. That's why I started doing parrots."

Parrot Trooper's father pleaded with him to forgo smuggling, even offering to give him money. "I said, 'Dad, it's a challenge. I know what I'm doing.' Running birds has been a high-adrenaline rush. It's the most euphoric sensation you could ever experience—something you want to tell your grandkids: '*I swam the Rio Grande with fifty parrots.*'

"I'm starting to turn my part of the business over to other people now, teaching them how to cross the river and such. This way if something happens, they'll get caught—I won't have to suffer the rap. You'd have to be a fool to get caught, though. There's really only a three percent chance of being busted— that's when you're dripping wet with a cageful of birds under one arm and an inner tube under the other.

"I made a chart once—Saturdays and Sundays the Border Patrol checkpoint near my crossing point is usually down. One time we did hit a checkpoint, but they just waved us by. They were looking for Mexicans. I know how police think. I'm majoring in criminal justice. I want to go to law school."

Parrot Trooper talked as though he would soon retire. All profit, all thrills, no errors. Yet he had that one characteristic endemic to all smugglers: He wanted to make that One Last Deal. When we spoke again a few months later he was ebullient as ever, enthusiastic over how well business was going.

"I've found a number of people interested in scarlet macaws," he said, "so this summer I'm going down to the Canal Zone and bring back about ten of them. I can get them all for about fifty dollars there. When I get to the border I'll call in my crew and have them bring the birds across. They sell for more than eight hundred dollars apiece wholesale north of the border. 'Long about Christmastime, the pet shops are just cryin' for them."

En Route

November signaled a change in the weather, and the border changed seasons with us as we headed west. Cool winds braced the evenings, rangeland lined the highways. Just west of Lake Amistad the Pecos River enters the Rio Grande. Reyes Ortiz, employed by the International Water and Boundary Commission, works above the Pecos, literally. His job is to go out in a small metal buggy suspended from a cable between two sheer canyon walls and measure the flow, speed, and depth of the river just before it joins the Rio Grande. He relies on two two-and-a-half-inch pitons lodged in the canyon walls to secure the cable holding his little car 125 feet above the water. The buggy is a metal-bottomed container with three-foot steel beams rising from each of the four corners to crossbars connected to the pulley. The buggy has no motor; to get out to the middle, Ortiz releases it from the canyon wall, allowing it to slide along the 325-foot cable back and forth, back and forth, until it settles in the center of the expanse.

Ortiz invited us to join him in the buggy. The sensation of swinging free between the canyon walls wavered between breathless euphoria and stark fear. The railing and side beams were all we could hold onto. As the three of us adjusted our weight, Ortiz confessed, "The first time I went out in one of these things I was scared. The height didn't bother me, though. The buggy did—it seemed so fragile."

We agreed with that assessment as he continued: "Sometimes a hotshot Border Patrol pilot will fly his plane *underneath* the cable, between it and the river. I think that's crazy. My friends think *I'm* crazy for doing this job." He smiled. "Well, maybe I am, but I bet I'm the only guy around who gets paid for watching the river flow."

We thanked Ortiz for frightening us and quickly returned to the relative safety of our car. The highway signs reminded us that we were nearing Langtry, where the legendary Roy Bean declared himself the "law west of the Pecos." Despite all the hoopla about Bean's "even-handed justice," he left his finest mark as a fight promoter.

In 1896, the heavyweight boxing championship match between Australian Bob Fitzsimmons and Irishman Peter Maher scheduled for El Paso was canceled by Texas officials at the last minute. Mexican authorities refused to allow the fight in Juárez. New Mexico and Arizona, both territories, were likewise declared off limits.

Roy Bean stepped in, inviting the boxers and impatient fight fans milling about El Paso to Langtry. At Three Mile Bluff, a stretch of land along the Rio Grande in Coahuila, Mexico, Bean set up a boxing ring. A hastily constructed pontoon bridge served to carry the crowd across from Texas. Texas authorities were helpless to stop the fight in Mexico and Mexican officials were too far away to halt it themselves. After the fight, in which Fitzsimmons knocked out Maher in the first round, Bean invited the boisterous crowd to his Jersey Lilly Saloon where he took in more money in one night than he normally did in months.

The much-ballyhooed Terlingua Chili Cook-Off was fast approaching, and we headed over to watch the festivities. Weekend after weekend, chili cooks pack up their Coleman stoves and cooking pots, their spices and meats and their chili, and head for the nearest cook-off. Attending the Terlingua affair, the most touted event on the cook-off circuit, has become a tribal ritual within the cult of chili aficionados.

Terlingua, Texas, lies in the parched land just west of Big Bend National Park, about three miles north of the border in what Woody Guthrie called "mesquite rawbone country." Once a thriving mining camp, Terlingua now caters to ghost-town tourists and, once a year, to chiliheads. To reach the cook-off, we had to drive down a one-lane desert flattop and along hairpin curves on unpaved mountain roads.

The cook-off gave rambunctious Texans an excuse for a weekend party. The crowd of four thousand was entertained with pre-cook-off patter by a steady stream of entertainers, such as television personality Mark Shaw. "I've traveled all over the country," said Shaw, "and let me tell you—there's no people more fun-lovin' than Texans." The crowd, which would have cheered on the last word alone, let out a war-whoop at his compliment. Other preliminaries included a wet tee shirt contest and a fair fanny display.

Cooks were busy preparing their brew in the exhibit area for the judging later in the afternoon. I asked Judy Wimberly of the *Goat Gap Gazette*, the chilihead's bible, what makes good chili. "I've tasted some of the best soups, stews, pizza sauces, barbecue sauces, and spaghetti sauces that people call chili. They just aren't it!" she exclaimed. "If you can't eat it with a fork, it's not chili. This is a meat dish."

A "Mexican Fence-Climbing Contest" was the last event prior to the chili-tasting. The contest, a spoof of the government's controversial plan to build up the chain-link barrier between Mexico and the United States at El Paso–Juárez and Tijuana–San Ysidro, tested entrants' ability to scale a ten-foot wire-mesh fence placed in front of the stage. Anglo contestants, some donning sombreros ("so the government can see what a Mexican looks like," said the announcer), scaled the barrier as the crowd cheered them on. "Basically, most chili-eaters are opposed to plans for the new border fence construction," explained Tom Tierney, the contest's organizer. "It might adversely affect our supply of chili—but more important, the fence is downright unfriendly."

What the crowd did not know was that their fence actually had been built by the only Mexicans in attendance a few days prior to the festivities. Every year the workers, natives of Ayo El Chico, west of Guadalajara, cross the Rio Grande upriver at Lajitas to work at Terlingua for two months helping prepare for the cook-off. They are paid five dollars a day plus meals and lodging—a one-room adobe shack shared with a burro. After the cook-off they pick up the beer cans and the rest of the trash.

To reach Presidio, our next stop, we traveled the Camino del Rio, the most spectacular, winding, twisting highway of our entire journey. We spotted our first roadrunner at Redford, an adobe town whose only significant buildings appeared to be a Roman Catholic church and the Outlaws Cafe.

In 1913, during the Mexican Revolution, journalist John Reed wrote that Presidio was "a straggling and indescribably desolate village." Reed's words are still appropriate for this town of two thousand. Presidio's chief notoriety is that it often boasts the highest daily temperature in the United States. Until 1975 Oliver Harper kept track of such things at his hardware store on Route 67, Presidio's main street. A cheerful white-haired man, Harper showed me where the thermometer rested on the side of his store until vandals broke it. Back at his desk he reached inside a drawer and pulled out a piece of cardboard, down the left side of which ran a list of years dating back to 1949. Neatly written next to each year were its high and low temperatures. "Let's see," Harper said refreshing his memory, "in 1952 we hit one hundred seventeen degrees. In 1956 we did it again, and also in 1960. But don't forget—it gets cold here, too. We had four degrees in 1962," he said with pride, "and back in 1949 it got down to eight degrees."

From the front of Harper's hardware store we could see La Sierrita de la Santa Cruz, a mountain in which local legend says the devil lives, two miles south of the border. *El diablo* comes out of his cave periodically to perform evil rites using a swing on the mountainside to propel him over to the U.S. side. Every May, local people make pilgrimages to the chapel atop the mountain, carrying religious gifts to leave for Satan so he won't bother them in the coming year. "Yup," Norah remarked, looking at La Sierrita, "if I were the devil I'd probably live near Presidio, too."

Later we spoke with Hank Murphy, a member of the local school board. "We have trouble recruiting teachers—no one wants to teach here more than a year or two. For many years," he told us, "some government agencies considered Presidio a hardship post because of its isolation and climate.

"Our bilingual teachers are inexperienced. In Presidio, 'bilingual' means inept in both English and Spanish. My child is in the fifth grade and her teacher asks *her* how to pronounce words. If my little girl gets a word wrong, the entire fifth grade mispronounces it for the rest of their lives."

The bridge linking Presidio to Ojinaga, Chihuahua, is the only privately owned and operated bridge between the two countries. It is also the most poorly constructed and the highest priced. Americans who drive across to the town of thirty-five thousand pay sixty cents for the car and driver plus four cents for each passenger. Mexican citizens, under a curious clause in the original contract, pay a reduced rate of forty cents per car. We paid our sixty-four cents and crossed over.

The food, the clothing, the skin tone, the accent—everything told us we had at last arrived in the Mexican West. There were more cowboy hats than wide-brimmed sombreros, more flour tortillas than corn, more Indians from the interior than in any other town we had visited, and more cowboys, too. Ojinaga, called San Francisco de la Junta de los Ríos until 1865, when Benito Juárez rewarded supporter Manuel Ojinaga with his own town, is the border town least affected by American culture or commerce. One curio shop is more than enough to satisfy any tourists. Far removed from major cities in either country, Ojinaga has the rhythm of a *pueblito* in Mexico's interior rather than of a town facing its northern neighbor.

After a tasty chicken *mole* at La Fogata, I drifted across the sun-drenched plaza to the lottery office inside a candy store on Zaragosa Street. Bingo! My most recent ticket scored *reintegro*. Since I was reimbursed twenty-five pesos, and the next drawing, which I bought into, was a fifteen-peso contest, I considered that I had actually won ten pesos. We decided to stay an extra day.

9

BIG BEND

VALENTINE, TEXAS, twenty-five miles east of the border, has a friendly freight yard where Mexican immigrants often hitch rides to Houston. Getting to Valentine from the border—or to Midland or Odessa—requires crossing through Big Bend country, the land which forms that hump on maps along the border in the western part of Texas. Big Bend country is particularly treacherous to travelers on foot because of its desolation, rugged terrain, cold nights, and lack of shelter or water. To find Mexican workers headed for Valentine and elsewhere, the Border Patrol uses planes, whose pilots act as spotters for patrol cars below. The best of these pilots, Johnny Williams, offered to show us two hundred miles of the border from the air.

Our flight started at Marfa Municipal Airport, and we were soon looking down upon the Sierra Vieja mountain range. "There's an old man who homesteads down there named Evans Means," Williams told us. "He looks a little like a Mexican bandit hiding out in the mountains. He's got some livestock and somehow he makes a living from them. He's a total recluse, a real hermit." Williams swung the plane around and jockeyed it into a cushion in the mountains. Below us a rock house dug out of the mountainside came into view. "Every now and then some rookie patrolman will spot him somewhere on the ground and ask him for his papers. It's all part of breaking in the new recruits out here." At the beginning of 1980, Means, eighty-eight, fell off a ledge, broke his skull, and died.

So much water from the Rio Grande is diverted by irrigation for farming in New Mexico that by the time it flows past El Paso and Ciudad Juárez and down into Big Bend country, it is hardly grande and certainly no río. When we banked south, the river was no more than a trickle flowing through a twenty-foot-wide riverbed. From five hundred feet the border seemed a narrow, dried-up mud puddle with brown cracks running back and forth between the two countries. You could drive a car across the Rio Grande there and barely get your tires wet.

We were cruising over the Mexican settlement of Barranco de Guadalupe when we spotted the village cemetery. A crowd was forming inside the entrance while dozens of pickups, horses, and burros were parked outside. "Some important person in the community must have died," Williams supposed as he steered the Cessna-182 farther down the river. Soon we were flying over Vado de Piedra and noticed that all of its townspeople, too, were gathered at their village cemetery around the local priest. Williams couldn't figure out why both cemeteries were full at the same time on the same day.

"Maybe a double suicide?" I ventured.

"I've got it," Norah exclaimed. "Yesterday was All Saints' Day so today must be *El Día de los Muertos,*" The Day of the Dead.

"Yup." Johnny bobbed his head in confirmation. "Gives the *padre* a chance to pass the basket two days in a row."

Cerro Alto. Paradero. Buena Vista. Esmeralda. From the air the Mexican *pueblitos* took on a surreal quality. The only sign of life was laundry hanging out to dry. We saw more homes abandoned than occupied—mainly *jacales,* thatch-roofed, mud-plastered adobe huts—and more goats and burros than people and cars. Everything was in hues of brown. The settlements looked as they must have fifty years earlier.

We continued a bit farther downriver where parched rangeland still filled the U.S. side. Across the border, however, an expansive irrigation project resembling a spider web spread out through the countryside using water from the Río Conchos, a muscular river which flows north from central Chihuahua.

Ejidos and private farms alike benefit from the irrigation project resulting in cotton, grain, and corn.

The Río Conchos refortifies the Rio Grande just above Ojinaga, where once again the Rio Grande becomes a certifiable river. Elaborate levees built in 1976 hold the two rivers in place, but even these are threatened during heavy rainfalls.

At eight hundred feet the Rio Grande appears a rich chocolate color as it prepares to enter the massive canyons of the Big Bend. Scrub brush and the remains of abandoned *jacales* dot the hill country on the Mexican side. Little islands of silt appear in the middle of the river, constantly being built up and washed away by the river's flow. The borderland of the Big Bend was as deserted a stretch of the frontier as we had yet come across. Pilot Williams was disappointed we didn't have the Piper Cub, a smaller plane, which he would have flown between the towering canyon walls above the Rio Grande. Instead, he angled in and out of the beginning and end of each canyon.

The magnificent Santa Elena Canyon came into view at the southwestern corner of Big Bend National Park. Sheer rock rose from the river on both sides, carved by centuries of constant flow. The sun hit the upper parts of the walls but was blocked from the lower walls. Only around high noon does the sun's light cut straight through the narrow slit. Above the canyons on both sides were plateaus of rock and desert brush.

Fifty feet from the South Rim of the canyon was the Mexican village of Santa Elena. Families at Santa Elena row across the Rio Grande to the Castelon Trading Post for weekly provisions. The area is also a favorite with marijuana smugglers who consider the sparsely settled region ideal for importing contraband by truck, boat, and plane.

As the canyon walls shrank, more light entered the river channel and greenery filled the sides of the Rio Grande. At the very end of the canyon the walls gradually turned into rock slides, and Williams descended slightly. The Chisos Mountains, the north-south range in the National Park, connect to the Sierra del Carmen and Fronteriza ranges in Mexico, bisected by the slender, twisting river.

Soon we came upon Mariscal Canyon, second of the three spectacular chasms along the Big Bend. Mariscal marks the actual bend itself where the Rio Grande starts its flow northward. Its walls were so straight and narrow it seemed we could lie down atop them with our heads in the United States and our feet in Mexico. Between Mariscal's 1,600-foot sides the Rio Grande changes from a docile and tame river into a wild animal, clawing to be let out. When the canyon walls finally diminish, the river heaves a sigh of relief—free again.

Next we passed over San Vicente, a crossing where wax is smuggled into the United States. *Candelilla*, as the substance is known, is a strong natural wax with a high melting point, making it particularly useful in cosmetics, polishes, waterproofing, and paint remover. Its main use, however, is in chewing gum. *Candelilla* puts the chew into the gum.

Candelilla grows in the deserts of Chihuahua and Coahuila as well as in Durango and Zacatecas to the south. The plant, a pencil-thin cactus, is yanked up by its root and hauled in burro-powered wagons to wax camps where *candelieros—candelilla* workers—dump the raw cactus into steel tanks filled with water and boil it. After sulfuric acid is added, wax floats to the top and is skimmed off for shipment to the Mexican government's central processing refinery at Saltillo, Coahuila. A government agency, the Banco Nacional de Crédito Rural, imposes strict quotas on *candelilla* production and controls its price and export. American manufacturers who want to buy the wax must go through an agent for the Mexican government—in Millburn, New Jersey.

That's the way the business is supposed to run. But at the border, supply and demand circumvent law and order. When the wax camps near the Rio Grande produce more than their quota the balance often goes to Jim Casner, a businessman in Alpine, Texas, who pioneered the practice of smuggling *candelilla* into the United States. Casner's clandestine activity, when it was in full operation, rewarded the *candelieros* for overproduction and, by underselling the official Mexican price of *candelilla*, affected the international wax market. In the

1950s the contraband wax trade was so well developed that a complex system of drop points and independent truckers was established to haul the illicit material up to Alpine, where it was refined and shipped out to buyers throughout the world. The Mexican government sent police to the area to try to reduce the black-market trade.

Candelilla smuggling, which started before World War II, is now a nearly extinct industry. When I visited the area, Casner, approaching ninety, complained that the *candelieros* he relied on in the past had gone to work in the United States, earning more than he could ever pay them for supplying him with wax. But he still found an occasional buyer for his limited supply.

"From time to time Casner will call and say, 'I can get you some wax for a couple pennies cheaper per pound than the official rate,' " one East Coast wax broker explained, "so occasionally we'll buy what's called 'Texas *candelilla*' from him. We're down to a truckload a year, though. He's really the only one left in the business. The last of a breed."

The most spectacular of the Big Bend canyons is Boquillas. Its slightly sloped walls are tinted with brilliant reds, browns, and yellows, while an occasional strawberry cactus brightens plateaus at the canyon's top. Williams put the Cessna in slow flight above Boquillas. Except for the steady drone of the plane, all was peaceful for miles around. The landscape looked like this in the nineteenth century and will in the twenty-first.

We stayed with the Rio Grande until Heath Canyon where we turned northwest back toward Marfa. "I've got a surprise for you," Williams announced as we left the Rio Grande behind. "I've saved the best for last. It's coming up right below us." Looking down we saw the most magnificent land formation we had yet encountered, a seemingly endless series of canyons more grandiose than the Grand Canyon and more colorful than the Painted Desert. Narrow slivers of rock pointed straight up, shaping a formation like the moon's landscape. To the side, fingers of parched desert were frozen in mid-gesture. The contrast with the surrounding vegetation was so stark we felt transported to another world. At one time the entire area had been thick with rivers. Now there was one stream, trickling with the force of a leaky faucet. No roads, paved or otherwise, were nearby. The desert canyonland below was in pristine condition. The only way to see it was from the sky.

As we descended to the airport some antelope galloped beneath, frightened by the roar of the engine. Our six-hour flight had ended, and Williams nodded with satisfaction: "Cheated death again."

We had driven the border, flown over it, and walked alongside it. Now we were ready to float down it. In the Big Bend area a number of trading posts will take you rafting on the Rio Grande, and we signed on with one at Villa de la Mina near Terlingua.

Rod Ponton, one of the Big Bend's premier river runners, was our guide. The stretch of border between Redford and Heath Canyon—more than a hundred miles as the fish swims—encompasses virtually all of the river's moods, from calm pools to angry rapids. We decided on the Colorado Canyon section, a stretch just west of the National Park. Cookie, a college student from Houston, and Leon, a diesel mechanic from Sierra Blanca, Texas, joined Rod and Norah and me.

This would be my first experience at river running, and just the previous day Rod had spilled while shepherding a party of ten through the considerably more difficult Boquillas Canyon. Even though he insisted the spill was the only mishap of its kind he'd had while leading hundreds of tours downriver, I still approached the trip with some trepidation.

I had also been reading the journal of Major William Emory written during his visit to the same area more than a century earlier. The Big Bend stretch of the border was so rough that he and his crew chanced carrying their gear around the canyons rather than risk life and limb floating through them. "Bold Emory," as he was called, wrote of "the impassable character of the river; walled in at places by stupendous rock barriers, and escaping through chasms blocked by huge rocks that have fallen from impending heights, where, if the traveller should chance to be caught in a freshet, inevitable destruction would be the one consequence."

This part of the Rio Grande remained uncharted until Robert T. Hill, brother of labor organizer Joe Hill, set out to run the Rio Grande in 1899. Hill too had seen Major Emory's account: "Since I first read the narratives in early childhood, they have excited my desire to try this passage," he later wrote. "For years I have longed to launch a boat upon the river." Setting out at Presidio with a five-man crew, Hill took three weeks to travel the 350 miles to Langtry.

A few miles upriver from Lajitas we belted on life jackets, and Rod once again assured me that today's trip would be no trouble. Just a few mild rapids and lots of scenery. We could relax.

Leon, big Leon, shoved us off from the muddy bank and jumped in. Rod maneuvered the twelve-foot craft a little to the Mexico side and pointed us downriver. All my misgivings dissolved quickly as the sensation of floating between countries took hold. I exchanged knowing glances with the water as we became best of friends. Finally, I knew how the river itself felt looking out at both countries at once. This was the simple and joyful anarchy I'd been searching for on the border. Free at last!

The thunder of an approaching rapid reached us. Little peaks of white water swirled along the rocks near the banks, but with forty feet of river between countries to float about in, they posed no problem. Leon popped out some Lone Star as the current dragged us slowly downstream. Rod's job looked easy. All he had to do was steer. The water, which had appeared so muddy from the air, took on a multitude of colors. From above the flow looked even. On the river itself the current was alternately stubborn and yielding, tugging and releasing.

After a few minutes Rod suggested we stuff our gear in a plastic bag, sit tight, and grab the metal handles alongside the raft. The twisting funnel of our first rapid was directly in front of us. Rod entered it at a forty-five-degree angle, waiting for the surface current to take us over the undercurrent tugging from below. "Get your goose pimples ready!" Cookie shouted from

the rear as we took a rocking roller-coaster ride over the harder
waves and gently cushioned into the softer ones. Rod stroked
hard to the left, then forward. Seconds later we emerged from
the rapids relieved and somewhat wetter. The drop—a few feet
—was small as rapids go, but my respect for Rod soared. His skill
was obvious yet he managed the rapid effortlessly. "There's no
such thing as an easy rapid," he said when I mentioned this to
him. "Some are just less difficult than others."

The most important factor in our trip was the sun. Being in
the shade meant a drop in temperature of twenty degrees.
Since we were traveling east by southwest, the Mexican side of
the river became shady as the afternoon progressed, while the
American bank lingered in the heat. Ocotillo, carrizo, and salt-
cedar were the only vegetation sturdy enough to survive the
mixture of riverbank and desert soil. From time to time deer
would appear on the U.S. side. Little peninsulas covered with
lush golf-course moss reached out as we floated by. We beached
on a sandbar on the U.S. side before entering the canyon.

"If you follow the small streams up a way," Rod told us, "you'll
find Indian pictographs on the walls." Centuries ago many
tribes crossed back and forth along the Rio Grande in Big Bend
country. More recently Comanches lived here until Anglos and
Mexicans combined to drive them out. Names in the area speak
chapters of local history: Comanche Crossing, Contrabando
Creek, Smuggler's Creek, Las Vegas de los Ladrones (Meadows
of the Thieves).

Colorado Canyon was wide compared to the others we had
seen from the air. Its walls were jagged, sloping outward rather
than shooting straight up. The afternoon sun was turning the
north wall a deep watermelon red above the quiet listless river.
A couple of cows had managed to wander through the seemingly impenetrable canyon walls and lazily raised their heads to
gaze at us. This was an area Rod knew well. Since his initial trip
down the river at age eight, the first of an estimated one thousand such trips, the river had taken on intangible qualities for
him. "The Rio Grande is my great sewer," he said. "It cleans me
out. It becomes spiritual to me. When I go down the river here
I become part of this country, part of the river itself."

Leon, who had just completed his first six-pack, took over the rowing chores for Rod and immediately we were headed for a rock on the north bank. Rod barked out directions: "Point your nose *towards* the rock and head *away* from it," he instructed. We avoided the rock and proceeded on our way.

As we continued floating down the river, millions of Americans were busy voting politicians in and out of office. It was Election Day, and I felt certain we were doing our part for democracy by drifting along the outer edge of America. I wished every Election Day could be like this. Leon cocked his head back. "Sheeyit. Our five votes wouldn't make a difference anyway."

We came upon another rapid and Leon navigated us through it perfectly. The water, which at first appeared to be boiling, simmered and finally relaxed.

After stopping for a rest on the Mexican side, Leon turned the helm over to me for the final stretch of the trip. This experience would be my showdown with all those interminable rafting articles in outdoors magazines about taming the Tennessee and conquering the Colorado. My first problem, however, was conquering the nine-foot oars. "You mean if I stop rowing on *this* side we start drifting to the *other* side? I've got to sit *backwards* to row *forward?* If I pull the *right* oar toward me the raft *turns* to the left?" The basic rule seemed to be that whichever direction we wanted to go I had to row the opposite way. My respect for Rod grew further.

My tenure at the helm went smoothly with neither rocks nor rapids to test my mettle. The river and I giggled and whispered to each other. I thanked it for a safe trip, and a few minutes later, as our seven-mile float came to a close, it invited me back for a longer stay.

En Route

During our airborne tour of the border we had noticed what seemed to be a vast mining operation on the Mexican side of Heath Canyon. Before heading up to El Paso we drove over to see the mine firsthand and met its manager, Brick Parrish. The rocks in the area, Brick explained, are rich with fluorspar, a prime ingredient in fluorocarbon. La Linda, as the operation near Heath Canyon is called, is an immense network of mines, processing plants, barracks, homes, and offices. The Dow Chemical Company started the mine in the early 1950s and sold it to the DuPont Company of Wilmington, Delaware, in 1971. A Mexican government program to "Mexicanize" U.S.-owned industries required DuPont to relinquish control of La Linda, and in 1978, 51 percent of the operation was sold to investors in Mexico City. La Linda remains one of forty-five companies owned either partially or outright by DuPont outside the United States.

Parrish, a husky Texan who had worked at La Linda for ten years, was anxious to show us the mine. We put on hard hats, hopped in his pickup, drove across the company-built bridge at the Rio Grande, and bounced down some dirt roads toward the Cuatro Palmas mine. On our way we stopped to pick up Andy Kurie, a geologist and the only other American on the grounds.

Cuatro Palmas is an open-pit mine, 120 yards deep and almost as wide at the top. We drove halfway down its side over a precarious road which spiraled around the outer edge of the pit. At the very bottom, mammoth Caterpillar tractors shovel loads of sludge into the backs of trucks which chug up and around the pit to the top and on to a flotation plant. There the raw material is crushed and ground into a fine powder and trucked seventy miles northwest to Marathon, Texas, where it is shipped out to buyers by freight train.

At the nearby Agua Chile mine four miners, suspended by safety harnesses from an overhang one hundred feet in the air, were jamming jackhammers into the walls of a mineral deposit. When they were through they planted some dynamite in the wall, left, and ignited the fuse by remote control. Stenciled on their equipment was a slogan: SEGURIDAD—PRIMERO CUIDA TU VIDA Y LA DE TU COMPAÑERO. Safety—first take of care for your life and that of your companion.

In the early 1970s aerosol-spray cans with fluorocarbons were found to be unsafe and were taken off the market in the United States. The workers at La Linda, however, were surrounded by similarly hazardous material all the time, a situation which Brick was quick to defend. "Our miners are required to wear respirators in very dusty areas," he explained. "We sample the dust they are exposed to. We have a company doctor and a full-time safety engineer. We make sure our new employees wear different color hard hats when they start work so we can spot them. (The ones he had given us for the day were for initiates.) We require ear protectors where there's noise. We use a spirometer up at the clinic—it measures the vital capacity of your lungs. Mexico's safety standards are usually four or five years behind the United States', but we enforce safety pretty strongly here."

As we traveled farther down the rutty back roads of La Linda, Brick mentioned that the land contained enough fluorspar to last into the 1990s. Do you ever reforest areas already mined? I asked. Andy and Brick looked at each other quizzically as if I had asked if the sun sometimes sets in the east. "We don't have those laws here," Brick finally replied. "We have no EPA standards to meet. When we're through with an open-pit mine we simply put a fence around it as a safety measure to make sure no one falls in."

Driving on, we passed an *ejido* where the residents were tending goats. Under Mexican law the mine had to turn over a fraction of its profits to the *ejido* and give work to some of the *ejidatarios.* Whether miners or not, most *ejidatarios* use the company doctor, often paying him in chickens or goats or a service such as welding.

At the foot of Agua Chile, a mountain which figures prominently in local *ejido* legends, are the barracks for miners who have hired on from all parts of the country. Although fairly small, the miners' quarters are clean. They sleep nine to a room in army-style bunk beds. Nowhere at La Linda can miners spend their wages except at the junction of two dirt roads when, on weekends, a merchant from Múzquiz, Coahuila, 150 miles southeast, comes over to sell beer from the back of his truck. To fight the boredom, miners watch movies brought in from Monterrey in the barracks' rec room. Some play in a binational semi-pro baseball league against teams from Ojinaga, Fort Stockton, Múzquiz, Alpine, and Marathon. The bachelor workers are given ten days' leave for every two months at the mine.

La Linda recruits its miners through radio and newspaper advertisements around the country. Newly hired workers arrive on a daily company flight from La Linda's office in Ciudad Acuña. The conversation shifted to the miners' salaries.

"Don't we pay a pretty fair salary, Andy, to our *peón* workers as far as the *peón* wage is concerned?" Brick asked.

"Oh, I think for the average worker's wage in Mexico we pay a very good wage," Andy replied. "But I don't know what the average wage *is* in Mexico." Andy stopped to tote up the miners' pay, figuring in a recent raise. "We pay six dollars a day," he said with finality. "Plus they get work clothes and their meals and the dorm rooms—in addition to the six dollars a day."

"And these guys get an extra two weeks' salary at the end of every year," Brick added. "What do you work 'em, Andy?"

"Well, they work eight-hour shifts, then they start in on overtime. Sometimes they'll work two shifts straight, but normally if they go into overtime a shift and a half is the most we work 'em."

"Some miners come over, work for two weeks, pick up their paychecks, and go wet," Brick explained. "That starts to add up when you're supplying each miner with a set of clothing and shoes. But if one of our miners goes wet and looks for work in the area near here, the Border Patrol doesn't care. The main thing immigration people want to make sure of is that our workers don't end up somewhere north of Highway 90."

Like Chicago.

Across the river in the company-furnished Parrish home at Heath Canyon, Brick and his wife described the novelty of the relatively recent innovation, television. In 1975, TV came to La Linda by way of newly installed signal relays from Alpine which cost DuPont a thousand dollars a month. For that money workers and management can watch two stations, both originating in Odessa, Texas. The Parrish children attend school in Marathon, commuting 140 miles daily. Except for television, isolation for the Parrishes matches that of any family on the border. To their west is Big Bend National Park. South of them is the mine. A wilderness preserve lies to the north. A vast desert stretches east.

To elaborate upon the isolation, Brick described the fifty-dollar pizza. "The pizza doesn't taste like a fifty-dollar pizza— actually it's just an ordinary pizza—but it costs us that much to have one. First there's twenty dollars in gas to drive up to Alpine and back. Then five dollars for the pizza and a little more for drinks. Well, we can't just drive up, eat, and turn right around, so we have to pay another fifteen dollars or more for a motel room. And of course there's breakfast the next morning. That comes to fifty dollars a pizza."

We chatted some more, bid the Parrishes good night, and pushed on to the Chisos Basin Campground in Big Bend National Park to spend the night before continuing to El Paso. No sounds were in the air, no one else was on the road. We opened the windows so the night chill could blow through the car. We stopped once, got out, and gazed skyward. Only a few dark spots could be seen between the stars.

10

ROSA'S CANTINA

"EL PASO" is the quintessential borderland cowboy ballad. The tune itself is one of the most recognized melodies in American music. It tells the story of a cowboy who falls madly in love with Felina, a flirtatious dancer at Rosa's Cantina.

> One night a wild young cowboy came in,
> Wild as the West Texas wind.
> Dashing and daring a drink he was sharing
> With wicked Felina, the girl that I loved.
> So in anger I challenged his right for the love of this maiden.
> Down went his hand for the gun that he wore.
> My challenge was answered. In less than a heartbeat
> The handsome young stranger lay dead on the floor.

Only two verses into the ballad and already we have interracial love, insane jealousy, a barroom shoot-out, and a dead body. The cowboy ("shocked by the foul evil deed I had done") runs out the back door, steals the fastest-looking horse, and rides

> . . . just as fast as I could from the West Texas town of El Paso
> Out to the badlands of Old Mexico.

We have a murderer and a horse thief on our hands who, in the tradition of other borderland outlaws, crosses the frontier to escape punishment. (The song's original lyric has him ride off to Old Mexico; on record this was revised to *New* Mexico. We'll stay with the original.)

Despite the obstacles preventing their reunion, the cowboy longs to see Felina ("My love is stronger than my fear of death. . . . Maybe tomorrow a bullet will find me. Tonight nothing's worse than this pain in my heart") and saddles up for his return to El Paso. As he begins the final approach to the bar, a posse surrounds him. His only option is a suicidal dash for his loved one: "Shouting and shooting I can't let them catch me. I have to make it to Rosa's back door."

Finally:

> I see a white puff of smoke from the rifle,
> I feel the bullet go deep in my chest.
> From out of nowhere Felina has found me,
> Kissing my cheek as she kneels by my side.
> Cradled by two loving arms that I'll die for,
> One little kiss and Felina goodbye.

"El Paso" is complete unto itself, but to true lovers of borderland mythology many gaps remained in its story. Marty Robbins obliged these aficionados with "Felina from El Paso," in which he describes Felina's background and the forces that led her to Rosa's Cantina. "El Paso" ends with her lover's death. "Felina from El Paso" completes the tragedy:

> Quickly she grabbed the six-gun that he wore.
> And screaming in anger and placing the gun to her breast,
> "Bury us deep and maybe we'll find peace!"
> Pulling the trigger she fell 'cross the dead cowboy's chest.

Highway signs for El Paso, the most populated American city on the border with 450,000 residents, start hundreds of miles away. Every time I see a mileage sign for the city, I unconsciously hum the tune to "El Paso." Soon I start singing the words, and by the time the signs read

EL PASO 20

I am literally shouting the lyrics along Interstate 10. To learn whether "El Paso" is based on something other than Marty Robbins' imagination, I checked local newspaper files, where the only mention of the song was in a concert review. A woman at the public library reference desk laughed and said that every now and then someone inquires, but no, the song is strictly fictional.

If the song had had historical validity, then the drama would have unfolded on the west side of town, most likely on the edge of a barrio where both Mexicans and Anglos would frequent the cantina. The Rio Grande must be nearby so the cowboy can quickly ride back and forth. And Rosa's must be near the bottom of a hill (". . . at last here I am on the hill overlooking El Paso, I can see Rosa's Cantina below"). I spent hours driving the streets of El Paso until I found the truth: Rosa's Cantina lives.

It is on Donaphin Road near Sunland Park Race Track in a curious stretch of land where the states of Texas, New Mexico, and Chihuahua, all bump into each other. Any one of the three states is only steps away from the other two. A cowboy could gallop from Rosa's across the Rio Grande into Old—or New—Mexico in less than a minute.

From a distance Rosa's appears a forgotten building from another era. Donaphin Road, a major thoroughfare until the parallel strip of Interstate 10 was completed, dead-ends in the next block. White paint covers Rosa's adobe walls. Unpaved parking space adjoins the building. The bar's name, spelled out in large, red plastic letters in front and again in wrought iron on the front door, is all that indicates life within.

Inside, Rosa's Cantina is magnificent. The dimly lit barroom is spacious, with enough room for Felina and a hundred other dancers. An unfinished mural depicting El Paso's history covers part of the west wall. The opposite wall sports a string of chile peppers shadowed by a ten-point buck. Trophies won by Rosa's entry in the Upper Valley Little League line another wall. A pool table sits to the side. Next to a plastic palm and below an American flag is the jukebox, with artists from Glenn Miller to Johnny Rodriguez, Eydie Gorme to the Righteous Brothers, the Platters to Freddy Fender. (Yes, Marty Robbins' "El Paso" is there too.)

Roberto Zubia, an industrious and friendly man in his fifties, owns Rosa's Cantina. That was its name when he bought it in the early 1960s, he said, and had been for as long as he could remember. Zubia worked in maintenance at a downtown hotel to support his family and the cantina until the bar started to break even. When he was pointed out to me, I asked him if he was, in fact, the owner. "Rosa, hah!" came the reply. "She owns *me!*"

Rosa's opens for lunch daily with meals prepared by Anita Zubia, Roberto's wife. Each table has a handwritten menu on lined paper listing specials of the day such as *chili con queso*, short ribs soaked in red chile, tostadas, or hamburger steak. The meals come with rice, refried beans, soup, tortillas, and iced tea, and cost $1.75 complete. Food is served up quickly to accommodate nearby factory workers on forty-five-minute lunch breaks.

After lunch Rosa's is empty until the afternoon shift change at the ASARCO (American Smelting and Refining Company) plant. "It's a good bar, Rosa's," explained Jesús Martinez, a maintenance foreman for ASARCO, sitting with three fellow workers. "We always come here. After a day at ASARCO we need to."

The four workers discussed a recent hunting trip. Jesús motioned to the deer head on the wall. "You want to hear a good one?" he asked of no one in particular. "I once brought back a deer bigger than that! That's when I was a bullfighter."

"You mean a bullshitter," nudged Ken, sitting to the right of Jesús.

Two mailmen from the nearby Coronado Post Office watched a little Sony television broadcast the afternoon news. "This morning," intoned the anchorman, "the President said the time is right—" He paused.

"—for revolution!" spouted one mailman. The others nodded their heads, smiling. Everyone lifted his beer, ¡salud!

Hernando and Bob, also from ASARCO, ordered up another Pearl. Jesús was showing them photos from his recent fishing trip to the Amistad Reservoir. "We got drunk in Acuña afterwards," he laughed, tucking the pictures in his pocket. "By the way, anything new on the 'tortilla curtain'? "

The "tortilla curtain" is the reinforced steel mesh wall which the U.S. government was planning to install between El Paso and Juárez to keep Mexicans from crossing over illegally. The western edge of the restructured fence was supposed to end along the river near Rosa's.

"Nobody 'round here likes the idea."

"Besides, they'll just cut holes through the new fence."

"Sure, and it won't stop the workers who come through the underground tunnel from Juárez every morning, anyway."

"Hey, I've got an old friend who used to be a wetback. Gary is his name. He ran Canadian Club into the U.S. during Prohibition across the river. Only it was the St. Lawrence River, not the Rio Grande. He was a Canadian wetback!" We all toasted Canadian wetbacks.

"I know Gary," Jesús bragged, "but I don't think he's ever been to Rosa's. Here you find Anglos, Comanches, Mexicans, Dagos, Germans, and anyone else who works at ASARCO."

ASARCO, which processes zinc, lead, copper, and antimony, is one of the region's major industries; for years its smokestacks have coughed up noxious fumes which blanket both El Paso and Juárez, making it the center of controversy about binational air pollution. "All that talk about pollution has pretty much died down," Bob said. "The people who were complaining about the smog? Hah! They've all been voted out of office. Defeated!"

Owner Zubia spoke with pride of the rich history he has seen unfold in the area. "You're going all the way to Tijuana?" he asked. "Tell me, does Tijuana have a history? I don't think so. Not like here. That's why they call it El Paso. Let me show you something."

We hopped in my car and drove a mile to a flat stretch of barren land directly beneath the ASARCO stacks. The Rio Grande was at our feet no more than fifty feet wide and only a few feet deep. "This is where I grew up," Zubia explained with affection. "About nine hundred people used to live here. In the early 1970s the last of the houses was torn down. Everyone called the community Smeltertown.

"There was only one industry in Smelter in the old days: smuggling. My daddy was involved in it—and so was everyone else. The Mexicans used to bring whiskey and tequila across by the sackful in *latas*, the kind of cans you store lard in. Smelter families would hide the booze in their homes waiting for it to be picked up.

"The Mexican smugglers had to contend with the *fiscales*"— law enforcement officers—"to get the contraband across. Sometimes there were three-day fights between the smugglers and the *fiscales*. People would die, but the contraband usually got through. Nighttime was best for moving the goods.

"The whole scene was crazy. U.S. customs agents would try to catch smugglers who got by the Mexican authorities. If the smugglers killed an American customs man, they'd drag his body back to the Mexican side and leave it there. If the *contrabandistas* killed one of the *fiscales*, his body would be brought over to the U.S. side. In the mornings we'd all go down to the riverside and see who was killed and who survived. I was only nine when Prohibition ended but I remember these things. Many *corridos* were written about the smugglers and how brave they were. I have one on the jukebox; it's called 'El Contrabando de El Paso.' Today the smugglers bring drugs across. I don't like that."

Back at the bar Roberto played "El Contrabando de El Paso." Anita, busy arranging tables for a private wedding party that night, came over to show me a souvenir she kept next to the cash register: a day-sheet from the movie *When You Comin' Back Red Ryder?* The interior of Rosa's was used for some scenes in the film.

Another movie was shot in El Paso about the same time. This one, *El Paso—City by the Rio Grande*, was filmed at the behest of the city's Visitors and Convention Bureau. Marty Robbins was hired by an advertising agency to write the title song and narrate the script. The movie opens with Robbins in front of an old, abandoned adobe building. A crooked sign on the building says ROSA'S CANTINA. The film boasts about El Paso's history of bandits and barroom shoot-outs, balancing them with modern tourist attractions to draw future business.

"I heard about the film when they were making it," Zubia said. "They went to the race track. They went to Ranger Peak. And they went to the bullring in Juárez. But they didn't come here." Zubia looked around his cantina and shrugged. "I guess this isn't the image they wanted."

En Route

We crossed over to Ciudad Juárez, which, after Mexico City, Guadalajara, and Monterrey, is the most populated city in Mexico. Our drive around town started on Lerdo Street, a thoroughfare lined with dental clinics screaming for patients: PAINLESS EXTRACTIONS—$4 begged one. FILLINGS WHILE U WAIT boasted another. Giant replicas of teeth hung in their doorways.

Soon we arrived at ProNaF, the busy culture and convention center where arts and crafts from the interior are sold. The Programa Nacional Fronterizo, for which the complex is named, was founded in the early 1960s in an attempt to make border towns more respectable. Nearby a billboard advertised a new subdivision for Juárez's burgeoning middle class: MUY CERCA DE LA CIUDAD PERO MUY LEJOS DEL RUIDO Y EL SMOG. Very close to town but very far from the noise and smog.

Downtown Juárez seemed a healthy center of commerce with bookstores, movie theaters, department stores, and restaurants. A line was forming at one theater showing John Travolta in *Vaselina*. Next door was a lottery outlet where the previous Monday's winners list revealed I had won again—that is, I was reimbursed for the price of my ticket. Back in the car I was telling Norah I sensed a winning streak when a young traffic cop pulled us over. The left-turn arrow had not been flashing green when I turned off Avenida 16 de Septiembre, the officer said. I looked back and noticed that there was no left-turn arrow to begin with, so of course it could not have been flashing green. "May I see your license please?" he asked courteously. An old Firesign Theatre routine came to mind.

"I have to give you a ticket," he said in perfectly good English. I pretended not to understand. He was almost apologetic as he repeated himself syllable by syllable in Spanish: *"Ten-go que dar-te un bo-le-to."* In either language his words were a polite request for money. A pregnant silence followed while I reached for my wallet and fished for a twenty-peso note.

I wasn't sure of the etiquette in a situation like this. If twenty pesos was not enough he might be insulted. If it was too much I wanted change. Every Mexican official I have ever seen take *mordida* uses a graceful and smooth motion for grasping and pocketing money. One *inmigración* officer in Ojinaga performed sleight-of-hand tricks with *mordida;* I wanted to applaud him.

I flicked a twenty-peso bill toward the Juárez cop. In one sweeping motion the bill disappeared in his right hand while his left hand returned my driver's license. As we prepared to pull away the officer patted the roof of the car. *"¡Tengan más cuidado!"* he cheerfully told us. Be more careful!

We headed south past some working-class *colonias,* then blocks and blocks of junkyards. Eventually, we arrived at an open landfill which spread out for acres. As in many Latin American cities, the dump in Juárez has become a valuable source of income for citizens who scavenge through the discards searching for recyclable goods. The ragpickers, as they are sometimes called, have unionized in their attempt to bring order to an unsanitary profession. The city dump co-op organizes its members according to the material they rummage for —nylons, glass, wood, cardboard, bones, bottles, aluminum, and so on. The ragpickers gather their specialties in piles inside the dump and truck them to buyers in town. Bones go to make glue, rags are sold as fabric, cardboard is used for packing. Some families have lived at the dump for generations, jealously protecting their little domains. The scavengers are an embarrassment to Juárez boosters, made all the worse by their institutionalized desperation.

In five minutes we were at Campestre Juárez, home for the city's bankers and industrialists. Opulent modern houses lined hidden cul-de-sacs; two-car garages sheltered Jaguars and Mercedeses. Across the street from Campestre Juárez bales of cotton were stacked in a field waiting for shipment to a warehouse across town. The noise and hustle of the city could have been a hundred miles away.

On our way to the west side we passed Juárez's penitentiary. In front youthful guards lazily leaned back in metal folding chairs, submachine guns in their laps.

In a few more miles we arrived at the land of the *paracaidistas*, literally parachutists, people who drop in at the border from the interior. Juárez attracts the unemployed, the poor, and the upwardly mobile of Mexico's midwest. A comparatively high minimum wage ($1.33 per hour), proximity to the United States, and American-owned assembly plants are among the reasons they come, hoping to find here what they can't in the interior: enough money to support a family. This northward migration overtaxes the limited services of Ciudad Juárez and other border towns, so the *paracaidistas* form *colonias* outside the city. New shantytowns such as Alta Vista, Francisco Villa, and Felipe Angeles have no services such as gas, water, electricity, or paved roads, but they have already taken root. Attempts by the government to alleviate conditions make the *colonias* more inviting; ignoring them worsens their situation. The forces of push and pull have spawned a perpetual dilemma.

Workers on the Mexican side line up along the four-mile cement culvert through which the Rio Grande trickles, waiting for the most opportune moment to cross over. Some do it daily, commuting, as it were, to jobs in El Paso. Others hope for longer residency deeper in the U.S.A., and still others cross just for the thrill. The Border Patrol spreads its men along the riverfront highways intercepting as many of these people as it can, yet when groups of ten, twenty, or even fifty at a time make a dash for the American side, *la migra* is helpless. A festive atmosphere settles over the Juárez riverfront as the two sides square off. Husbands kiss their wives goodbye before leaving for work. Friends and relatives come to wish their loved ones *buena suerte*.

Andrés and Raúl sat on a guardrail watching the ritual, taking note of the actions of the Border Patrol on the other side. The two, both in their twenties, had met on the 230-mile bus ride from Ciudad Chihuahua the previous evening. In Chihuahua, Andrés had worked in a poultry plant chopping heads off chickens; Raúl was a mechanic. Andrés had never been to the United States; Raúl had worked in a factory in Pennsylvania, picked fruit on the Gold-Mar ranch west of Phoenix, and been part of a construction crew in Houston. He was happy to learn that Mexican workers at Gold-Mar had struck successfully for better working and living conditions. When he worked there he had been picked up by the Border Patrol and sent back across the line at Nogales.

The two new friends talked about what they wanted to do in the United States. "We can always find construction work," Raúl told his younger companion. "See that car over there?" he asked, nodding toward an open boxcar in the freight yard across the river. "It's going to Houston. We'll be on it tonight. God willing, we'll have jobs tomorrow."

Javier, another Chihuahuan, came to pass the time. He had recently returned from five months' work in Los Angeles. Before entering the United States from Tijuana he paid a *coyote* one hundred dollars to deliver him safely to L.A. The investment was worthwhile, he claimed, "but next time I'll be able to cross on my own."

A bit farther upriver Juan and César Hernández sat on the hood of their pickup with no intention of crossing. They simply enjoyed looking at the best free show in town. They had brought binoculars with them so they could watch the Border Patrol watching them through binoculars.

Next to the Hernández brothers a small crowd formed around Adolfo Gutiérrez. For many years a heavy equipment operator at Guadalupe, Arizona, Adolfo was now in semiretirement, selling peanuts and oranges by the river. "Juárez is like a *ciudad trampolín, ¿verdad?*" he smiled.

The Tigua Indian Reservation lies on the U.S. side of the Ysleta-Zaragosa Bridge east of El Paso–Juárez. In the mid-eighteenth century the king of Spain awarded the Tigua thirty-six square miles, a land grant confirmed in 1864 by President Abraham Lincoln. Unfortunately for the Tigua, Texas was in the confederacy at the time so the land was never officially theirs. In the following decade Texas opened the same parcel of land for settlement, a move later rescinded. The damage was done, however—the Tigua ended up with thirty-six acres.

Over the years the Tigua worked as scouts for the Spanish, the Mexicans, the U.S. Cavalry, and the Texas Rangers. Except for occasional intermarriage with Mexicans they became socially isolated, and relations with their ancestral brethren, the Pueblo Indians of New Mexico, were virtually nonexistent.

By the mid-twentieth century Tigua tribal identity barely existed. Other than some small farms, they had no industry and only limited formal education. Soon eviction proceedings began against them, an action which spurred tribal member Pablo Silvas and a local lawyer to launch what amounted to a revolt against the foreclosings. Eventually, the state government recognized the tribe, confirmed their landed status, and assumed responsibility for Tigua health and welfare. Today the Tigua have reinstituted a tribal junta and other ancient forms of Pueblo government. Tribal affairs, however, are run by the Texas Indian Commission.

"There is a stigma attached to being Indians in this area," complained Ray Apodaca, the Commission's supervisor at the Ysleta del Sur Reservation. "We're not accepted by whites, blacks, or most Mexicans. They think we're all drunken thieves. They put our kids in special-ed classes. The average educational level for Tigua now is six-point-nine years. Almost forty percent of the Tigua on tribal rolls"—six hundred in all—"are unemployed."

With guidance from the Texas Indian Commission and encouragement from civic boosters, the Tigua have entered a new industry: tourism. They are El Paso's pet tribe.

Highway billboards promote the Tigua Craft Center where, for $1.50, tourists watch real Indians string beads, package herbs, bake bread, and throw pots. A Tigua youth group stages tribal dances and chants on the craft center's patio. Because the tribe knew virtually none of its own rituals, anthropologists from New Mexico were brought in so the Indians could learn their customs anew for tourists. The young Tigua, who receive $2.65 an hour to perform for the tourists—paid in part from federal CETA funds—learned their tribal chants from phonograph records.

Elsewhere in the craft center, plastic "Tigua Indian" snack trays are sold, along with coffee mugs, tee shirts, ashtrays, and a dozen other items with the tribe's name on them. The Tigua also have a boutique at El Paso International Airport. "The tribe is like most tourist-oriented businesses," supervisor Apodaca said. "We do well in the summer. In the winter the crowds slack off." After three centuries on the Rio Grande, the Tigua have become, in effect, a reconstituted Indian tribe.

The Rio Grande part of our journey, 1,243 miles, was complete, and we felt a sense of accomplishment. What we had traveled was not the Texas of John Connally, Neiman-Marcus, or Don Meredith; it was the land of Jacinto Treviño, Virgilio Guerra, Jack Stockley, and the Zubias.

According to *Great River*, Paul Horgan's epic chronicle of the Rio Grande, the river has had seventeen different names since the early sixteenth century, beginning with Río de las Palmas. At El Paso, the great river wound north while we headed west for the New Mexico–Chihuahua border towns. The Pacific Ocean was only 690 miles away.

11
VIVA VILLA

THE PANCHO VILLA CANTINA, on the main street of Columbus, New Mexico, is a comfortable saloon lined with photos of its namesake, the Mexican revolutionary who plundered the town in March 1916. Hunched over a beer at the end of the bar was a cheery-looking mustachioed man, his denim cap displaying the U.S. and Mexican flags entwined. Next to him sat a clean-shaven fellow who nodded thoughtfully at the barroom banter. The bartender was pacing back and forth, wiping the bar, cleaning out already spotless ashtrays, moving bottles from one case to the next and back again. Now and then he'd look up, flash a smile, and add his two cents' worth to the conversation. The bartender's wife, who managed the local motel, was pacing the floor. Ignacio from the Standard gas station on the corner was shooting pool. Near the opposite end of the bar, the only Mexican national present, a construction worker from Palomas, Chihuahua, three miles down the road, sat by himself. He wore a cowboy hat and a hand-tooled belt.

The big news at the Pancho Villa Cantina was that the beer distributor now carried Pearl. Everyone ordered a bottle to test its contents. "No different from any of the rest," the clean-shaven man commented. The others mumbled their agreement.

The man with the binational cap introduced himself as Carlos Ogden, a transplant from Los Angeles who moved here because his daughter had come down with a mild form of tuberculosis. The climate was just what she needed. Carlos was serving his first year as mayor, a position whose function he described in three words.

"I eat shit."

I stared at him. "How's that?"

"That and beg. The state government thinks we're in Chihuahua, and the county commissioners won't do anything for us— we beg them to pave our roads, but with two Republicans on the board they ignore us. We're in a gray zone between the United States and Mexico. Our most important asset is our twenty-four-hour border crossing.

"Last year customs was going to cut us down to sixteen hours a day and we raised hell! Petitions to our congressmen, statistical analyses, economic profiles, the works. We even urged tourists to drive back and forth through the port-of-entry to demonstrate the volume of traffic we have." He laughed. "On a per-capita basis we have as many night crossings as El Paso. But they'd never close down El Paso, now would they?"

He bought a round of Pearl.

"Oh, by the way, this is my town council." The clean-shaven man next to him, Ramón Garcia, nodded. Ramón managed the U.S. Market, owned by the former mayor, Sus Carreon, approaching seventy-five and in ill health.

Narissa Ferrer sauntered up to Carlos and Ramón. "Are we having a meeting?" Narissa, the motel manager, was also on the council, elected on the same slate as the other two earlier in the year. "We make all our decisions here," she announced.

Mayor Ogden smiled. "There's one little old lady who keeps saying, 'How come I never know what's happening?' We claim it's because she doesn't drink beer!" We toasted the little old lady in absentia.

Steve Ferrer, who has a pronounced British accent, served up a Michelob. "You lookin' for a small town to move to? Columbus is the place." He peered at me intently. "Wait a minute. You have a talent? We don't encourage talent. If someone with talent moved here it'd shame us all." Steve and Narissa came to Columbus from Spain via Costa Rica and now have grand plans to develop tourism here. In addition to the Pancho Villa Cantina and the Pancho Villa Motel, they own the Pancho Villa Museum and a restaurant, La Frontera. A few months back La Frontera's cook left town. Until a new one showed up Columbus was without a place to eat.

"This town is unique," the mayor continued. "You've got your tourist thing, and your wetback thing, and your old-time rancher thing, and your floater-drifter-newcomer thing—like me. I'm called 'the hippie mayor' because I drive a VW van. When I was in my late twenties I served in the Peace Corps in Sierra Leone, West Africa. My wife says now that I'm in my forties I'm doing Peace Corps work again here in Columbus.

"I started out as the city maintenance man, which was a CETA job, but I turned it into a white-collar position. Finally, I went to Sus and told him that since he wasn't standing for re-election I was going to run for mayor. He'd been mayor for thirty years. He said, 'Wait a minute. Who told you I wasn't going to run?' I reminded him that *he* had. Things used to be very simple here—if you didn't vote for Sus he'd cut off your credit. With him out of the race, winning was a lot easier, but I couldn't have done it without this fellow's support." He slapped Ramón on the back.

On Election Day, Carlos won by a landslide, 93 votes out of 129.

"Y'see, the way a border town this size is run, you have to balance your rednecks with enlightened citizens. Rednecks can't say they're anti-Mexican anymore, so they have to find other ways to get that feeling across. My job is to placate everybody. For instance—every *pueblo* in Mexico has a city hall which says 'Palacio Municipal' out front. I thought that'd look nice here, a friendly gesture, so I had PALACIO MUNICIPAL painted on the entrance to our village building. I warned the painter that if he charged more than fifty dollars I'd have to get approval from the town council, and then the rednecks around town would have their say. The painter made sure the job came to just under fifty dollars."

We carried on into the evening, talking about the tacos in Mexico City, movie reviews in *The New Yorker,* travel through Latin America, and jet flights to Guadalajara. "I'd like to travel by yacht," Mayor Ogden fantasized. "You could see the entire coast that way. Yes, a yacht. Or a private railroad car. Imagine the scenery traveling in your very own railroad car. That would suit me fine."

Finally the Mexican construction worker spoke up. "It's best to travel by burro. That way you see *everything.*" He took a final draw on his beer, slowly stood up, and left. For a long while the sound of Ignacio's cue stick hitting balls into the corner pocket was the only noise.

Celebrating Pancho Villa in the town he attacked seems a bit unusual, but few appear to mind. Villa felt an affinity for the border, buying weapons in the United States and conquering towns in Mexico. The raid on Columbus, his only military foray into America, was the last attack on mainland United States by foreign troops. Eighteen Americans were left dead, as were scores of Villistas; horses were stolen and buildings burned. The predawn raid prompted a jingoistic outcry from the nation's press. Typical was the *New York Evening Journal:* "What has been done in California and Texas by the United States can be done all the way down to the southern bank of the Panama Canal and a few miles beyond." Texas Governor James E. Ferguson urged President Woodrow Wilson to "enter Mexico and assume control of that unfortunate country."

Wilson dispatched General "Black Jack" Pershing to hunt down Villa. On its way down, Pershing's "punitive expedition" camped at Columbus; it returned eleven months later, empty-handed.

What tourism Columbus has results from Villa's invasion and the subsequent search for him. The Pancho Villa State Park—formerly Camp Furlong—is forty-nine acres of cactus, parking spaces, shower and cooking facilities, and historical markers commemorating the American soldiers stationed there. Every March, on the anniversary of the raid, townspeople gather for a combination memorial service and fiesta. Survivors—they number less than five—recall for visitors the horror of that day. Pictures of the photogenic Villa hang in the Pancho Villa Museum, along with artifacts from the raid. Narissa spoke fondly of her museum and her hopes to expand its exhibits. "We have all of Dr. Braddy's books," she said proudly. "He's the leading expert on Villa."

Columbus' love-hate relationship with Pancho Villa is best left unexplored, as I soon discovered when I good-naturedly asked, "What would Columbus do without Pancho Villa?"

There was dead silence before Narissa finally replied, "Well, there was also General Pershing."

It was my turn to buy a round.

Mayor Ogden will use any excuse to visit Tillie's, the best restaurant in Palomas, Chihuahua, and its social center as well. "As mayor you get your real dividend when you visit Palomas. In Columbus you're just the mayor, a dollar-a-year job that doesn't mean much. But in Palomas my stature soars. All the men introduce their wives and buy me drinks—in fact, that's the biggest hazard of this job. And there's no way I can get a parking ticket in Palomas. One time I was parked illegally and I was about to rush outside to move my car, and everybody laughed. 'You can't get a ticket,' they said. 'You're *el presidente!*' I'm glad the job means something to someone.

"The people of Palomas also like us because we put out their fires. We're a small town, less than five hundred, but Palomas, which is nearly ten times our size, has no fire protection, so when we learn there's a fire across the line we just can't refuse, international border or no. The less enlightened in Columbus don't like us to go there; they say, 'What if you dent a fender on a car? They'll confiscate our fifty-seven-thousand-dollar truck!'

"Like hell they will; there're too many people in Palomas who have family in Columbus. Our fire chief is Mexican-American, but his wife is from Palomas.

"Anyway, we love to go there, roaring down the three-mile

stretch way too fast, hangin' on to the back of the truck. When we hit the border we don't even slow down—Mexican customs knows we're comin' and wave their arms for us to drive on in. "Usually the fire is someone's car burning or a stovepipe set somebody's roof on fire. They haven't had any really bad fires because the houses are so far apart a fire can't spread. "Once we've put the flames out, a crowd gathers. In Columbus a fireman is, well, interesting, but on the other side we're heroes. We have to keep someone on the back of the engine just to keep the kids from climbing on when we pull away. We hope there's never another fire in Palomas, but if we have to go, it's exciting."

Cattle is the major industry in Chihuahua. Three months out of every year Palomas fills with cows, cowboys, ranchers, and cattle-barons delivering cattle to American buyers. U.S. Department of Agriculture veterinarians go over to Mexican corrals to inspect the animals, dipping them for fever ticks, checking for traces of disease, stamping and tagging each one, and making sure they are all neutered. Rejected steers are sprayed on the forehead with red paint and sent back to the interior; those that pass inspection continue through a maze of wooden chutes west of the port-of-entry, crossing the border on the hoof to waiting trucks on the U.S. side. The entire process, in fact, bears a striking resemblance to the way in which *campesinos* were herded across the border during the Bracero Program, 1941–1964, to work in rural America. The chief difference is that the cattle are assured of being well fed and cared for on arrival, while the *braceros* had no idea what lay in store for them.

En Route

Before pushing on we returned to Tillie's for one last meal. This time we tried the special plate lunch—*nopales* omelette with frijoles, hot sweet bread, Spanish rice, and tortillas. To

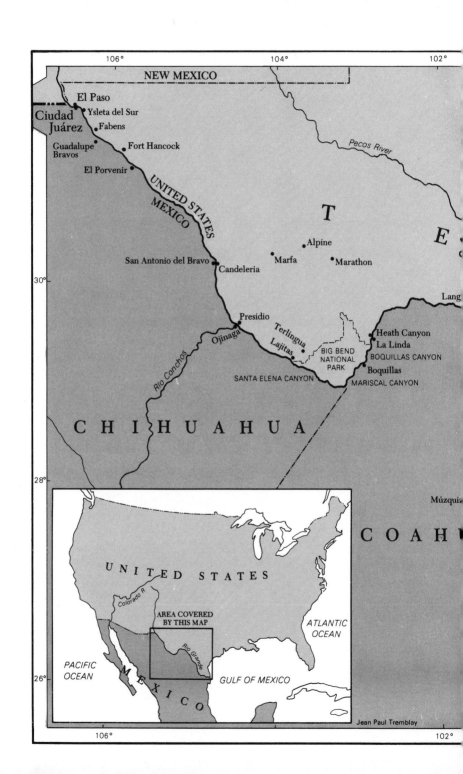

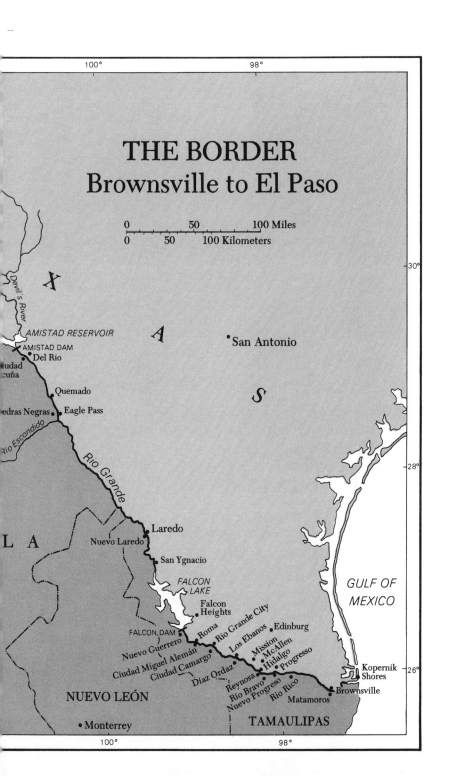

THE BORDER
Brownsville to El Paso

0   50   100 Miles
0   50   100 Kilometers

100°

98°

Devil's River

X

AMISTAD RESERVOIR

A

San Antonio

30°

AMISTAD DAM

Del Rio

iudad
cuña

Quemado

S

Rio Escondido

edras Negras

Eagle Pass

Rio Grande

28°

L A

Laredo

Nuevo Laredo

San Ygnacio

FALCON
LAKE

GULF OF
MEXICO

Falcon
Heights

Rio Grande City

FALCON DAM

Roma

Edinburg

Nuevo Guerrero

Los Ebanos

Mission

Ciudad Miguel Alemán

McAllen

Ciudad Camargo

Hidalgo

Progresso

Díaz Ordaz

Reynosa

Nuevo Progreso

Kopernik
Shores

26°

Rio Bravo

Río Rico

NUEVO LEÓN

Matamoros

Brownsville

Monterrey

TAMAULIPAS

100°

98°

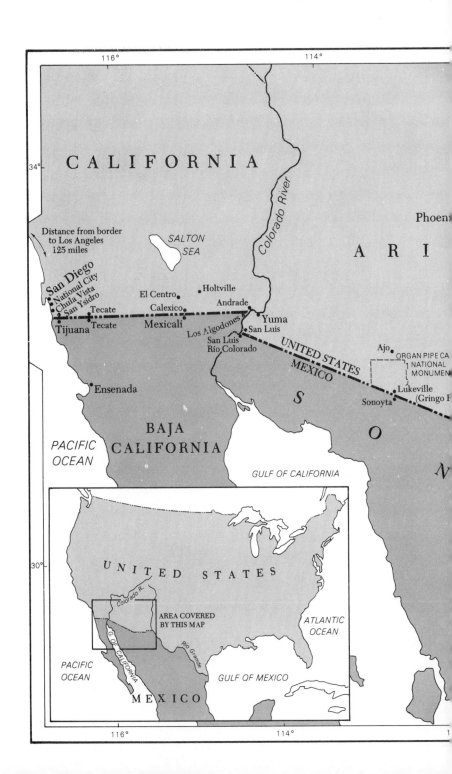

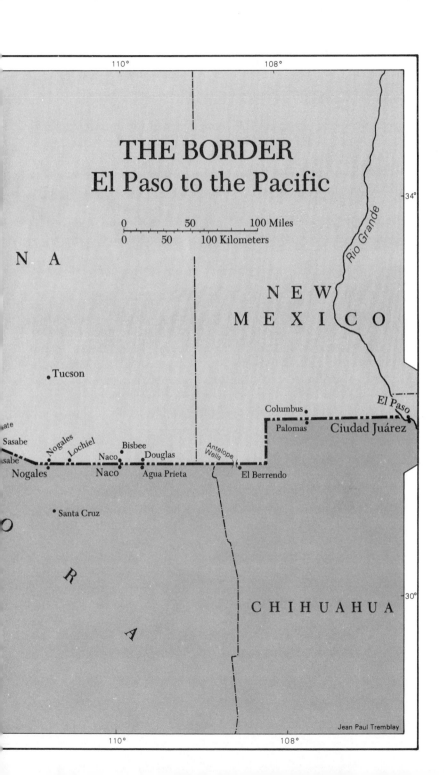

THE BORDER
El Paso to the Pacific

0   50   100 Miles
0   50   100 Kilometers

N A

NEW
MEXICO

Rio Grande

34°

Tucson

ate

Sasabe

sabe

Nogales

Lochiel

Naco

Bisbee

Douglas

Antelope Wells

Columbus

El Paso

Palomas

Ciudad Juárez

Nogales

Naco

Agua Prieta

El Berrendo

Santa Cruz

O

R

A

CHIHUAHUA

30°

Jean Paul Tremblay

110°

108°

make the specialty, finely dice the pads of a young prickly pear cactus, add chiles, and toss into an omelette. The plate lunch was a rare delicacy, all the more unusual for its price: $1.50.

Our destination was Douglas, Arizona, via Antelope Wells, New Mexico's only other port-of-entry. From Columbus we drove west on Route 9 through open rangeland. The two-lane road, not entirely paved, took us by an old water tower which once served the community of Hermanas. Black paint covered a portion of the tower's front, not quite blotting out some lettering. We swung around to read it:

WHITE IS RIGHT
KKK

In the western section of the border Ku Klux Klansmen had been making noise about rousting Mexicans who came across the frontier illegally, but the lonely tower at Hermanas was the only visible sign of their racism. The area was sparsely populated save for some cattle on the range; neither Anglo nor Mexican lived for miles around. Farther on we bought some soft drinks at Hachita's one grocery store and turned south into New Mexico's bootheel.

The mostly gravel forty-five-mile road to Antelope Wells was so hazardous that I questioned my determination to visit each border crossing. Had we been sensible we would have turned back after five minutes. No cars passed us in either direction during the entire two-hour drive. The only road sign we encountered pointed east into the Big Hatchet Mountains; it said HIGH LONESOME and we believed it.

An average of three people a day enter the United States at Antelope Wells, making it the least used port-of-entry along the entire border. Two officials are assigned to the crossing, commuting in five-day shifts from Deming, eighty miles away; each has a mobile home behind the customs house. Antelope Wells has no other residents, nor, I noticed, either antelopes or wells.

We arrived there after four o'clock, at which time the gate closed. The customs station itself was empty, and there was no sign of life nearby. Just before leaving we chanced a knock on the door of one of the trailers.

"Come in, come in," a friendly voice said as the door opened. "Don't have many visitors here. Can I get you a drink?" Ed Willis was busy slicing vegetables for his dinner. His partner was back in Deming; he was alone, enjoying the solitude and peace his job afforded him.

The border fence was twenty-five yards away with a hole big enough for a body to slip through. I asked Willis if I might cross over for a minute to walk around. Stepping on Mexican soil there was vitally important in a way I found difficult to explain; Willis understood. He wouldn't grant me permission, but he did say that if I bought anything on the Mexican side to declare it upon my return.

The Mexico side of the fence was called El Berrendo and consisted of two shacks: one for the *aduana* official and the other for the *inmigración* man. Their nearest neighbors lived on some *ranchitos* a few miles away. The closest stores were at Janos down a thirty-mile dirt road.

Outside the U.S. customs station was a brightly colored sign four by six feet welcoming visitors to the United States. The sign, one of a series posted at all ports-of-entry, was a kaleidoscopic Technicolor splash designed by painter Peter Max. When the series was formally unveiled in 1978 in Washington, D.C., an official said that "Peter Max has captured . . . the warmth and excitement we hope will be felt by all people entering this country—visitors and residents alike." Willis and I agreed that the Antelope Wells sign, a sort of pop art "Have a nice day!" happy-face in the midst of the desert, was hopelessly incongruous. In all, the government paid $300,000 for the signs. We felt sure that plenty of people would be willing to tear them down at no cost.

We left Willis to his dinner and headed back up the road. At Hachita we turned west, and within thirty miles crossed the twisting Continental Divide three times. There was nothing of scenic note at any of the three points, but the Divide was yet another landmark achieved, and that gave us a sense of satisfaction. We drove past Rodeo, New Mexico, and down through the Chiricahua Mountains to Douglas, Arizona, and its Mexican companion, Agua Prieta, Sonora. We were in the transition zone between the Chihuahuan and the Sonoran deserts, which surveyor John Bartlett characterized as "sterile plains, where no tree offered its friendly shade, the sun glowing fiercely, and the wind hot from the parched earth, cracking the lips and burning the eyes. . . . As far as the eye can reach stretches one unbroken waste, wild and worthless. . . ."

The intervening years had done little to change the view.

12

HANIGAN'S GRAVE

MANUEL, BERNABÉ, AND ELEAZAR felt confident Wednesday morning, August 18, 1976, as they crossed the fence separating Mexico from the United States. Bernabé knew where they could find work in the Sulphur Springs Valley and Manuel was anxious to locate his last employer, who still owed him money. The three walked through mesquite and scrub brush, resting occasionally and sipping from their plastic water jug. As they circled around the smelter stacks west of Douglas, Arizona, Bernabé, who knew the countryside best, spotted Highway 80, the first major landmark of their journey. Just then a plane flew overhead and the three dove into the hip-high Johnson grass nearby. *La migra* is everywhere, they knew, even in the air. Eleazar pointed to a man on a tractor in the distance, but his two companions shrugged. They were busy refilling the jug at a windmill.

As they sipped some water a yellow pickup with a white camper shell headed toward them, and the three jumped back into the grass. The truck passed them—then stopped, backed up, and came to a halt. An Anglo with a black mustache, wearing work clothes and a baseball cap with an H on it, hopped out brandishing a pistol. He was the same man Eleazar had seen on the tractor.

"OK, mojados, pa' arriba," the Anglo commanded. OK, wetbacks, get up. Slowly the three came out from the brush as the

armed man demanded in Spanish: "Where are you going?"
"We're going to Elfrida to work," Bernabé replied.
The man pointed to a paper bag they were carrying. "What's in there?"
"Just food and clothing," Eleazar answered.
"All right, you fucking wetbacks," the young rancher continued in Spanish. "You're not going anywhere. All you wets do is come here to rob and then you go back to Mexico." Manuel protested. "No. We're not here to do any damage, we're here to work. There's no work in Mexico."
"There's lots of work in Mexico," the man countered angrily as he motioned them into the camper with his gun and shut the door.
"I guess he's going to turn us over to *la migra,*" Manuel said, recalling his previous departure from the United States a few weeks earlier. "Well," added Bernabé, "we'll just have to start all over again tomorrow."
The truck carried them to Highway 80 where it turned west, then into a driveway leading to a ranch house north of the highway. The driver got out and went into the house.
The mustachioed man returned fifteen minutes later and opened the camper door. "Are you hot?" he asked. The temperature hovered just under ninety degrees, and the three nodded quickly. The gunman led them over to some shade next to the house. Again he asked why they were in the United States. "We can't find any work back home," Bernabé replied.
A blue pickup, also with a white camper shell, pulled into the driveway and a well-dressed elderly businessman carrying a rifle emerged. He glared at the three. "Wetbacks?" he asked the gunman. The young man nodded and the two talked in English. The old man, a stocky fellow with a weather-beaten face, went into the house. When he came out a short time later he wore denim pants, a plaid shirt, a red kerchief, and a straw cowboy hat. "*¿Entienden inglés?*" he asked the apprehensive Mexicans. Do you understand English? They did not. Just then a third pickup arrived, hauling a cow in a trailer behind it. A tall baby-faced cowboy hopped out, a handgun tucked in his waist-

band. His right wrist was wrapped in a white bandage.

"Ah, *mojados!*" the newcomer smiled. He turned his attention to Manuel. "I know you. You stole three rifles and a pistol from me."

Manuel furrowed his forehead. "No, that's not true. I've never been here before."

"I know you by the shoes you're wearing," the baby-faced cowboy charged. Manuel was wearing the only pair he owned —a black patent leather pair with platform heels.

"These shoes were given to me by Don Antonio Hernández of Agua Prieta," an old family friend at whose house Manuel had been living and in whose junkyard he had worked.

"Liar," Baby-Face spat out. "All Mexicans are thieves."

"You're crazy! I've never been here before."

"Shut up!" Baby-Face shouted back.

"OK, back in the truck," their original abductor ordered. Manuel, Bernabé, and Eleazar sensed that the Border Patrol was not coming after all.

As the three Mexicans watched from the camper, Baby-Face took some rope from his pickup and got into the cab of the yellow pickup with *el bigote,* the mustachioed one. With the old man following in his truck, *el bigote* and Baby-Face drove the Mexicans to an arroyo near the original windmill site. They told Manuel to get out and lie down.

Manuel García Loya resisted at first. The eldest of ten children, twenty-five-year-old Manuel had hitchhiked to the border seven weeks before from Ciudad Chihuahua, where his father worked on construction crews. He crossed near Naco and found a job at seventy-five cents an hour cleaning out treewells at the Pride of Cochise apple orchard near Willcox, Arizona. He figured to send some money home and work his way north until he got to Chicago, where he had heard Mexicans could earn high wages. His dream ended abruptly when the Border Patrol raided the apple orchard twelve days later and shipped him back to Mexico before he even got paid.

The three *norteamericanos* were insistent. Manuel stubbornly refused. As *el bigote* held him, Baby-Face took some rope and tied Manuel's wrists behind him. The two threw him to the ground while the old man stood guard with his shotgun and laughed.

Eighteen-year-old Bernabé Herrera Mata was next. The eldest of seven children, Bernabé had been on the road since leaving his home in Durango, Mexico two years earlier. The slight *muchacho* with Indian features had lived in Tijuana and occasionally crossed into Southern California, had crossed the Sonora–Arizona line many times, the Chihuahua–New Mexico border once, and had even slipped into the United States as far east as El Paso. Sometimes the Border Patrol picked him up, other times he returned to Mexico on his own. His most recent job at Mission Valley Farm near Elfrida, twenty-five miles away, had paid a dollar an hour, and his boss had told him he was welcome back to help with the peanuts, wheat, alfalfa, and corn.

That seemed unlikely now, as *el bigote* and Baby-Face beckoned him to lie down next to Manuel. Bernabé's hesitation ended quickly as he was grabbed, had his hands tied behind him, and was forced to the ground.

Eleazar watched in horror. Born twenty-four years earlier in Mocorito, Sinaloa, Eleazar Ruelas Zavala helped his family of fifteen by working in the fields near Culiacán. At twenty-one he decided to travel to the United States, but found a job instead at a limestone quarry in Sonora. Soon he moved to Agua Prieta, where he worked for two years at an American-owned textile plant. In early 1976 he lost his job and started crossing into the United States. Eleazar's last boss, for whom he weeded cotton, was particularly impressed with him. When he left his common-law wife and their three-month-old son to travel with Manuel and Bernabé, Eleazar had been full of optimism.

Eleazar meekly complied with the Americans' orders, allowing his wrists to be tied behind him, then lying down near the two others. Baby-Face knelt and tied Manuel's ankles together, and then tied them to his hands so all four limbs were immobile behind his back. Bernabé and Eleazar received the same treatment.

The three Americans talked in English, then the younger ones searched the Mexicans' clothing. "Oh, you have money!" the tall cowboy smiled as he pulled close to seven dollars from Manuel's pocket. His shoes yielded thirty dollars more. Bernabé had a dollar, which was taken from him.

"Why are you coming to the United States?"

Manuel cried out that he had only come to find work, and that the money was to buy food. The armed Americans kept laughing as their captives looked up in horror.

Baby-Face and *el bigote* methodically stripped each of the tied-up Mexicans, using a knife to slice off their clothes. Baby-Face lit a mesquite wood fire some yards away and tossed strips of clothing into it. The paper bag with food and clothing the Mexicans had been clutching all morning was tossed toward the fire; bread and bologna scattered all over. While Manuel, Bernabé, and Eleazar were bound and naked, their heads were yanked back and a knife slashed through their hair. "Why are you coming here?" *el bigote* asked as he hacked at Eleazar's hair, tossing clumps of it into the fire. *"Pinche* Mexicans, we never go to your country. Why do you come to ours?"

Bernabé screamed: "Why are you doing this?"

"Mexican crybabies," the old man said in disgust. He got a knife and threatened to cut the Mexicans' throats. Baby-Face put a pistol to Eleazar's head: "Let's see if your Virgin of Guadalupe can help you now," he laughed.

The young tormentors took turns dragging the Mexicans by the ropes close to the fire. "You're not going to live a minute longer," *el bigote* announced. "You're not going back to your damn Mexico. You're going to die here."

"Are you thirsty?" the old man asked. The three nodded their heads, tongues hanging out. Baby-Face approached them with their own water jug and, laughing, poured water on each of them. With his boot he turned each one over on the 135-degree desert floor. Dirt and pebbles and stickers clung to their bodies. "We don't like Mexicans," Baby-Face said as he finished rolling the third one, "because all Mexicans are thieves."

Bernabé was dragged still closer to the fire but squirmed

away enough so he didn't feel the worst of the heat. *El bigote* took a long metal rod out of the fire and passed its hot end over the bodies of the three. The tall cowboy took the hot bar from *el bigote* and touched it to the bottoms of Eleazar's feet, burning them again and again. The odor of his own burned flesh filled Eleazar's nostrils, and he could see the smoke rising from his soles. His scream began in his feet and worked its way up.

The old man had been looking at young Bernabé, particularly at his penis. He took a knife from *el bigote* and, grinning, grabbed Bernabé's testicles in one hand and slowly drew the knife next to the sac with the other. "I like your balls," the old man said, "I want to cut them off."

Bernabé screamed "No!" and started praying. He was convinced he was about to die. *El bigote* ran up and pulled the old man's arm away, pleading with him to stop. The old man relented.

Eleazar was dragged along the hard ground by the rope binding his hands and feet until at last he was deposited at the bottom of the arroyo. One end of another rope was placed around his neck. The other end was thrown over the branch of a tree growing at the arroyo's edge. Baby-Face pulled on the rope and Eleazar's body lifted a little bit off the ground. To relieve the pressure around his neck Eleazar maneuvered himself to the bank of the arroyo and propped himself up on his elbows.

Bernabé could see Eleazar's shoulders and head above the arroyo wall. "Please let me loose," Bernabé begged. "I'll never return to the United States again."

"Of course you won't," Baby-Face said as he cut Bernabé's ropes, "because in another minute you're going to die. Let's see how good you are at running." Bernabé froze.

"Run!" the *norteamericanos* yelled. Bernabé ran, heading in the general direction of Mexico, while Baby-Face climbed on the hood of the nearest pickup and fired after him. To Bernabé the shotgun pellets felt like a swarm of bees stuck to the backs of his arms and legs. He let out a screech and looked over his shoulders to see the Americans laughing. A second shot missed as the barefoot and naked Mexican zig-zagged through the brush. Eventually he reached the border fence and threw himself over it.

The noose around Eleazar's neck was cut and his hands and feet were untied. "You're next," the old man told him. "The same thing is going to happen to you as your partner. He's dead." Eleazar ran down the arroyo which slanted toward the border as Baby-Face charged after him, gun in hand. Dashing up one side of the arroyo, Eleazar tripped over a small gully. Shotgun pellets whizzed overhead as he fell. His hand hurt from the fall and a rock ground into his knee on impact. He hid behind some bushes. After a short silence he began crawling then walking, bent forward at the waist so he wouldn't be seen. Dirt and sharp rocks dug into the blisters covering the soles of his swollen feet. He paused twice to pull off dead skin before arriving back in Mexico.

A rope was tied around Manuel's neck and he was dragged forty feet toward a pickup. Next his hands and feet were freed, and Baby-Face motioned toward Mexico. "Run in that direction, because your friends are dead over there." The old man stood by and laughed some more.

"Why should I run?" Manuel asked the cowboy. "I haven't harmed you in any way." His protestation ended quickly as a rifle butt slammed into his shoulder. After running a few yards he felt a shotgun blast in his back. He thought his life was coming to an end. He picked up speed and another blast of pellets struck him. Finally, out of shotgun range, he shouted for his companions: "*¡Muchachos! ¡Muchachos!*" In his terror he had forgotten their names. Manuel, like his friends, ran 1½ miles in a southeasterly direction until he too reached the fence. Exhausted, he stepped into Mexico and fainted on an anthill.

"That was a dastardly thing George Hanigan did yesterday," Jerr Jones said, describing what he had learned of the torture incident to Bill Curtis on the streets of Douglas the next morning. Douglas police had learned from Mexican authorities the night before that three badly injured Mexicans had been brought to Agua Prieta's Hospital Civil and reported that they had been tortured by three Americans west of Douglas. From the descriptions of the torturers and the location, police suspected sixty-seven-year-old George Hanigan, a stocky rancher-businessman with a weather-beaten face, and his two sons, Pat, twenty-two, and Tom, nineteen.

While news of the incident spread around town, officers from the city police and the county sheriff's department took Douglas High School yearbooks from the previous spring, when Tom Hanigan graduated, and from 1972, when Pat graduated, to the Mexicans' hospital room in Agua Prieta. Pat Hanigan, a tall baby-faced cowboy, was identified by the victims as one of the younger tormentors. Tom, who sported a black mustache, was identified as the other.

The Hanigan land had been homesteaded by George's father in 1900, a year before Douglas was founded and twelve years before Arizona became a state. In Douglas' early years ranching and the copper industry thrived, and "the second Denver," as some called the town, grew to a population of twelve thousand.

Soon after George was born, July 4, 1909, his father turned from vegetable farming to running a dairy. One of George's chores as a youngster was to watch over the family cattle to make sure no Mexican herded them across the border into Sonora. In the mid-1930s George took over the ranch from his dad and continued supplying Douglas with bottled milk from Hanigan's Dairy. Fifteen years later the family dairy business faded out.

George maintained the 2,200 acres as a cattle ranch and started investing in Dairy Queen ice-cream shops, but his real prominence came from political activity. In 1956 he was a delegate to the Republican national convention; he was an alternate to the following two conventions, supporting Richard Nixon and Barry Goldwater. George became known as "Mr. Republican of Cochise County" and started a chapter of Americans for Constitutional Action, a conservative organization. "If Adolf Hitler were running for office," said the dean of students at

Douglas High School, a Hanigan friend for twenty years, "he'd be George's man."

George Hanigan's attitude carried over to local fraternal lodges. "The Elk's Club has an unwritten law that 'no Mexican will ever cross these portals,'" the Douglas city attorney at the time of the torture incident explained. "Three NO votes are needed to blackball a prospective member, and Hanigan can always muster up two others to keep a Mexican out. A long time ago when Dr. Mike Gomez was in line to become president of our Kiwanis Club, George ran another candidate to make sure no Mexican became an official. He's got a mean temper. He's been known to turkey-tromp a few people."

Born and raised on the family ranch, Tom and Pat grew up in an Anglo society surrounded by a Mexican majority. Tom's first awareness of border problems came at age seven when he was riding horseback near the Phelps-Dodge smelter and saw a group of Mexicans readying to steal some scrap iron and take it back to Agua Prieta to sell. For the *campesino típico*, however, the family often left food and water at the windmill site, a resting spot well known among Mexicans hiking into the Sulphur Springs Valley for jobs.

Tom and Pat were worked hard by their dad from an early age, both around the ranch and at the Douglas Dairy Queen. Because they lived on a ranch and their dad owned a string of forty-two Dairy Queens throughout the state, the brothers' classmates thought of them as rich kids, a sentiment which sometimes provoked fights with Chicano boys. In high school Pat was a center on the football team but his heart was in the rodeo club. Students like Pat in the vocational-agriculture program and the Future Farmers of America were known as "stompers." Pat and the other stompers hung out at Silver Creek, Dawson's, and the Red Barn, drinking, shooting pool, and carrying on. Sometimes they'd cross over to drink at the Vegas Club, a bar in Agua Prieta's red-light district. Pat was an apprentice good-ol'-boy.

Tom joined the band at Douglas High and, like Pat, Future Farmers of America and the rodeo club. A knee injury sidelined him from varsity football but he made spending money phoning game results to the Tucson and Phoenix newspapers. Growing up in Pat's shadow, Tom noticed a gap between himself and the Mexican-Americans at school and wondered if Pat had done something in prior years to cause it. He found that if he became too chummy with Mexican-American students his Anglo friends became stand-offish. When a Hispanic friend came to Tom's senior-year party, daddy George insisted the guest leave right away.

The family's attitude toward Mexicans coming across the fence changed in the early 1970s as an increasing number of their neighbors became the victims of burglaries. Sometimes footprints from the burglarized homes led back to the border, beyond which American police were powerless to hunt for suspects or stolen property. When Pat Hanigan's mobile home, down the highway from the family ranch house, was broken into on July 4, 1976, he and Pamela, his wife of two years, found the trailer in a shambles. Gone were his weapons and her jewelry, some cash, and other possessions. Footprints from the trailer led south.

Pat told Pam and Tom that the family had never bothered "wetbacks" crossing the property and in return none should bother them, either. But because of the burglary they would make it known that from that day forward Hanigan property was off-limits. The next night the brothers armed themselves and rode Tom's Kawasaki across the ranch patrolling for Mexicans. If they came across any, Pat threatened to "knock them around a little bit, steal their money, and turn them in to the Border Patrol." Tom said anyone who would commit a burglary like Pat had suffered "deserved to be shot."

The patrols continued almost every night for the next few weeks. A state trooper caught them once, but they said they were just hunting rabbits. A few days later, Pam, pregnant, left Pat; he beat her and she had had enough. The torture took place soon after.

Bernabé and Manuel were too injured to travel, but Eleazar, now in a wheelchair with his burned feet bandaged, was taken back into the United States by investigators and driven up

Highway 80. Five miles west of Douglas, Eleazar pointed to a ranch house with a big sign out front reading HANIGAN'S. The ranch house, he said, was the same one he and the others had been taken to the previous day. Two pickups were parked nearby, one yellow and the other blue. Both had white camper shells. A short distance east the car turned south and Eleazar pointed to a windmill on the Hanigan ranch as the spot where the previous day's ordeal had begun.

Cochise County sheriff's deputies drove to the Hanigan ranch house with a search warrant that afternoon, and Mildred Hanigan answered the door. A Hanigan for twenty-six years, Mildred was a strong woman who kept busy with ranch work, a music club in town, and looking after the three men in her life. Tom was sick that day and awoke as Detective Ritchie Martinez approached his room. After reading Tom his Miranda rights, Martinez asked him if he had had contact with any Mexicans from across the line. "So what if I did?" Tom blurted out. His mother hushed him up.

Tom waited a few minutes and spoke again. Why, he asked Detective Martinez, was he being investigated when the Mexicans have no right to be in the United States? Tom tagged along as the deputies took three shotguns, ropes, clothes, and his baseball cap with an H on it from the house and dusted his camper for fingerprints. "There was a time," Tom told the investigators, "when you could employ someone from across the line and they'd be grateful and put in a hard day's work. But now you don't find any that are willing to work. All they want to do is rip you off."

Five miles away at the Agua Prieta hospital the three victims were besieged by officials, reporters, investigators, lawyers, and nuns. In Mexico City the Ministry of Foreign Relations sent a note to Cochise County officials demanding punishment for the attackers, a sentiment also voiced by President Luis Echeverría. The Ministry of the Interior labeled the assault "racial sadism." "What was on the minds of those who tortured three Mexicans?" *Excelsior* asked in an editorial. "Was it to cause more friction on the border?" One columnist wrote in *El Día* that the torture must be analyzed as part of a campaign to prevent Mexico from achieving complete independence, while a colleague at *El Universal* said the beating was motivated by U.S. allegations that American prisoners are mistreated in Mexico. A third columnist called the affair "barbarism in Yankee civilization." A Hermosillo, Sonora, newspaper reported that "a series of diggings on the Hanigan property" would soon begin to look for secretly buried Mexicans. U.S. Ambassador Jova expressed "regret" over the attack and assured Mexico that justice would be served.

Others were not as quick to condemn. When three Chicano Douglas city councilmen asked other officials to join them in conveying "deepest sympathy" for the "vicious and sadistic acts of violence," without mentioning any suspects by name, Mayor Ray Willcox called the statement "rabble-rousing and scandalmongering." The Douglas *Daily Dispatch* refused to print photos of the hospitalized victims, fearing the effect upon public opinion. The Hanigan incident, as the events of August 18 soon became known, allowed Cochise County ranchers to vent their anger at Mexicans by supporting George, Pat, and Tom. The incident legitimized their frustration at a recent rash of unsolved burglaries in outlying areas.

"We have a backlash of the Anglo-Saxon baboon types here who want vigilante-style justice," explained County Attorney Richard J. Riley. "Many people feel the Hanigans are justified in what they did. I don't think George Hanigan was trying to kill the three Mexicans. He could've done that and buried them on the ranch. No, I think he was trying to say, 'Don't come this way.' "

"The worst thing the Hanigans could have done was to torture them and send them back to Mexico," said Douglas Police Chief Joe Borane. "My men have killed Mexicans—I've shot people too and spent many sleepless nights over it—but to torture them? I can't figure that out." Senior Border Patrol agent Drex Atkinson felt the same. "I can see shooting them, you know, blowing their heads off. But torturing them makes no sense."

Among Douglas' 70 percent Mexican-American majority, the Hanigan incident provoked reflections of growing up in a polarized town. "In high school they used to seat us alphabetically so the teachers could learn our last names better," a native said one afternoon to some friends in Charro's Plumbing Shop on Eighth Street. "I could sit next to an Anglo kid for four years and I'd meet him on the street and I didn't exist. In forty years I have been invited into an Anglo's house once—and that was just last year."

Charro, who sat on the Douglas city council, was irate. "I don't care if it was three Mexicans who tortured three gringos. Those motherfuckers ought to be hung."

Pat Hanigan bragged of the episode. "We fixed those son-of-a-bitchin' wetbacks, " he boasted one night at the Gadsen Hotel coffee shop. "We horsewhipped 'em."

"Did you read about the Border Patrolman who got five to life for shooting a wetback?" a friend asked. "They said his gun went off accidentally. Twice!" Everybody laughed.

The Hanigans were indicted by a Cochise County grand jury in December on three counts each of assault with a deadly weapon, three each of conspiracy to assault, three each of kidnapping and conspiracy to kidnap, and two counts each of armed robbery. (An August indictment had been thrown out for procedural errors.) The trial was scheduled for March 29, 1977 in Bisbee, the county seat twenty miles west of Douglas, before Judge J. Richard Hannah of Tucson. Hannah was brought in after the local judge, a close friend of George Hanigan's, disqualified himself. Prosecuting would be Lawrence Turoff, a top criminal prosecutor "on loan" from the Maricopa County Attorney's Office in Phoenix. His assistant would be Pat Elliston from the local county attorney's office, whose subdued style and flat Texas drawl contrasted sharply with Turoff's big-city ways. "My job," Elliston explained, "is to sit next to Larry, look things up in law books, and say 'Mes'can' every now and then."

Alan Polley and his father Wes, the grand old man of Cochise

County law, represented the Hanigans. Wes studied law in the mid-1930s as a guard at the state prison in Florence where his father worked. His authority is such that judges have been known to halt a trial in mid-witness to ask him how other judges have ruled in the past on procedural matters. A bishop in the Mormon church, Alan Polley's statewide notoriety was limited to the football field where in 1957 he captained the University of Arizona Wildcats to one win in ten games, their worst season ever.

Manuel, Eleazar, and Bernabé moved to Hermosillo where the state found them menial jobs and places to live. They became accustomed to the status the case had thrust upon them, finding irony in the attention paid them by high government officials of both countries. They heard themselves compared to Cuauhtémoc, the last Aztec emperor, whose feet were burned by the Spanish in the sixteenth century. *Alarma!* devoted a full page to their torture. Radio stations throughout the north played "Los Tres Mojados," a *corrido* immortalizing their ordeal. Every couple of months they were shepherded to Bisbee for pretrial interviews, but privately they began having doubts that their case would ever come to trial.

The charges also changed the Hanigans' lives. A few days after the incident, a bullet fired from Highway 80 just missed hitting George in the head. Anonymous telephone threats were common. The prison grapevine at Florence spoke of the Hanigans' deaths should they be sent there. Old friendships became strained. People would whisper and point when any of them entered a cafe. Tom, described by friends as a mild-mannered boy, toughened up quickly after August 18, 1976. Pat got taunted in barrooms despite his six-foot-two frame; he only felt completely relaxed at the rodeo grounds. The joke went around that the Hanigans were holding a Mexican barbecue; bring your own.

A week before the trial was to begin, sixty-seven-year-old George Hanigan died in his sleep of a heart attack. His friends and family held public services for him at a church, then a bigger private gathering at the Elk's Club. Most of George's friends said the strain of his legal problems did him in, but in the Mexican-American community they knew better; *lo castigó Díos,* they said. God punished him.

The death of George Hanigan delayed the trial another four weeks, during which prosecutors Turoff and Elliston argued that the case should be moved from Cochise County. At a hearing to determine the extent of prejudice in the county, Jim Wilson, whose twelve years as sheriff had elapsed a few months earlier and who had lived his entire life within a half-mile of the border, told Judge Hannah, "Of the people I've talked to, the Hanigans were justified in doing what they allegedly did," because of border burglaries. Hanigan attorney Wes Polley asked Wilson if, after the U.S. Border Patrol routinely picks up Mexicans, they "just dump 'em across the line."

"I think it's called 'voluntary return,' " Wilson answered.

"Then they [the Mexicans] voluntarily return to this side for another raid a few days later?"

"That's right."

Witness after witness took the stand acknowledging widespread sentiment supporting the Hanigans, adding that a "fair and impartial" jury could be impaneled in the county anyway. Charro, the Douglas plumber and city councilman, took the opposite attitude, explaining that he and other Mexican-Americans were violently anti-Hanigan. The prosecution failed to convince Judge Hannah; the trial would stay in the county.

The April trial date was postponed to May, and the May date to June. As the summer wore on, legal briefs from the Hanigans caused some delays while prosecution scheduling problems caused yet others. A seventh continuance was granted after Wes Polley complained of hemorrhoid problems.

La Raza Law Students Association, which had been following the case from Washington, D.C., began writing to Beverly Jenney, the new county attorney. What's taking so long? they demanded. The delays appeared to be part of a giant conspiracy to thwart justice by letting the case fade away. United Farm Workers president César Chávez wrote to authorities urging immediate prosecution. The Secretariat for the Spanish Speaking of the National Council of Bishops asked U.S. Attorney Griffin Bell to investigate. The National Council of Concern for Alien Rights began to lobby with the Carter White House. Surely an administration advocating human rights abroad could see the issues raised at home in the Hanigan case, they argued. The Mexican consul in Douglas, veteran diplomat Raúl Aveleyra, grew cynical at how slowly the case was progressing. The rumor of impending amnesty for undocumented foreigners already in the United States brought an increase in the number of Mexicans coming north, and a corresponding hysteria in the media about the "brown peril poised at the border." Finally on September 15, 1977, more than a year after Manuel, Eleazar, and Bernabé met terror in the desert, jury selection in The State of Arizona versus Thomas and Patrick Hanigan began.

The Hanigans' strategy was to keep Mexican-Americans off the jury. The prosecution's was to strike long-time county residents and those from border communities. The county voter rolls, from which potential jurors are randomly selected, showed twenty-six thousand registered voters, eighty-three hundred of whom were Mexican-American. Eight of the original jury pool of sixty-four were Mexican-American, and some of them were disqualified when they admitted prejudice in the case. One had read of the incident in *Alarma!;* another told the judge, "It's wrong what they [the Hanigans] did." Two of the twenty-six final panelists were Mexican-American; neither survived the cut.

Most of the twelve jurors and two alternates were from the Sierra Vista area—at twenty-seven thousand, the county's most populous area. Others came from St. David, a Mormon community forty-five miles north of Bisbee; Tombstone, a tourist trap twenty-five miles north; Sunizona, a retirement community in the Sulphur Springs Valley; and Pomerene, Bowie, and Willcox, three towns at the north end of the county. Pat Elliston sized up the all-white jury and took a deep breath. "Well," he whispered to co-prosecutor Turoff, "if we win we vacation in Mexico. If we lose we vacation in Texas."

Manuel, Eleazar, and Bernabé were the first witnesses. Respectably attired and healthy after a year of steady employment, they appeared more the products of city life than victims of desert sadism. As Manuel, who took the stand first, described the events of thirteen months earlier, an interpreter repeated his testimony in English. Pat and Tom, wearing conservative suits, sat at the defense table taking notes. They looked up briefly when Manuel walked over to identify them, then continued writing.

Manuel told the jury that his hands and feet had been tied together behind his back "like when you tie a calf"; that the Hanigans had rubbed strips of his clothing in his face; that after writhing away from the fire he was threatened with the hot metal rod. At last, he said, he ran back to Mexico shouting for Eleazar and Bernabé. "I didn't know if they were dead or what."

The jurors were riveted by Manuel's account, delivered with confidence over a three-hour period. They grimaced at hospital photographs taken the night of the incident showing his backside peppered with buckshot pellets, his face bruised, and his hair matted in clumps.

The Hanigans' cross-examination covered the same ground, only sharper and in more detail than the prosecution questioning. In the thirteen months between the incident and the trial, Manuel and the other two victims had described the events of August 18, 1976, to Douglas policeman Ted Dabovich, Cochise County sheriff's detective Frank Gonzales, a grand jury, a Mexican government lawyer, and in preliminary hearings, to the Polleys. The trial was the sixth account of the ordeal to be officially recorded. Alan Polley's goal was to find inconsistencies between the five earlier accounts and the courtroom testimony and to accuse the Mexicans of changing their story. Because the initial police reports were sketchy, incomplete, and by the investigators' own admission, replete with errors, finding inconsistencies was easy. So was implying that the Mexicans were lying. When Manuel said that Tom Hanigan chased Bernabé, after Bernabé had been let go, Alan Polley asked him if he had

said differently before. Manuel said he didn't remember, and
Polley read from an earlier interview showing the story
changed. Confused, Manuel admitted the discrepancy.

Polley used the same technique with Manuel about his description of Eleazar being hanged, about shotgun blasts aimed
at Eleazar, about being struck by the rifle butt, and about shots
fired at him.

Manuel was asked if he expected some money as a result of
a personal injury suit to be filed against the Hanigans on the
three victims' behalf. He was unsure; he understood little of the
civil suit, only that his government had approved it, that an
American lawyer planned to file it, and that if the lawyer won,
the three victims might profit. "Has the thought of your receiving some money from the Hanigans made you testify any differently at this trial?" Polley asked.

"No."

"Then why have you changed your testimony so many times
from before?"

After a full day of questioning Manuel was beginning to feel
that he had done something wrong to warrant such suspicion.
His account of the incident had been turned around on him.

Eleazar was next and, like Manuel, he took the jury through
the events of August 18, 1976. On the courtroom floor he
demonstrated how he avoided strangulation by hanging. Pictures of Eleazar's burned feet were passed among the jurors.

Polley's cross-examination of Eleazar duplicated his questioning of Manuel. Eleazar's testimony diverged from earlier accounts on how he traveled to the border on the morning of the
incident, the hour the torturing took place, where he met Manuel, George Hanigan's clothing and weapons, the distance from
which he had been shot at, and Tom Hanigan's characteristics.
Eleazar, who had difficulty understanding the interpreter, felt
compelled to answer even if he wasn't sure. How he got to the
border mattered little, he thought, only that he got there and
crossed. The time of day he was tortured meant less to him; the
important thing was that he was tortured. How he met Manuel
was inconsequential; that they were friends was all that mattered. How would he know the distance from which he was shot

at? All he knew was that he heard pellets go by just above his head.

Polley ended by asking Eleazar if he expected to get some money from the Hanigans through the impending civil suit.

"Yes," Eleazar replied.

The jury sat up and took notice.

Bernabé told the jurors of his experience, as had his companions before him. He lay down on the courtroom floor to show how Pat Hanigan had tied him up. And again, Alan Polley showed discrepancies between the initial police reports and the witness's testimony. Although the reports had little credibility, by the time Polley was through with him, Bernabé had even less. At last the lawyer asked Bernabé if he was after the Hanigans' money. "The way I look at it," Bernabé replied, "I don't want their money. The only thing I want done is justice."

The doctor who treated Bernabé at the hospital on August 18, 1976, was the next witness. Bernabé, who had been clothed, fed, and taken to a Red Cross station by ranchers who found him in the border area west of Agua Prieta, arrived at the hospital at five o'clock. According to Doctor Ramón Barroso García, he had rope burns, as well as forty-seven pellets stuck in him, the twelve most painful of which were removed right away. Eleazar, whom Agua Prieta police found wandering near the border, got to the hospital an hour later. Manuel arrived at eight o'clock after having been driven to his friend Don Antonio's house by some farm workers. His back was peppered head to heel with one hundred twenty-five shotgun pellets, some of which Doctor Barroso brought with him to court. The injuries sustained by all three, the doctor said, were consistent with their description of the torture. When Doctor Barroso detailed the burn wounds on Eleazar's feet, prosecutor Turoff asked, "You weren't able to read the letter 'H' or the word 'Hanigan' in those wounds, were you?"

The jury was unimpressed with the prosecution's chief investigator, sheriff's deputy Frank Gonzales. Were the footprints found at the torture site photographed? No. How about footprints in the arroyo heading toward Mexico? No. Did you tape record the initial bedside interview with the victims? No. Were the .357 Magnum shells found at the scene mentioned in the written report? No. What happened to some plaster casts made at the scene? They broke. What name did you call Eleazar Ruelas in your first report? Ernesto Robles. Did you identify the weapons correctly? No. Did you tell the grand jury the same things the victims told you? No.

Gonzales' best evidence was a key on a ring and a belt buckle retrieved from the fire near the arroyo. The key fit Eleazar's suitcase back in Agua Prieta; the belt buckle came from the Mexicans' clothes.

The state's case closed with two criminologists. One said that dried blood found in the dirt at the torture site was the same type as that of Manuel and Eleazar. The other said that a shotgun shell found nearby had been fired from one of the Hanigans' guns.

The Hanigans' defense was a series of alibi witnesses for Pat. If Pat's friends and neighbors could show that he had been away from the ranch on August 18, 1976, then the Mexicans' story would crumble.

Pat's day, according to witnesses, started after ten o'clock when he bought a cow from Elona Panzer in Double Adobe, fifteen miles from the Hanigan ranch house. Pat had trouble loading the animal into his stock trailer, and the cow horned him on the right wrist. The gash started bleeding, and Mrs. Panzer dressed it in a bandage. Pat left the Panzer place by eleven-forty for the drive—just under nineteen minutes—back to the ranch house.

A little more than an hour of Pat's time is unaccounted for before Betty Lucas, a nurse at the Cochise County Hospital— a seven-and-a-half-minute drive from the torture site—redressed his wound shortly after one-fifteen. At one-forty-five Pat dropped by the family Dairy Queen outlet in Douglas, then left to get his wound sutured by the family doctor. He returned to the Dairy Queen afterward, and spent the rest of the afternoon with a friend at a local motel lounge and cafe.

That was the defense. Neither Pat nor Tom took the stand.

For most of the two and a half weeks the courtroom had no more than ten spectators, half of them reporters. For the closing arguments it filled with Hanigan supporters. "I believe you have seen a smoke screen," Larry Turoff told the jury before recounting Manuel, Eleazar, and Bernabé's testimony. He reconstructed Pat Hanigan's day, which allowed more than an hour for the kidnap, assault, and robbery to take place. Tom and Pat, along with their late father, George, tortured the three Mexicans on their ranch on August 18, 1976, Turoff insisted. All the evidence points to conviction.

Alan Polley's summation opened with the biblical tale of David and Goliath, with David, "D," the defendants, and Goliath, "G," the government, the governors, and Gonzales. The whole case against Tom and Pat was a fabrication to get the Hanigans' money. The three Mexicans were nothing more than burglars who repeatedly perjured themselves. The three knew about the Hanigans because they were lying in wait in the weeds across from the Hanigan home and saw the family pickups and Pat's bandaged wrist. Or else Frank Gonzales and the other officials fed them details about the Hanigans and their land. Evidence found at the arroyo could have been planted. The Mexicans kept using the phrase "more or less" because they were never sure of their facts. One had the incident starting at ten-thirty, another guessed it ended after four o'clock. The wounds must have come from a rancher who caught them burglarizing his home. Whoever made up the castration story, "it shows their character and it shows the evil mind they have and it shows how debased and perverted they are." By the end of Polley's argument, his clients were no longer on trial. Manuel, Eleazar, and Bernabé were.

The jury set up its deliberation room as the Hanigan ranch and tried to reenact the allegations. The jurors' bathroom became the Mexican hospital room where so much of the initial information came from. Time charts following the accused and the accusers from breakfast to nightfall hung on the walls; courtroom exhibits covered the floor.

They questioned the lack of evidence: Where were the

burned clothes from the fire? a Sierra Vista man asked. And the metal rod? a woman from the Sulphur Springs Valley wanted to know. How about clumps of the victims' hair? queried another. Why didn't they hear from any of the Mexicans who found the three and took them in for medical treatment?

The jury's most arduous debate was over the "assault with a deadly weapon" charge. Most felt that the Hanigans did attack the Mexicans, but not with a "deadly weapon" as defined in their instructions from Judge Hannah. They sent a note to the judge: "If there is reasonable doubt that assault with a deadly weapon (to wit: a gun) occurred, can the lesser charge of assault be considered?"

The judge replied, "No."

While jury deliberations continued into a third day, seventy demonstrators from Tucson, Bisbee, and Douglas celebrated Mass next to the courthouse, calling for an end to border violence. Inside, the Hanigan clan paced the lobby like a family anticipating the death of a relative. "You know," Tom Hanigan said, "something like this happens and you never know how good you had it before. You wonder if you'll ever recover."

The jury returned its verdict: not guilty of kidnapping; not guilty of conspiracy to kidnap; not guilty of assault with a deadly weapon; not guilty of robbery.

In parks and bars, on the street and in people's homes, wherever Arizonans gathered over the next few weeks, the subject was the Hanigan verdict. Some were content to let the matter rest; others were outraged. Three days after the trial, Margo Cowan, director of a Tucson agency advocating rights for Mexicans in the United States, handed the Justice Department a petition with two hundred signatures from Cochise County calling for a retrial in federal court. The following weekend fifteen hundred demonstrators gathered at the Douglas–Agua Prieta crossing and, in an attempt to pressure businessmen to support the retrial plea, agreed to a boycott of merchants in all Arizona border towns "until justice is done." The boycott ended after ten days when its organizers received bomb threats and the City of Douglas threatened legal action.

David Duke, a national leader of the Ku Klux Klan who had been advocating that Klansmen patrol the border for Mexicans, came to Tucson and urged sympathizers to converge on the Douglas area. The Mexican government dispatched troops to its side of the border in response. No Klansmen were seen in the area and the Mexican army soon withdrew. The Border Patrol, concerned about a possible Klan–Mexican Army standoff, picked up fewer people than ever crossing north. A Border Patrolman amused his fellow workers one night by showing up in a white sheet and hood, with a homemade sign reading BORDER PATROL KLAGENT.

Mexican consul Raúl Aveleyra called the acquittal a declaration of "open hunting season on every illegal alien," and informed Manuel, Bernabé, and Eleazar of the verdict. They couldn't figure it out. "They had the crime on their hands," Eleazar said. "Maybe," Bernabé suggested, "the judge and jury didn't like Mexicans." Perhaps, Manuel added, the Hanigans got off "because they have money and power, and because we were in the country illegally. It was as if we were the ones who were found guilty."

With tension still high, Douglas residents accustomed to shopping in Agua Prieta were reluctant to cross the line, fearing hostility. Police Chief Borane urged Tom and Pat to leave Douglas until the controversy surrounding their case subsided, and Tom soon went to visit relatives in New Mexico. At a hotel bar in Santa Fe one night he chatted with some strangers. "Oh, you're from Douglas?" one of them said. "That's the same town where those rich ranchers killed four illegals, bought off the jury, and got off. Killed 'em! First degree!"

"Yeah," replied Tom, who had started to grow a beard. "I know the Hanigans. I don't think it was quite like that."

In Washington, D.C., Antonio Bustamante was upset with the verdict. A Douglas native who was president of his 1970 high school senior class and played on the football team, Tony had gone to Stanford University and the Antioch School of Law in Washington. Tony's briefings had alerted La Raza Law Students Association to the case earlier in the year, and now, angered at what the acquittal told him about justice for Hispanics, he set out to have the case presented anew in federal court. Fellow law students pitched in, and soon Antioch approved a clinic whose goal was to research the case and present the Justice Department with its findings.

Right after the initial incident the Justice Department said it had no jurisdiction, and concluded the same after an FBI investigation following the state trial. Yet at every turn Department lawyers were met by members of the National Coalition on the Hanigan Case, a group comprised of Hispanic and other civil rights organizations. The Coalition lobbied on Capitol Hill, at the White House, with the U.S. Commission on Civil Rights, anywhere people in power would listen. Petition drives called upon Attorney General Griffin Bell to reopen the case. The "Hanigan clinic" at Antioch combed transcripts of the state trial. "The government prosecutes people for shooting bald eagles," Bustamante complained, "but not for shooting Mexicans."

Telegrams, letters, and resolutions arrived at the Justice Department. The Town Council of Guadalupe, Arizona, asked for a new prosecution; the Iranian Students Association at the University of Maryland did likewise. So did the Disabled American Veterans of Kansas, and AFL-CIO president George Meany, who wrote that "justice has not been done" in this case of "inhuman brutality." A Douglas High School student told the Attorney General that "the rights of the Mexicans were stepped on and the Hannigans [sic] brothers rights were greeted with open arms." All the correspondence called the state trial a travesty of justice which the federal government had an obligation to correct.

In late 1978 the National Coalition on the Hanigan Case filed a lawsuit to force the Justice Department to take action. Its spokesmen testified about the case in Congressional hearings, and it picketed the White House during a National Hispanic Heritage Week ceremony.

Bustamante and fellow law students visited Hermosillo, Sonora, to interview the victims. Other coalition activists met with community leaders in Arizona to organize mass support. Heading west on Highway 80 after a round of conferences in Douglas, Coalition members left one of their leaflets in front of the Hanigans' ranch house. They drove on to Phoenix to meet with U.S. Attorney for Arizona, Michael Hawkins, telling him how to handle the case. Hawkins was not impressed; he remembered his own college days in the thick of the antiwar movement and felt like a college president dealing with student demonstrators. "Vigilantes from the opposite side," he called them.

Mexican President López Portillo, whose Foreign Ministry kept him current on the case, mentioned the incident during a 1978 visit to China. In his February 1979 trip to Mexico, Jimmy Carter pledged that he would protect "the basic human rights of all those, who, for whatever reason, are within the boundaries of our country." *Excelsior* endorsed the drive to reopen the case, labeling the incident *"sadismo texano."*

The Hanigans followed their fate through newspapers and television news. They grew used to snide remarks, wild punches, and blank stares. Their cattle were shot at. Pat's trailer was broken into once again. When a judge in Washington dismissed the Coalition's lawsuit against the Justice Department, the brothers took it to mean that they weren't going to be prosecuted. They had learned in civics class that no one could be tried twice for the same crime.

Bernabé drifted back to Durango, but Eleazar and Manuel continued to work at state jobs in Hermosillo. Pedro Flores, the songwriter who recorded "Los Tres Mojados," met them and told of grand plans to make a movie about the case. Their story appeared in a five-peso *novela* which portrayed the "Flanagan" family torturing three *campesinos,* then leading a Ku Klux Klan assault upon Mexicans at the border.

The Hanigan clinic at Antioch turned its research over to the Justice Department, suggesting six possible statutes under which to prosecute: three immigration laws; two civil rights laws; and the Hobbs Act, which prohibits interference with interstate commerce.

By June 1979 more than forty U.S. congressmen and senators —including Dole of Kansas and Tower of Texas—had written Attorney General Bell about the case. At the end of June a federal grand jury started investigating. Four months later, two years after they had been acquitted on state charges, Tom and Pat Hanigan were indicted on three counts each of violating the Hobbs Act.

The Hobbs Act, according to its namesake Samuel Hobbs, a congressman from Alabama in the 1930s and 1940s, was meant to "protect the freedom of freeborn Americans on their way to market." The law itself speaks of "interference with commerce by threats of violence," which the courts have interpreted to include potential interference with commerce. The farms to which Manuel, Eleazar, and Bernabé were headed all dealt in interstate commerce; hence to interfere with potential employees of these farms was to violate the law. The three workers, since they were seeking jobs, were themselves considered commerce. Their status in the United States was not an issue because no law prohibits employers from hiring undocumented labor.

For their legal team in federal court, the Hanigans added Tucson attorney Alex Gaynes, an aggressive and inventive lawyer who resembles Woody Allen. Gaynes enjoyed unpopular causes even in his youth, when he was once expelled from school for refusing to say the Lord's Prayer. Now, taking on the most unpopular case in the state since Cochise County Sheriff Harry Wheeler was tried for shipping all of the striking Industrial Workers of the World out of Bisbee in boxcars in 1917, Gaynes was in his element. He asked U.S. District Court Judge Richard Bilby, who took office the same week the Hanigans were indicted, to throw the case out for misapplication of the

Hobbs Act and because it constituted double jeopardy. Conceding that "this is about as far as you can stretch the Hobbs Act," Bilby denied Gaynes' motion. As for double jeopardy, since the charges and jurisdiction were different from the 1977 trial, the judge let the indictment stand.

Hanigan sympathizers in Douglas, outraged that a band of noisy Hispanics could influence the U.S. Justice Department, formed a Hanigan support group, whose acronym, ENUF, was conceived before its title, Enlightened Nationals United for Freedom. ENUF raised money to help pay attorneys' fees and petitioned the government to drop the charges. They wrote letters to local newspapers. "We will wake up one day soon as an extension of Mexico," warned rancher Mary McGoffin at one ENUF meeting. "Why, if you ask for a drink of water in Mexico, they give it to you from a toilet. Now I don't begrudge the little Mexican kids using our schools, but the rest of this illegal alien stuff is subversion. We're American citizens. We're the ones who built this country."

"Who is sponsoring this anti-Hanigan coalition," asked Morton Fagan, a retired engineer, "Mexico or Russia? The undermining of the American people couldn't be done better. With this Hobbs Act nonsense, anyone I catch vandalizing my property can say he's on his way to Elfrida and he'll get off. If this case stands, illegals can go where they want with impunity."

Most Hanigan supporters could accept that George, Pat, and Tom abducted, hogtied, stripped, tormented, burned, threatened to castrate and hang, and shot at the three Mexicans. They just didn't want the brothers tried a second time.

Members of the National Coalition on the Hanigan Case were not pleased with the indictment either; it was too lenient, they insisted, and avoided civil rights statutes with the potential to protect noncitizens in the country. Their continued demands for a diligent prosecution included a "parade for justice" by low-rider and van clubs.

The Hanigans, who faced twenty years in prison and a ten-thousand-dollar fine on each count, spoke contemptuously of the coalition bearing their name. "People think we're racist, but we have a Jewish attorney and a Mormon attorney," said Tom, who had married a Mexican-American woman a few months before the June 26, 1980, trial date. "They don't want justice. They want to see us hanging off some gallows in some bar."

Manuel and Eleazar were in Tucson ready for another go-round, but Bernabé had left Hermosillo a few weeks earlier with a traveling circus in which he had started an apprenticeship as a catcher in a trapeze act. A Mexican official in Nogales, Sonora, aware that Bernabé was needed in Tucson, noted a circus passing through town and found him there, shortly before the circus was to leave for Central America.

Bernabé wanted nothing more of this American justice nonsense. He had started to stutter as a result of the desert trauma. In a recurring nightmare he would be running, then look over his shoulder to see the Hanigans laughing at him. Manuel still had pellets lodged in his body, by which he could forecast a change in the temperature. Eleazar never again found his wife or their child, whose birthday he commemorates each year. For Bernabé, Manuel, and Eleazar, August 18, 1976, had been their holocaust.

The federal trial lasted four weeks. The jury, again all-Anglo due to defense peremptory challenges, heard the three Mexicans once more describe their beating four years earlier. Once again Alan Polley's cross-examination made their testimony suspect by comparing it to previous accounts. Eleazar, who was on the stand for three and a half days, appeared so disoriented that Judge Bilby asked a psychiatrist to assess his ability to withstand the trial.

The most devastating evidence against the Hanigans was presented when an FBI fingerprint expert testified that one of the prints lifted from Tom Hanigan's pickup on August 19, 1976, the day after the incident, positively matched Eleazar Ruelas Zavala's right thumbprint. The match was the first clear independent physical evidence linking the Hanigans with the three Mexicans.

Prosecution witness Pamela Hanigan, who had not seen her former husband since 1977, nervously told the jury about Pat and Tom's "wetback hunting trips." Other new witnesses included some of the Mexicans who found the three victims and took them in for treatment.

The defense added two new alibi witnesses, Mareva and Bill James, long-time Hanigan friends who lived between Highway 80 and the Panzer place where Pat had bought the cow that gored him. They said that Pat had stopped to chat with them for fifteen to twenty minutes. Again, neither Pat nor Tom testified.

Mexicans and Mexican-Americans, lured by announcements over Spanish-language radio stations on both sides of the border, filled the courtroom every day. Teachers brought their classes, and farm-worker organizers bused in *campesinos.* For *la raza,* bearing witness at this historic trial was almost a religious experience.

Outside the courthouse it remained a political one as well. Demonstrators, dissatisfied with the Justice Department's lawyers, vilified the Hanigans and accused the prosecution of giving the case away. On the final day of the trial four hundred people marched through downtown Tucson behind a banner reading: HUMAN BRUTALITY + HANIGANS = WHITE CANCER.

"What big brave cowboys these guys are," prosecutor Linda Davis said in her final argument. "Armed with shotguns, they terrorize. They take three defenseless young men, rob them of their money, their clothes, and their dignity." She repeated testimony about the Hanigans wanting to warn Mexicans to stay away from the ranch. "Perhaps that message was conveyed by these acts. But if it was," she implored, "I ask you to hold Pat and Tom accountable."

Her summation impressed the most antagonistic of Coalition members—San Antonio attorney Ruben Sandoval, who monitored the entire trial. "I think I'll go to church," he said afterward, shaking her hand, "and light a candle."

Alan Polley's final argument was a prolonged accusation that the three Mexicans were liars pressured by their government to continue their convoluted story. Their testimony, he said, was "like pouring a cup full of black paint into a bucket of white paint—how do you separate the truth from the lies?" He suggested that Eleazar's fingerprint found in Tom Hanigan's truck showed that the other two "were never in that yellow pickup."

The Mexicans were credible, said one of the four male jurors once deliberations got under way. How else would they know the layout of the Hanigan ranch? The cartridge found at the site, the fingerprint from Tom's truck, and the gap in Pat's day all pointed toward conviction.

Not so, argued another man. Maybe the three were really robbers, especially since they had all been in the country before and knew the territory. Acquittal is in order, the man insisted, because the pattern of pellets on Manuel and Bernabé's back was not consistent with the distance they claimed they had run before being shot at; because an initial police report said Bernabé described George Hanigan as having a mustache; because so much time is unaccounted for between the torture and the Mexicans' hospitalization; because American investigators may have told the three about Pat's wrist bandage; because no charred clothing from the fire was in evidence. All that the fingerprint evidence showed, the juror reasoned, was that Eleazar may have taken a peek inside Tom's pickup earlier in the day.

A woman agreed, adding that the police could have planted what evidence existed. This juror, who resented that a law student in Washington had persuaded the Justice Department to reopen the case and who called attorney Sandoval "the fat mariachi player," said the victims must have been watching the Hanigan house to rob. And if a fire had been built in the desert, why didn't the shrubbery nearby burn too?

Jurors favoring conviction replied that the essential truths remained: who the three Mexicans encountered, how they were abducted, where they were taken, their ordeal, and their wounds. As for the lack of evidence, the Hanigans were smart enough to clean up the site before leaving. Finally, why didn't the last alibi witnesses, who claimed to have spent a crucial time period with Pat that day, come forward before June 1980?

In their sixth day of deliberation eight jurors were convinced that the Hanigan brothers had tortured the Mexicans; the rest favored acquittal. They told Judge Bilby they had no hope of breaking the deadlock. He thanked them for their time, declared a mistrial, and sent them home.

A month later the Justice Department announced it would retry the case. A burst of public sympathy for the Hanigans erupted, something lacking in the prior four years. A third trial seemed unconscionable to many, even as they conceded the likelihood of the Hanigans' guilt. Tucson businessmen raised ten thousand dollars to help out Tom and Pat, whose lawyers' fees had reached $160,000. "Everything we have," said Mildred Hanigan, "has gone to clear our name." They put some of their Dairy Queen holdings up for sale.

The retrial lasted four and a half weeks. Held in Phoenix, which Judge Bilby considered less volatile than Tucson, two juries heard testimony, one for each Hanigan. When evidence incriminating to one brother was presented, the jury for the other was excused. Manuel and Eleazar repeated their oft-told account, and again defense lawyers attacked their credibility. In Hermosillo, Bernabé had drunk daily until he passed out in the evening. Once he commandeered an unattended Pepsi truck, driving it through the streets until he careened into a streetlamp. After a short jail term, he continued drinking, and by the time he arrived in Phoenix he appeared zombielike. The two juries were simply told he was "unavailable" and a transcript of his Tucson appearance was read to them.

Prosecutors A. Bates Butler and José Rivera produced a new witness who told Pat's jury about the boast at the Gadsden Hotel; another witness told Tom's that in a late August 1976 conversation about the incident, Tom said that the press "had blown it out of proportion." The Pat Hanigan alibi was again presented and once more neither defendant took the stand.

The two all-white panels returned their unanimous verdicts on February 23, 1981, after a sequestered weekend of separate deliberations: Thomas Hanigan—not guilty; Patrick Hanigan— guilty as charged.

Some of Tom's jurors felt that he had tortured the Mexicans but they all agreed that a Hobbs Act violation wasn't proven. "What I don't understand," one juror said afterward, "is how they can call this interstate commerce. They weren't carrying any commodities." Together, the verdicts satisfied no one.

Back at the border, Mexicans continue to cross into Arizona, undeterred by the legend of *los tres mojados* and how they suffered at the hands of the Hanigans. A favorite spot to cross is a tear in the fence on the east side of Agua Prieta, from which a path goes through Douglas' Calvary Cemetery, leading to a pickup point northeast of town. As a new generation of migrants takes its first steps in America, the trail they follow takes them right over George Hanigan's grave.

En Route

Naco is an Arizona–Sonora border town of 6,800, all but 800 of whom live on the Mexico side. The biggest boost to Naco in recent decades resulted from the Watergate scandal. When a new U.S. president takes office, the first foreign head of state he sees is either the prime minister of Canada or the president of Mexico. After Gerald Ford assumed the presidency following Richard Nixon's 1974 resignation, he and Mexican President Luis Echeverría agreed to meet in October at Nogales, the Arizona–Sonora border town south of Tucson. Echeverría arrived the afternoon before the summit to politick with Sonoran businessmen and office-holders. When Dr. Antonio Romo, Naco's mayor, addressed Echeverría, his talk went something like this: Mr. President, my little town of Naco is in such decay it is almost beyond redemption. The only paved street has potholes bigger than many cars. Our children are poorly educated because the school is so bad. The train no longer comes through. What little industry we had has abandoned us. *Norteamericanos* don't come over and spend money anymore, and why should they? The town has nothing to offer them. We have so many unemployed that keeping track of the job holders is easier. A new highway is planned from the south, but that could make matters worse: Naco's young will have a road to leave on. I'd join them but somebody has to turn out the lights. Mr. President, you'd have to see it to believe it.

A good idea, thought Echeverría, and so at eleven-thirty P.M., the president of the Republic of Mexico, the mayor of Naco, the state governor, and a contingent of press boarded a bus for Naco. The safest and most direct route between Nogales and Naco covers eighty-five miles over smooth highways. But these highways are in Arizona; for Echeverría and his party to ride them would be a tacit admission of Mexican inferiority and a breach of international diplomacy. So Echeverría's bus churned through the middle of the night over narrow, twisting, washboard Mexican roads, arriving in Naco at two A.M., October 21. The town's leading citizens, alerted by telephone, joined the entourage for coffee and a walking tour of Naco by moonlight. Before reboarding the bus two hours later, Echeverría promised Naco industry, money, construction, and welfare.

The promise was kept. Soon Naco had new shirt, shoe, and furniture factories. An abandoned lime quarry was reopened. Streets were paved—poorly, but still paved. A new community auditorium–gymnasium was built. The sign 21 DE OCTUBRE is prominently displayed on the front of all buildings constructed as a result of that visit, and every year on that day the Naquenses hold a fiesta celebrating Luis Echeverría's midnight mercy mission to their forgotten border town.

Lochiel is the next border crossing, named for the Scottish ancestral home of one of the community's early land-grant holders. The nearest Mexican village is Santa Cruz, seven miles south down a dirt road. Inexplicably, Boundary Commissioner Bartlett spent a lot of time in Santa Cruz in 1849 and '50. Norah and I spent none, since we arrived at the crossing five minutes after the gate had been locked for the day.

Paul Bond was just opening up his boot shop in Nogales, Arizona, when we arrived there the next morning. Bond, a former rodeo rider from Carlsbad, New Mexico, makes western boots from the skins of alligators, calves, camels, ostriches, lizards, buffalo, sharks, elephants, and anteaters. Most of his business is mail order but he maintains two Nogales shops for walk-in customers. Prices start at $265 for unadorned calfskin boots and run to $1,350 for a fancy alligator-skin pair. Unlike most bootmakers, Bond insists that every step of production be done by hand.

To fill an order, one of Bond's six Arizona workers designs the pattern, cuts the skin, and builds the wooden last, which copies the shape of the foot. The skin and last are carried to a companion shop a few blocks away in Nogales, Sonora, where thirty Mexican workers do the actual stitching and hand sew the welting for the sole and arch. The assembled boots are imported back to the U.S. shop for the final steps and shipped out. Bond's production line turns out boots at the rate of three pair a day, while customers, who have included John Wayne and Roy Rogers, wait up to two months for their footwear.

From the boot shop we headed down Morley Avenue to the foot-crossing into Sonora, a path Jack Kerouac followed in the 1950s. "The moment you cross that little wire gate and you're in Mexico," Kerouac observed on entering Nogales, "you feel like you just sneaked out of school when you told the teacher you were sick and she told you you could go home. . . . You walk thirsty through the swinging doors of a saloon and get a bar beer and turn around and there's fellas shooting pool, cooking tacos, wearing sombreros, some wearing guns on their rancher hips, and gangs of singing businessmen throwing pesos at the standing musicians who wander up and down the room. —It's a great feeling of entering the Pure Land, especially because it's so close to dry faced Arizona and Texas and all over the Southwest —but you can find it, this feeling. . . ."

Kerouac and Nogales were made for each other. Both romanticize the foolish and exaggerate the common. Since Kerouac's visit, Nogales has become the major exporting center for produce from northern Mexico. Tourists also contribute to the town, visiting for gifts, meals, dentists, clothing, groceries, drugs, prostitutes, and liquor. (I have known people to come for each of these, but never for all eight at once.)

A Nebraska family of five—Mom, Dad, Grandma, and sons Mark and Dan—came for the afternoon. As they left a curio shop near Obregón and Eighth streets, a Mexican photographer next to a striped donkey tied to a cart hailed them: "Want to get on the zebra?"

The man's name was David, and the donkey—whose stripes were nothing more than hair dye—he called Chico. David smiled at Mark and Dan. "Don't you want to ride the zebra?"

Confused, Mom whispered to Dad, "Do you think that's a real zebra?"

"Well," Dad shrugged, "maybe it's a cross between a zebra and a donkey."

Grandma nodded toward the photographer and asked an Anglo passerby, "Do you suppose he speaks American?" Assured that he did, Grandma asked David how much a photograph of her grandsons on the zebra would cost. Two dollars, he replied, quickly wrapping a *sarape* around Mark's shoulders and plunking a ten-gallon sombrero on Dan's five-gallon head. Against a backdrop painting of an Aztec warrior protecting a dying woman from circling vultures, topped by letters spelling out SOUVENIR—NOGALES, MEXICO, the children forced smiles for David's Polaroid camera. As Grandma paid him, David bowed slightly and hurriedly approached the next family walking down Obregón: "Want to get on the zebra?"

Eight blocks into Nogales the tourist district abruptly ends and the city of 150,000, a world apart from donkey carts and curio shops, begins. In front of a department store Luis Manzano, an Indian from the state of Oaxaca, played his wooden flute. His three children danced in front of him as walnuts tied around their calves clacked in beat. His wife walked through the crowd that had gathered, soliciting money with Luis' wide-brimmed sombrero. When Luis' tune ended, he and his children smiled and bowed while his wife collected the last of the donations.

In the next block another Oaxacan, Juan, an elderly man with Lee Marvin hair and a Charles Bronson face, played his clarinet while his small son accepted pesos. His music wailed, mournful and expressive as the Mexican soul itself. Originally from a *pueblito* near the highway connecting Oaxaca to the state of Guerrero, Juan and his family migrated north when their plot of land at home went fallow. He and most other Oaxacans in Nogales, he said, live in a small community on the east side of town. None of them wants to go north of the border. "What would we do there?" he asked. "This is as far as we understand."

The Papago Indian Reservation, three million acres in size, is the second largest reservation in America. Long before the area belonged to either Mexico or the United States, the Papago and Pima Indians lived west of what is now Tucson. Their land is sagebrush, cactus, and mesquite. Their homes and their food reflect that they are truly people of the desert.

Among the Indians' first Anglo visitors was Nathaniel Michler of the Army Engineer Corps, who in 1855 marked the international boundary which bisects their land. "As I sat upon a rock admiring the scene before me," Michler wrote, "an old grey-haired Pimo [sic] took great pleasure in pointing out the extent of their domains. They were anxious to know if their rights and titles to land would be respected by our government, upon learning that their country had just become part of the United States."

Today the Papago jealously protect that same land. (The Pima live farther north.) They are members of the Papago Nation first and Mexicans or Americans second. Gates in the fence allow them easy access by foot, horse, or pickup to neighbors on the other side. The seventy-five miles of U.S.–Mexico frontier which cuts across Papaguería, as the land is called, is not so much an international boundary as a fence to segregate Mexican cattle from U.S. cattle. Within the Papago nation the border does not exist.

South of the cattle fence in villages such as Pozo Verde and S'gogogsig (Many Dogs), Mexican Papago complain of broken promises by their own government. In 1979 the Instituto Nacional Indigenista—roughly the equivalent of the Bureau of

Indian Affairs—opened an office in northern Sonora to try to solve their problems. If the Mexican Papago—there are an estimated 250—need medical care or schooling, Papago on the U.S. side often provide it. Some of them use the address of tribal kinfolk north of the fence to register for government benefits in Arizona. Most Papago—about 18,000 in all—now live in the U.S.

The closest villages north of the cattle fence are Menegers Dam and Newfields. Daniel Juan, a heavyset Papago in his fifties, lives in Newfields, and every week rides his horse over to a gathering at a crossing point in the fence called Southgate. About one hundred Papago from both sides come to this isolated desert meeting ground by pickup, donkey-cart, and foot. Young tribal members—many from Sells, the most populated Papago town twenty miles to the north—sit on the fence in dry ninety-degree heat singing Mexican *ranchero* ballads and American country music. Fifty yards south of the fence merchants who have driven the dirt roads from Sásabe, Sonora, sell their wares from the backs of their pickups.

Daniel Juan looked over the selection at this most primitive shopping center on the border: squash, tortillas, fruit, peppers, cheese, lard, firecrackers, candy, and flour. He bought nothing but stayed the afternoon to chat with his brethren. He took pride in his tribe's land much as Nathaniel Michler's Indian had generations earlier. "I like to live here," Daniel smiled. "I like to be free."

The Mexican merchants also sell beer and bottles of whiskey. Although illegal on the Reservation north of the cattle fence, nothing prevents the sale of alcohol to its south. The practice is tantamount to bootlegging, though no one calls it that. The Papago still have their ways of adapting to the desert borderland.

13

SONOYTA INTERLUDE

SONOYTA, SONORA, one of the older western border towns, is the meeting place of three major Mexican highways, and the key passageway to Mexico's interior for travelers from the West Coast. One hundred fifty buses pass through daily. In the 1850s, Major William Emory's border survey team reported that the town was "a resort for smugglers, and a den for a number of low, abandoned Americans who have been compelled to flee from justice." Sonoyta's reputation has stayed intact: here more than a hundred years later, Ken Kesey bribed his way into Mexico after his LSD journeys through America.

A big, white adobe-walled building sits a few yards inside the border. The building's vacant high-ceilinged front room is big enough to have been a dance hall. The rear divides into a series of small rooms, each slightly larger than a broom closet. Some are locked, others have no doors at all. Eduardo Polín, a Mexican customs man in his early thirties, is part-owner of the building.

"Al Capone used to come here," Eduardo said. "He owned this place. His gang would come down during Prohibition and throw parties. But when there was trouble, they'd sneak out through a tunnel which goes underneath the border and ends up on the American side. They could also escape the United States into Mexico through the tunnel if they had to." He pointed with a finger. "I'll show you where the tunnel begins."

Inside, Polín took a long metal rod and started tapping the floor. "The tunnel starts around here," he announced, listening for hollow sounds. "No, maybe it's over here." He tapped some more. "You know," he said, continuing to tap, "there were actually two tunnels—one which went under the border to the American side and another which led across the street." *Tap-tap-tap.* "They'd use the second one if there was trouble in the bar itself." His eyes brightened. "I think the tunnel under the border starts in this room." Eduardo turned the handle to a door but it wouldn't budge. "Ah, Alfredo has the keys to all the locks here and he is in San Luis today. But the tunnels are here somewhere, of that I am sure." He kept tapping.

Eduardo planned to convert the building into a museum of Al Capone artifacts where tourists could come to see the famous gangster's borderland hideaway. The centerpiece of the museum would be the actual bar which Al Capone had ordered custom-made from France. The bar had been handcrafted from beautiful wood, and people came from as far as El Paso and Tijuana to see it. Eduardo's eyes glazed over and his hands swept through the air as if the bar stood right before him. It was like the tunnels under the border, however; Eduardo had never actually seen the bar. He had only heard stories about it from long-time Sonoytans.

He sensed that his story was losing credibility. "Pancho, the bartender at Vásquez Cantina across from the Post Office, he will tell you all about it. Why not go visit him?" He continued tapping his long metal pole down the hall, cocking his ear for the entrance to the tunnels.

At Vásquez Cantina Pancho nodded his head vigorously. "Yes, it is so—Al Capone used to come and throw parties." He paused. "At least that's what they say." He pointed to a pile of wood in the corner next to the jukebox. "That is part of Al Capone's bar over there." The wood looked like discarded timber, unfit for service as a small card-table, much less as a grandiose bar.

"Well, maybe that isn't Al Capone's bar," Pancho admitted. "Leonel, the owner of this cantina, would know. He will tell you all about the white building and Al Capone's bar when he returns from Mexico City next week. For now, perhaps Señora Vásquez, his mother, can help."

Leonel's mother lived in a small apartment at the rear of Vásquez Cantina. An aged woman born and raised in Sonoyta, she smiled broadly at the mention of the white building next to the border. "Years ago they would throw big parties there. People always talked about gangsters coming over from the other side, but I never saw any myself. Everyone called the place La Dorina. Come back in a little while and I'll have someone help you in your search for the bar. I know it is here somewhere."

Returning to the white building, I found Eduardo Polín gone, but his brother Manuel, the building's co-owner, was there. "In four or five years we will build a motel here," said Manuel, an artist from Mexico City. "We would like to help develop tourism in Sonoyta. But no one comes here because the border gate is closed between midnight and eight in the morning, and the Americans won't make it a twenty-four-hour port until more people come. A *círculo vicioso, ¿verdad?*

"There is a bar across the line in Arizona which stays open until after midnight. People from Sonoyta go there all the time. They always come home through a hole in the fence west of the crossing." He grinned. "The American authorities know all about it, but they say nothing. It's just local people."

Manuel was less sure than his brother about Al Capone and the elusive tunnels beneath the building. "Al Capone may have come here a few times, *¿quién sabe?*" As for the tunnels, Manuel thought they started in the bathroom, the last room down the hall on the right, but we never found any sign that the passageways began there. He furrowed his forehead. "Maybe they've been cemented over."

The legend of Al Capone's tunnels, so vivid and convincing, sank further a few days later when a man present at La Dorina's construction assured me that the only thing below the floor was hard ground. "La Dorina was originally built as a lodge for hunters on expeditions into Sonora," he said. "I played in it as a kid, exploring every nook and cranny. If anything as exciting as a tunnel existed, I would have known."

Back at Vásquez Cantina *la señora* was not surprised to learn that the tunnels could not be found, but she introduced me to Nacho, another Sonoyta native, who she insisted could lead me to the bar.

Nacho took me back through the barroom, around to a deserted dance hall, and up a flight of seldom-used cement stairs. The second floor of Vásquez Cantina was an unlit, seemingly abandoned storeroom sealed off with floor-to-ceiling sheets of plastic. Nacho ripped down the plastic; behind it lay dozens of old tables, chairs, and barroom fixtures blanketed by ten years of dust. "There is the bar." He pointed. "Under those chairs."

Climbing over piles of abandoned furniture, Nacho made his way back to a long slab of wood, wiped away the accumulated dust, and uncovered the twenty-foot-long mahogany showpiece from La Dorina. It was a marvelous piece of furniture with fancy handcrafted ornaments and curlicues carved into its side. "When the bar was in place at La Dorina," Nacho recalled, "it had a mirror behind it as big as the entire wall. On a pedestal at each end of the bar was a *mona*," a statue of a naked lady. "The two *monas* are over there next to you."

At my side were two handcarved statues, handsome, with delicate features, each standing six feet high and weighing close to one hundred pounds. We carried them out to a balcony overlooking the street and Nacho began carefully dusting them off, as if performing surgery. They appeared to be blinking in the sunlight.

"The *monas* used to be black," Nacho explained, "but the color was taken off with paint remover and a glossy finish applied to bring out the natural mahogany texture. Each part of the body was carved separately, then glued together. See this?" Nacho pointed to an indentation in the left breast of one of the *monas*. "It is a stab wound. Sometimes people would take target practice and throw knives at the statues from across the barroom, but they meant nothing by it.

"Leonel has had offers of five thousand dollars for the bar, including the *monas,* but he has always turned them down. There was another bar just like this one which also came over from France; some say it is in a private home in Tucson, others say it ended up down the border in Mexicali or Tijuana."

Nacho finished dusting off the *monas.* Free of dust for the first time in more than a decade, the two nudes looked positively splendid. Their rich mahogany luster sparkled in the sun. One's face was slightly different from the other's. The one with the stab wound looked slightly forlorn, while her friend had a hint of mischief about her. If either of them knew about Al Capone, she wasn't talking.

En Route

Organ Pipe Cactus National Monument, 516 square miles of desert full of ironwood trees, javelina, cactus, coyotes, roadrunners, ringtail cats, and thrashers, lies to Sonoyta's north. The founding of the monument was due more to hard-drinking politicians than to selfless wilderness preservationists. During Prohibition state legislators were getting most of their liquor from Sonoyta, Sonora. The well-traveled road from Phoenix to the border was in miserable shape; the final twenty-five miles to the border was nothing more than a bumpy culvert. Rumrunners often brought shovels along to dig their cars out. To get their route in better condition, state legislators in Phoenix donated the unused land north of the border to the federal government, knowing that one of the first actions the new owners would take would be to improve the road. Soon the federal government graded the road, Arizona's politicians got their liquor much more easily, and the public gained a wilderness preserve. In 1937 the land was officially opened as a national monument.

Organ Pipe Cactus National Monument is a favorite crossing point for those attempting to enter the U.S. illegally. Few border guards patrol the vast expanse, and footpaths traverse the monument like yard lines on a football field. Failure to dress appropriately or carry sufficient water for the harsh desert trek can be fatal.

Over the Fourth of July weekend in 1980 a group of refugees fleeing the civil war in El Salvador was not prepared for the trip through the rugged monument grounds. They wore city clothes, carried suitcases and had precious little water. Unorganized and weakened by the blazing sun—the temperature on the desert floor was estimated at 150 degrees—the Salvadorans drank any available liquid. They poured cologne, perfume, and after-shave lotion down their throats. They licked anti-perspirant roll-ons and sprayed deodorant in their mouths. In desperation they drank their own urine. Thirteen Salvadorans survived. An equal number were found dead; dirt and sand were found in their mouths from having gnawed the ground for moisture. Finding the bodies of foreigners who falter while crossing the desert is not uncommon; locating so many all at once is.

Adjoining Sonoyta on the U.S. side is a small shopping center for vacationers on their way to fishing villages on Sonora's West Coast. Officially called Lukeville, the pit stop is better known as Gringo Pass, a name given it by the stores' owner in the early 1970s. Gringo Pass is a "dull, uninteresting, hot, out-of-the-way place," according to its congressman Morris Udall, a characterization few would dispute.

Before we left the area, I stopped at Sonoyta's Lotería Nacional agency, located in a combination pharmacy and hardware store. A sign on the wall announced *el día del billetero*, the day honoring the lottery-ticket salesman. In Mexico, where almost every profession has its honorary day, that the neighborhood lottery agent should be recognized seemed more than appropriate. I chatted with the *billetero* and bought a ticket for the following Friday's drawing.

My lottery dealings were not as appreciated on the U.S. side, however. About this time I learned that I had been breaking U.S. law by shuffling back and forth across the border with my

Mexican lottery tickets. Specifically, Title 18, Chapter 61, Sec. 1301:

> Whoever brings into the United States . . . or carries in interstate or foreign commerce any paper . . . purporting to be or to represent a ticket, chance, share, . . . dependent upon the event of a lottery . . . offering prizes in whole or in part upon lot or chance . . . shall be fined not more than $1,000 or imprisoned not more than two years or both.

I was a borderland outlaw! I had joined the ranks of Jacinto Treviño and all the others whose crimes straddled America's southern frontier. I was a chronic offender. Rehabilitation seemed unlikely; I'd probably meet other lottery-ticket smugglers in jail and learn new tricks of the trade. Perhaps a *corrido* would be written about my bravery sneaking little pieces of paper into the United States past armed customs agents.

I stroll up to the bar in some small-town cantina. "What can I get you, *señor?*" the bartender asks. Two *vaqueros* shooting pool pause and stare. They whisper furtively and signal the bartender. "He is the famous lottery-ticket smuggler we have all heard so much about," they tell him. "Better be careful."

Meanwhile I'm over at the jukebox and play "El Corrido del Contrabandista de Billetes de Lotería Nacional." The title alone takes up half the record. The bartender has my drink ready.

"I am honored to have you in my humble cantina, *señor.* But you must beware: Another man has been here within the week, bragging that he too carries lottery tickets into the United States."

Competition! I grit my teeth. I'll show that *pinche cabrón* a thing or two about bringing tickets across the line.

The Camino del Diablo heading west from Sonoyta quickly brought me back to reality. Mexico's Route 2, the Devil's Highway, is a breathtaking two-lane road slicing through the Sonoran Desert. Black volcanic rock lines the south side of the highway; foreboding mountains roll north to the border. A forest of muscular cactus suddenly appeared to our north and just as quickly disappeared. Turning around for closer inspection proved impossible, since the blacktop has no shoulders or bank. The highway was chasing us all the way to San Luis and we were helpless. A bus passing at ninety miles an hour was the only other vehicle we saw for the entire 125 miles.

At San Luis Río Colorado, Luis Katsurayama showed us the town. Katsurayama was typical of Mexican middle-class businessmen on the border: he drove a late-model American car, listened to American music on the radio, and bought his groceries and clothes in the United States.

We drove by the new city jail, where three Americans were being held. "We used to have more Americans in jail here, but then there used to be more marijuana trafficking. The prisoner-release program a few years ago cleared a lot of the Americans out. American smugglers—they think because they are no longer under their own laws they are not under anyone's! It isn't so."

At San Luis' baseball stadium players were arriving for spring tryouts. The city's entry in the Liga Norte de Sonora, the Algodoneros—the cotton pickers—play their minor league ball against teams from Nogales, Agua Prieta, Magdalena, Caborca, Tijuana, and Puerto Peñasco. The team isn't especially good, Katsurayama admitted, but it is very popular.

Luis' father was among many Japanese imported to Sonora in the early twentieth century. "There was mesquite on the property where my father worked," Luis said. "His job was to prepare the land for farming."

After the Japanese attack on Pearl Harbor rumors circulated in the United States that Japanese in western Mexico were building landing strips and ammunition depots in preparation for an attack on California. The Mexican government rounded up the Japanese, Germans, and Italians on the border and sent them to Mexico City and Guadalajara.

"We weren't in camps there, but we couldn't leave, either. We were so far from our homes on the border that we lost all our land and our farming equipment. In 1945 we were allowed to return. By the time my family got back, we had to start all over again." Katsurayama described the ordeal in flat tones, devoid of emotion. "Today only about ten Japanese families are left in San Luis."

14

THE GREAT CANDY EXCHANGE

GANGSTERS AND SMUGGLERS, cops and conmen. Each knows his own role on the frontier and seldom oversteps his territory. To get other impressions of this country between America and Mexico we visited with fourth-, fifth-, and sixth-grade students at a Yuma, Arizona elementary school. Without hesitation they spoke their minds about the differences between Yuma and nearby San Luis Río Colorado, Sonora.

"The streets are made of dirt in Mexico!"

"Yeah, they're bumpy and they don't fix them up. They're full of holes."

"And they have a lotta rocks, too. They're too poor to pave them."

"The houses are smaller there."

"Yeah, they don't got no wood to build no houses."

"The schools are real tall. If you go there and you don't know Spanish, they put you in the first grade."

"And their teachers are real strict. My cousin is in school there and she told me."

Among the Yuma students were recently naturalized citizens as well as a number of green-card children, whose parents were Mexicans allowed to live and work on the U.S. side. Many of the students spoke English and Spanish interchangeably, and those who conversed only in Spanish learned English in special classes. One of the recently naturalized students preferred her

American school. "They don't have trash cans at the school I went to in Mexico. And we get more education than they do."

"They think different in schools down there," a boy said slowly. "They teach math but it's different. They know how to do it but they do it in a different way."

Most of the Yuma children had relatives or close friends across the line and visited them regularly. When they visit San Luis they bring something for their friends, such as—

"Shoes! Some kids over there don't have any shoes."

"Clothes!"

"I once brought my cousin a bike."

"I gave my old skateboard to Margo. She lives in San Luis."

"I have some cousins over there, and they said they would like to have our president."

"Money. Sometimes we bring money."

They all knew money. I held up a ten-peso note—worth approximately forty-five cents—in one hand and a dollar bill in the other, and asked which they would rather have.

"That one! The dollar!"

"But this bill says 'one' on it and the other says 'ten.' Wouldn't you rather have ten than one?"

"*Noooooooooooo.*"

"Why aren't they the same?"

"Their money's different because it's lower."

"Yeah, that's the way the president wants it."

"One time I was in a store with my Mom, and this Mexican man, he pulled out a Mexican dollar. He thought he could buy some bread."

"You can get stuff cheaper over there than here," chimed in a classmate. "Like if you only have a hundred dollars you can buy anything 'cause they only make seventy-five dollars a month."

"They don't have too much work over there. That's why."

"Yeah, they don't have any money. They have to go get their water outside the house and drink it."

"And the bathrooms are outside, some of them. And they're wooden."

"Their president steals too much from the poor people."

"I feel sad when I see people so poor," a girl added.

A sixth grader waved his hand frantically. "Sometimes people come across the border and they walk right by our house. The people who sneak across wear those big long things called *sarapes* and big hats. They eat beans and tortillas every day."

"I heard they swim across. But I don't know where they swim at."

"This whole school used to be an ocean," a neighboring fourth grader patiently explained. "And they used to swim across here."

A more knowledgeable classmate spoke up. "There's a dam. The All-American Dam, it's called. The people who come across hide in the bushes down there. We went down there once and saw the Border Patrol. If they see footprints, they'll follow them."

"Yeah, they pick up wetbacks. They pick 'em up and take 'em across the border."

"Sometimes when people are picking lemons and the Border Patrol comes around, everyone runs."

"My friend from San Luis told me they hit him with a belt," one Mexican boy said.

"Some of them get killed, I heard," another quickly added.

"They won't let you across if you don't have a *pasaporte*. Otherwise you have to stay in Mexico."

"The kids come across through a hole and they go to that park by the fence," said a boy as everyone giggled. "One of them put a *thing* on an old lady and they took her purse. Now they don't let them come across anymore." The giggling stopped.

"The Border Patrol is real strict. If Mexicans are walking down the street and they look like they're real poor, they get asked questions. If they don't speak English, the Patrol takes them in."

"They're *mean*, the Patrol," said a girl, making a face. "You're supposed to have papers to get by the border—I hate them. One time my brother was going to work and they were checking the little green cards, and my brother didn't have his and they brought him back to the border. And my brother said, 'I wish I could get a gun and shoot them.' They kicked him."

A classmate from Mexico nodded his head vigorously. "I think everybody ought to have the liberty to go anywhere they wanna. Mexico doesn't bother people from here going to Mexico. Not like the United States bothers us."

A shy girl in the second row spoke up. "I still can't get it why people from here go down there and Mexico doesn't do nothing to them. But people from down there come here and if they don't have no papers, they'll get in trouble by the *migra*."

"It's scary!"

"But all they're coming over for is jobs."

I asked if Mexico had a Border Patrol that picked up Americans who sneaked over looking for work. They laughed and laughed. Imagine, Mexico having a Border Patrol!

"A friend of my mom's got fired so a Mexican lady could work," said a tall girl in the back. "I don't think Mexicans should be allowed to come over and work."

A hush fell over the room. No one said a word.

The teacher broke the awkward silence. "You don't see so many of the little boys selling Chiclets and colored rocks any more. Why is that?"

"I guess they finally got fed up with not selling anything," one boy suggested.

I asked what some of the nice things about the other side were.

"Cheese! You can't get Mexican cheese here."

"They have a different kind of chocolate. I think it's called *cajeta*."

"Candy!" "Yeah, the candy!" "Mmm, I love their candy." "Their candy is different from ours." A chorus of *yums* went round the room. The feeling was unanimous. The candy was better on the other side.

"And Mexican suckers. I like Mexican suckers. My dad always buys me some when we go across."

"Yeah, they got sno-cones and stuff like that."

"And they have real nice decorated clothes."

"They dress different. Their shirts have pockets all over."

"I love their tortillas. They make good tortillas."

"And they have big Mexican flowers, paper flowers."

"They have different shoes."

"Yeah, their sandals are called *huaraches* and they all wear them."

"Also there's not any shoeshine boys over here, but there's plenty over there."

"And here you have to call on the phone for a taxi, but over there they have taxis all around."

"San Luis has lots of doctors and dentists. It's cheaper to go to one there."

"My Mom says they do a better job."

"Well, I like Mexico better," one recent immigrant asserted. "I was born there and grew up there."

"I like it 'cause you can get firecrackers there," said his neighbor.

"When you come back they check at the border to see if you're carrying any firecrackers or things like that."

"We get firecrackers over there for the Fourth of July," explained one girl. "When we bring them back we hide them under the pillows so the inspectors won't find them."

"Yeah? My dad hides them under the table in our camper."

"One time at the border they checked in the back of our trunk to see if we were bringing back a Mexican."

"They check in front, too. But we go through there all the time and they don't hardly check anymore."

"Once when we came back they checked the back of our van and we had our dog with us. They took the dog away for a while, so now we hide him. We put him down and pull covers over him."

"They also check to see if you're bringing any marijuana back with you."

"I know. Sometimes they pull your car over and put a search dog in it to look for drugs."

Lunchtime was approaching, and the children started talking about food again. Are the restaurants in Mexico very different? I asked.

"Yes. On all the walls they got big pictures of people on horses and things. They have those big forks and spoons which you can't get over here."

"When I walk into a restaurant there I notice the flies."

"They got little stools."

"A lot of their restaurants don't have menus, either."

"They don't got Burger Kings!"

"It isn't fair that we have so much and they have so little."

No matter what we talked about—food, clothing, schools, anything—in one form or another the children always commented on the poverty. Students who had family in Mexico said their relatives wanted to move to the United States.

"They should allow people to come in."

"Yeah, this is a free country. Isn't it?"

The bell rang and the children of Yuma scrambled for the door. A couple of them stopped as we prepared to leave. "Why don't you stay for lunch? You could eat with us."

"That's very nice of you. What are you having?"

"Let's see. Today is Monday. *Enchiladas quemadas, claro.*" Burned enchiladas, of course.

In San Luis Río Colorado, the state's oldest and biggest elementary school is named for Abelardo Rodríguez, a former governor and later president of Mexico. Professor Horacio Pompa, the school's principal, invited us to speak with his students at Escuela Abelardo L. Rodríguez about life along the border.

The students stood at attention when we walked into the classroom; that was the first difference. They spoke only Spanish; that was the second. But after that, the fourth, fifth, and sixth graders in Mexico had observations remarkably similar to their Yuma counterparts. Most of their mothers and fathers were employed, and over half of the parents worked in the United States.

"They prefer things that way," one student announced.

"There is more work in the U.S., and more money." The parents from San Luis who found work in Arizona and California toiled in lemon groves and lettuce fields, they drove tractors and made furniture. One sold car parts and another worked at Yuma Chevrolet.

Shy at first, the students soon began to voice their thoughts loudly about the other side.

"Their clothes—they have so many more of them!"

"Yes, and their clothes are much better. Our relatives are always bringing us some."

"They have more variety in what they wear."

"And their ice cream is good—we don't have it like that here."

"And you get good service in restaurants!"

"In our cafes all we have is chile and frijoles."

"We prefer the food in Yuma—"

"—'cause they've got Kentucky Fried Chicken!"

"They have candy over there we can't get."

"Oooo yes, our friends bring us American candy when they come over." "Their candy tastes delicious." "I like American candy." A chorus of *yums* went around the room. The feeling was unanimous. The candy was better on the other side.

The school's Drum and Bugle Corps was practicing outside the classroom window for the upcoming Yuma Rodeo Parade. Many of the students planned to attend. They liked listening to American music.

"American music is all John Travolta!"

"And the Bee Gees."

"All American music is rock 'n' roll and disco," a boy in front said. The class laughed when he said "rock 'n' roll."

"All we have is *ranchero* music."

I tried my money game again, asking whether they preferred the bill marked "10" or the one with a "1."

"That one! That one!" they cried out in unison, pointing to the dollar bill.

"Why are pesos and dollars different?"

"I know." A fifth grader on the side shot up his hand. "The peso is twenty-two-point-six to one!" No doubt a future financier. Or street vendor.

On and on our conversation continued through the morning.

"The roads on the other side are cleaner and wider," one student said, "with no holes." "They have green on the sides of the roads there," another added. "And most of them are paved, too," a third emphasized.

"They have fewer students in each classroom on the other side, and they go home from school earlier."

"We go over there to go shopping or to visit. But every time we cross," a girl complained, "we need papers."

"Sometimes we go over to play in Amistad Park on the border. We just go through a hole in the fence."

"It's easier for Americans to cross over here than for us to go there." Everyone nodded in agreement.

"Maybe we should hassle Americans like they hassle us."

"No," a classmate replied, "we need American visitors."

"Yeah, a lot of gringos go to our beaches."

They all had something to say about the Border Patrol: *"la migra!"*

"They watch people so they don't jump the fence."

"They catch the ones that don't have *pasaportes—*"

"—and take them away."

"It's better to work over there and live here," one boy proudly stated. "We're more used to living here. We're strangers on the other side."

When we finished, the students applauded in appreciation. As we were leaving the school grounds, we saw Professor Pompa tending the school garden. He came over to say goodbye and give us a flower.

En Route

Skip O'Dell was not pleased with America's shifting attitude toward Mexican immigration. "These Mexicans, they come up from the interior and get Anglicized in Mexicali and Juárez," the Border Patrolman complained as he drove through Yuma County in his pale green government sedan. "They learn a little English, then they think they have the right to come over here.

The government could take care of the problem if they wanted to, but they're afraid of how it affects our foreign policy. They're afraid of losing a quart of oil."

O'Dell's eyes narrowed to focus on a distant object. "After three or four years at this job you can spot an alien in a crowd," he insisted. "But when you're working a checkpoint, you can't wave all the cars with Anglos through and stop all the Mexicans. There've been decisions on that. We have to have 'probable cause' now, even if our instincts tell us they're wets—er, aliens. The courts make things worse and worse all the time."

That evening seventeen peasants from Jiquilpán, Michoacán, milled about the Yuma Border Patrol station where O'Dell works. An hour earlier they had sneaked across the border west of Yuma at Andrade, California. All of them—thirteen men, three women, and a baby—had traveled six hundred miles by bus to San Luis Río Colorado where a *coyote* convinced them to pay him two hundred dollars apiece to take them to Los Angeles, California. Now they were in the Border Patrol station occupying every spare seat and bench as if it were a bus station. Patrolmen acted like harried ticket agents writing up each one, then sending them on to a detention room to wait for the ride back to the border. Emmon Mann, the balding flat-topped agent in charge, gestured toward the crowd waiting in line to be processed. "They're over there now getting their story straight. If we can break 'em we'll find out who the *coyote* is. He can get five years in jail and a two-thousand-dollar fine for each smuggled alien."

The first twenty miles west of San Luis Río Colorado on the road to Mexicali was among the worst-maintained border highway we had yet traveled—bumpy, narrow, rocky, and thick with dust. The most insulting part of this stretch was having to pay a nine-peso toll to cross the Colorado River. We felt we deserved payment for merely negotiating that part of Route 2.

We were in a hurry to get to church in Mexicali that Sunday morning to learn how Roman Catholics there were responding to the visit of Pope John Paul II elsewhere in the country. Even the covers of Mexico's sex-and-violence weeklies paused between silicone-injected breasts and grisly slayings to acknowledge the presence of *el Papa*. Two days earlier, while blessing a plaza full of believers in Puebla, the Pope had said: "In the midst of suffering there are still the simple joys of the poor, in the humble shacks of the peasants, the Indians and the immigrants." Mexicali was a city full of immigrants, poor, and peasants in humble shacks. In short, it was the Pope's kind of town.

We parked near the Cathedral of Guadalupe, which was filling up for the eleven o'clock mass. At the side entrance Romana Meno Montaño was sitting on a metal folding chair, her lap full of posters of the Pope in the ten-peso size, a bigger one for twenty pesos, and the large economy-size Pope for thirty pesos. A slightly bent elderly lady who had been working for Romana came over and handed her some money. Couldn't she keep a bit more for each poster sold? she asked. Romana shook her head. The old lady reluctantly reached down in her stocking and pulled out some more pesos for her boss.

When mass let out the sidewalks filled. In the midst of the crowd we spotted a woman in a wheelchair, dwarfed by the throng. A towel around her shoulders was her shawl, a makeshift scarf protected her head. Her gnarled, outstretched hands begged for donations. To each passerby she showed a longing, forlorn gaze. In conversation she came alive. Her name was María González, and she had just moved to Mexicali from León, Guanajuato, fifteen hundred miles away. She had heard she could buy a good wheelchair in Mexicali, something she desperately needed. On arrival she bought a new one that was more comfortable to sit in and easier to maneuver than the one she used to own. A man strolling by dropped a five-peso coin in her Styrofoam collection cup. The outside of the cup said BURGER KING in bright red letters. She had found it just the day before.

Mexicali, Baja California, an agricultural and industrial center of 800,000, is off the gringo trail; as a result it was the only city we visited which looked more to Mexico's interior for its identity than to the border and the United States beyond. Mexicali was also the town in which we found the very best restaurant on the border, O'Lar Galego.

I employed rigid standards in my search for outstanding border cafes: the places had to be accessible to all; the prices under five dollars a meal; the atmosphere relaxing; and the help friendly. Tourist traps were out; I mistrusted restaurants where no Mexicans ate. The best cafes mixed character and salsa.

O'Lar Galego had the best of everything. In numerous visits I sampled practically every dish on the menu. My first meal there started with *champiñones rancheros,* mushrooms cooked in a light spicy salsa. The soup, a strong, clear broth with spinach, onion, and white beans, came next. My entree was *paella a la valencia*—saffron rice with shrimp, tomato, chorizo, egg slices, bacon, garbanzo beans, and ham. The next day I sampled the chicken casserole, baked with a tangy white wine sauce and served on a bed of rice. When I returned again I tried *tortilla de champiñones,* a delicate mushroom soufflé served up as an omelette. Each dish was prepared with obvious care and contained the freshest vegetables and meats. Pepe, the cook, had mastered the art of balancing *picante* spices with light greens. His was food to savor.

The atmosphere at O'Lar Galego is no less appealing than the food. The restaurant, located behind a laundromat at Justo Sierra and Carpinteros Sur, consists of one room with four tables, each of which seats four. A waist-high counter separates the dining room from the kitchen. Artwork from Mexico and owner Manola Joven's native Spain lines the walls. In good weather a few extra tables are set up outside. When the air is chilly, a fire in the corner pot-bellied stove warms the room. Señora Joven, who opened the restaurant in 1978, has established a warm and intimate *ambiente,* one in which you want to ask if you can do anything to help—set the table? Stir a simmering pot? When I started bringing friends to O'Lar Galego Señora Joven beamed with pride. She made us feel at home.

15

BAJA'S BLUES

BY SEVEN O'CLOCK, Baja California Norte Governor Roberto de la Madrid Romandía had already begun his two-hour exercise program with leg thrusts, bike pedaling, and sit-ups. Sporting a blue jogging suit, he was off on his daily two-and-a-half-mile walk through Mexicali's Colonia Nueva. Early risers on their way to work stopped him briefly: "Roberto, ¿qué tal?" Truck drivers slowed down to wave. De la Madrid paused in the chapel of Nuestra Señora de Perpétuo Socorro to kneel and pray, then returned to the streets. Two security cars and a jogging armed bodyguard kept a discreet distance.

"See this park here?" We were approaching Preparatoria Número Uno. "The high school students had appropriated the park for themselves. They held onto it for four years. The situation became so bad that the previous governor wouldn't come within four blocks of here. The first week that I was governor I came here and took possession of the park. The students rioted and everything. I told them it was a public park and from now on their brothers and sisters were going to use it too.

"One day I visited the park and some of the students were shooting baskets. They were amazed that the governor would come over to their court—they didn't know whether to fall flat on their faces or lynch me. I watched them play a little and noticed they were pivoting all wrong. By the time they had shot the ball all their energy had gone into bodywork and they had no momentum left for the shot. Their shots weren't half as strong as they should have been, and I told them so. They looked at me kind of strange and one guy says, 'OK, *you* shoot.'

"So I get the ball and go to the free-throw line, and I say, 'Is this far enough?' They all laugh and say, 'That's fine.' I say, 'No it isn't' and take another three or four steps back. Well, I hadn't shot a basketball in twenty years. I used to be pretty good—I was on two teams which went to the Pan American Games. And I thought to myself, Virgin of Guadalupe, help me now. I bounced it a few times and shot. The damn ball swished right through the hoop. The guys looked at it in disbelief, then they let out a big yell and ran over and slapped me on the back. I showed the guy who tossed me the ball how to make the shot and in a couple of tries he was doing all right. After a few sessions with them they named me their coach. For the first time in the school's history they won first place in the state."

It is a story de la Madrid loves to tell. A touch of macho, a dash of diplomacy, some fancy footwork, seizing a situation—the governor thrives on all of these. For a kid who dropped out of Sweetwater High School in National City, California, south of San Diego, Roberto de la Madrid has done quite well for himself. Born of Mexican parents in Calexico, California, in 1922, de la Madrid remained a binational citizen until his eighteenth birthday when he opted for Mexican status. A series of government jobs in the 1950s put him in touch with fellow bureaucrat José López Portillo, a man with whom he has remained close since. Through the years de la Madrid has assumed influential positions—Pemex distributor for Baja California, head of the Lotería Nacional, and state senator. At age fifty-five, two years after his friend José López Portillo became president, de la Madrid took office as governor of Baja California. Through considerable business and political contacts cultivated over the years, de la Madrid has emerged a pivotal personality in U.S.–Mexico relations. He is as much at home with America's decision-makers as he is with Mexico's. Baja California is the only one of Mexico's six northernmost states to have its capital on the border, and de la Madrid is the first homegrown son to govern

it since statehood was conferred in 1952. Brought up and educated in both Mexico and the United States, he knows how to
cut red tape in two languages. He is the consummate border
politician.

Elsewhere around the country the blue-eyed de la Madrid is
considered as much a gringo politician as a Mexican one. The
ease with which he slips in and out of American high society
amuses pundits in Mexico City. "Red Privada," the political
column in Mexico's major newspaper, *Excelsior,* refers to him
as "Roberto—'call me Bob, please'—de la Madrid." Instead of
gobernador, his critics label him *"el* bob*ernador"* and his administration, *"el* bob*ierno."* When they call him a *baboso* (blith-
ering idiot) it becomes "bob*oso."*

De la Madrid's name has been among those mentioned as a
possible successor to López Portillo. He claims no aspirations for
the presidency, though, and the Mexican constitution provides
that the president must be born in Mexico. "Ah, the laws,"
smiled a high official in de la Madrid's administration. "He can
always get around them. If I offer the presidency to you, would
you refuse? Anyway, when he was born, Calexico and Mexicali
were one city. There was no border then." A prominent Mexicali businessman hedged on de la Madrid's qualifications: "He's
a doer, not a thinker."

Public criticism of de la Madrid has emanated from only one
source in Baja California—Tijuana's afternoon daily, *ABC.* Its
articles, alternately aggressive and mocking, portrayed a state
administration beset by corruption and ineptitude. The newspaper once gleefully listed de la Madrid's relatives on the state
payroll, twenty-six in all. *ABC,* which often reprinted investiga-
tive pieces about Baja California from U.S. newspapers, so angered de la Madrid on one occasion that he said of editor Jesús
Blancornelas, "Insecticide ought to be applied to this insect of
journalism." *ABC*'s critical voice was stilled when a govern-
ment-backed union invaded its offices and ousted Blancornelas
and other editors. Blancornelas, who felt his life endangered in
Baja California, moved to Chula Vista, California; from there he
continues to irritate de la Madrid and other state officials with

Zeta, a new daily newspaper serving Tijuana and Mexicali.

Crisis has become an ongoing reality in Baja California. Nowhere is this more apparent than in Tijuana's Zona Norte, a crowded section of town adjacent to the tourist district. At the bus station *huarache*-shod peasants take their first hesitant steps in the fast-paced world of Tijuana. *Coyotes* and *enganchadores*—labor contractors—approach them, winning the confidence of the uninitiated. Flophouses and low-rent *casas de huéspedes*—rooming houses—swell with *campesinos* waiting for the opportunity to move north. Migrants looking for temporary work fill dank bars and two-table cafes before pressing on. Four-man *conjuntos* weave through the streets and cantinas, playing for anyone who will pause to listen. One block in the Zona Norte, Callejón Coahuila, is laughingly called "the largest consulate in the world" because so many border crossings are arranged there.

Typical of the new arrivals was nineteen-year-old Agustín. For three days and nights he rode buses and hitchhiked to the border from Dolores Hidalgo in the state of Guanajuato. The next ten days he lived in abandoned houses in Colonia Libertad, a rough section of Tijuana which crowds the border fence. At five o'clock in the afternoon of his eleventh day in Tijuana, Agustín stood at the fence pondering how best to enter the United States. He thought of the man who had given him a ride through Sonora and how he had told Agustín that in English the *g* in Los Angeles has a soft sound unlike the Spanish pronunciation. Agustín wanted to sound as much like an American as he could in case *la migra* picked him up. He smiled as he slowly said "Lawss AN-gel-es," then hesitantly asked if he pronounced it correctly. He pulled a few pesos from his pocket and asked if I had some American coins with me. We sat and compared their relative values. He wanted to make sure that when he got to Los Angeles no one took advantage of him.

As the sun started to set, Border Patrol agents drove by as close as twenty yards away. Agustín was considering paying some of the little money he had left to a *coyote* to help him across safely. A couple of *coyotes* were already lining up their *pollos* (literally, chickens) for the evening. One propositioned Agustín about crossing.

"Another *coyote?*" I asked after their conversation ended. Agustín nodded. "And I will be his *pollo.* And over there"—he gestured to the Border Patrol—"they are *cabrones*" (goats, but in slang, cuckolds or bastards). "We are all animals of one sort or another, *¿verdad?*"

With an estimated one thousand arrivals like Agustín a day, Tijuana's population has reached nearly one million. The unemployment rate hovers at 70 percent. Fully one-fourth of Tijuana's population is transient, making it the leader among the *ciudades trampolines* along the border. Attendant crimes —robbery, prostitution, drunken and desperate violence, and police corruption—abound.

"No state in the world can cope with a situation like this," de la Madrid admitted. "The people who come, they are so temporary they don't know how to handle themselves as citizens. Where do they live? Old shacks, maybe, with a color television because they can take that with them. The kids go about the streets, soon they become delinquent, and then they become addicted to drugs. These people lifted up their roots where they came from, but they have not planted them here."

Baja California's overpopulation and unemployment problems stem from its greatest asset: It has the highest minimum wage in Mexico and borders on a country where the wages are higher still. The most ambitious attempt to stabilize Baja's economy is the Border Industrial Program, commonly called the *maquiladora,* or assembly plant, program. As originally conceived when the *maquiladora* program began full operation in 1967, American manufacturers would establish plants in Mexico and hire Mexicans to assemble parts shipped over from the United States. American companies would then import the finished product back to the United States, paying U.S. duty only on the value of the added labor. The theory was that the *maquiladora* program would pump money into border-town economies, reduce unemployment, and thus lower the number of migrants crossing to the U.S. for work.

The program hasn't worked out that way. Some of the runa-way shops, as they came to be known, relocated across the border to avoid environmental or safety regulations. All came for a vast pool of cheap labor. Baja California, with approxi-mately 170 *maquilas,* has roughly one-third of all U.S.-owned assembly plants in Mexico, employing more than twenty thou-sand workers. Although everything from batteries to goggles is made in the *maquilas,* their two main functions are to assemble tiny electronic circuitry and sew clothing for sale in the United States.

In 1968 the Certron Corporation of Anaheim, California, opened a cassette-assembly plant with 13 workers in the base-ment of a run-down Mexicali building. That enterprise has grown to become a showcase *maquila,* operating around the clock in Mexicali's Parque Industrial with 680 employees. Giant fourteen-thousand-foot spools of uncut recording tape shipped from Anaheim to Mexicali are broken down into individual cassettes, each made in complex assembly-line fashion. Eigh-teen components make up each unit, from a little piece of paper that cushions the tape to five tiny screws that hold it all to-gether. Workers package two grades of tape and paste on "Cer-tron" or "Realistic" or "Pay 'n' Save" labels according to which order is being filled that day. Then the tapes are trucked back to the United States.

Complicated machinery fills the plant, and workers hardly ever shift positions. One group of six, for example, sits on stools dabbing glue in four spots on the inside of each cassette casing to hold the plastic window in place. Each worker puts in twelve thousand windows per eight-hour shift, meaning forty-eight thousand dabs of glue—enough to get the most sober workers stoned from the fumes, if they aren't already deaf from the surrounding noise. In normal operations Certron Audio churns out 110,000 cassette tapes each day. Certron of Anaheim pays most of its Mexicali workers 180 pesos a day ($8.09), the mini-mum wage.

Xavier Rivas is in charge of recruiting industry for Mexicali. He pitches U.S. companies—especially those in Los Angeles and

Orange counties, California—on the advantages of "offshore assembly." When a company expresses interest, he checks the import duty it would pay, the space it would need, worker skills it requires, and its credit rating. Rivas, a well-spoken man who attended American business schools, explained how his Comisión de Desarrollo Industrial—Industrial Development Commission—works: "We try to make sure the companies aren't running from the EPA [Environmental Protection Agency] or OSHA [the Occupational Safety and Health Administration] or avoiding upgrading equipment. We ask the companies to send their most recent health and environment records and we turn them over to the local health department for review. Of course we aren't as strict as the EPA but at least we want to make sure the workers' health isn't impaired." In Tijuana, no pretense of environmental standards is made. "We're trying to bring as many plants here as possible," an officer in the state's industrial development office explained, "so we have no restrictions at all."

Over 75 percent of the *maquiladora* workers in Mexico are women. Plant operators say they prefer female employees because they have better manual dexterity for intricate assembly. The main reason, however, can be found in a 1971 primer for businesses setting up *maquilas, The Border Industrial Program:* "From their earliest conditioning, [women] show respect and obedience to persons in authority, especially men. The women follow orders willingly, accept change and adjustments easily, and are considered less demanding. . . ."

Aside from the manufacturing companies, it is the American border towns that profit most from the program. Calexico, California, across from Mexicali, estimates that fully 85 percent of its trade comes from Mexicali, and most of that from the *maquiladora* workers. An experiment conducted by the *maquilas* themselves—marking pesos paid to employees—revealed that 65 percent of the wages were spent in the United States within twenty-four hours.

Consider: American plants get enormous tax breaks for locating on the border, they pay their workers the bare-minimum wage, for the most part the low wages aren't even spent in

Mexico, the American companies pay import duty on the added value only, and the products are not sold in Mexico. Border town factories attract people from the interior, the overwhelming majority of whom cannot land jobs at the *maquilas*. Those without jobs either further crowd the cities, move north to the United States, or return home humiliated. As a result, border town populations have not stabilized, and northward migration and joblessness have increased dramatically—which poses a not very humorous riddle: Would you rather be unemployed in Guadalajara or on the border?

"You must remember, about thirty-five percent of the pesos we pay out stay here," Rivas countered. "And if we open a plant with two hundred employees? That's two hundred Mexicans who won't go to the United States. And it's a free school for us. We'd never know how to make a garment or a cassette without the plants. We get the know-how. We had a stuffed-toy company once which gave jobs to these people. They left after three years. But the plant manager said, 'Hey, I know how to make stuffed toys.' Now he runs a stuffed toy company that's all Mexican."

Each year members of Congress, usually from garment manufacturing districts, try to repeal the sections of the U.S. Tariff Schedule permitting *maquiladoras*, and each year the bills have less and less chance of success as the Border Industrial Program continues to expand. The AFL-CIO, worried about American jobs being exported to Mexico, is unalterably opposed to the *maquilas*. "Once you get General Motors, General Electric, and RCA thriving in the border areas because they can't afford to pay American wages," complained an AFL-CIO economist, "you have a whole new grip of political pressures. It's a very ugly situation."

Another way Baja California tries to attract U.S. dollars is to encourage real estate investment by Americans. Foreigners are not allowed to own property within thirty-two miles of the seacoast or sixty-four miles of the international border. Strictly interpreted this would leave only a pencil-thin strip of land down the middle of the state available for foreign investors. But loopholes abound and through lease deals Americans can control property on the state's West Coast, turning parts of an impoverished section of Mexico into a sort of propertied *gringolandia*. Investment money goes mostly to developers, banks, and the government. The only impact it makes on Baja California's considerable poverty is to make it more obvious.

The most common method of acquiring property is through bank trusts, in which a Mexican bank holds title to a parcel of land. The American investor is the beneficiary of the trust for thirty years, which allows him to use, lease, or sell the property during that time. When the trust expires, the land reverts to its original owner.

Baja California's eight-hundred-mile West Coast is breathtaking, undeveloped for all but the far north and far south. Mobile-home parks have proliferated in the northern strip, however, and an estimated ten thousand Americans have moved into the area. California real estate forecasters see the area south of Tijuana as ripe for enclaves of Americans, treating the move across the international frontier as if it were as simple as expanding into a neighboring county.

Baja California officials are doing their best to facilitate the impending population shift. Full cooperation is given developers whose new homes will attract American wealth and reflect north-of-the-border taste. Some of the more modern developments along the coast are carefully designed, such as the celebrated and expensive ocean-view Bajamar complex with its eighteen-hole golf course.

The contrast between Bajamar and the nearby coastal community of Ejido Primo Tapia is stark. Primo Tapia is an agricultural cooperative, and its few hundred residents earn their living from beans, wheat, corn, and other staples grown in small plots surrounding their shacks. The *ejidatarios* travel on bumpy dirt roads, and services are at a minimum. Conditions are similar at La Misión, another *ejido* closer to Ensenada. In fact, the rule of thumb throughout Baja California seems to be that the roads are paved wherever *norteamericanos* are likely to travel and unpaved in the areas which are *puro mexicano*.

The United Farm Workers' lettuce-pickers' strike was on everybody's mind at Calexico across the border. In the week since the strike began blood had already been shed. A few days later one striker would be shot to death in the lettuce fields as he protested the presence of *esquiroles,* of strike-breakers. The lettuce-pickers, many of whom are green-card Mexicans who cross daily from their homes in Mexicali, wanted higher wages and side benefits. The growers insisted that they had offered raises in keeping with federal wage guidelines, while the farm workers showed that their pay was so low it was exempt from federal directives. But the strike, as always in a United Farm Workers struggle, took on significance far greater than nickels and dimes. It became a rallying point for stoop labor, those on the bottom rung of the farm-to-market ladder. No one could articulate their cause better than the founder and president of the United Farm Workers, César Chávez.

Chávez came to Calexico to calm his supporters after the initial violence. Field hands had thrown rocks at trucks carrying lettuce picked by strike-breakers a few days earlier, shattering windshields and bloodying truck drivers' faces. The Imperial Valley lettuce growers quickly improvised a "Volunteer Harvest Day" to capitalize on anti-union publicity, and invited local housewives and schoolchildren to the fields to pick the crops themselves. The event took on the air of a community strike-breaking day, with the clear implication that the union picketers were un-American.

At nearby Holtville, where farm workers picketed a lettuce-shipping center, a short, wiry striker from Mexicali holding a flag with the UFW eagle on it started to explain the union position. After a couple of minutes two men took him aside for a hurried conversation. "They told me to be wary when I talk to reporters," he said when he returned. "They said the reporters who cover the strike always seem to be on the side of the growers, that they don't take the time to understand our position.

"That violence a few days ago? That's what happens when the people get angry. When the growers bring in the dogs and have them charging at us, when the sheriff's deputies are swinging clubs and start calling people names, well, we can only take so much race-baiting, you know? That's how the violence starts."

As truck driver Dennis Balkham saw things, "It was like Geronimo charging at us the way those strikers threw those rocks. I got them to chunk the rocks at me as a decoy so the bus drivers could get out of the fields without getting hit anymore. I got it through the windshield." The glass on Balkham's truck resembled a jigsaw puzzle.

"I came out on the main road between Holtville and the freeway. There was a Mexican man that had a rock about this big." He connected his thumbs with his forefingers. "He handed it to a woman behind him and she threw it at me. And hit me! I was there in the 1970 strike when the Chávez people first started up in Salinas. They weren't as bad as this." Balkham noticed an American flag on a nearby truck. "That's the one we're trying to live under, instead of their commie one with the buzzard on it."

The morning after his arrival César Chávez toured twenty picket lines scattered throughout the area. Strikers who were clustered around small fires in the predawn chill welcomed him with cheers and crowded around as he chatted with them about previous struggles and missing *compadres.* Together they sensed a long fight ahead. Chávez walked down each picket line like a general inspecting his troops. "*¡Adelante, comandante!*" his aides would say and they'd leave for the next site. As he departed each picket line the strikers shouted through their scarfs: "*Huel-ga, huel-ga, ¡viva la huelga!*"

End of the Route

"It was always a borderland I had lived on," thought Danny Deck in Larry McMurtry's *All My Friends Are Going to Be Strangers,* "a thin line between the country of the normal and the country of the strange. Perhaps my true country was the borderland anyway." The border had been our true country for two thousand miles, a land which tugged on the extremities of life and sheltered them from the elements. We had crossed the frontier some four hundred times—more than anyone had a right to and still emerge with a sense of optimism.

I had one more mission before we were through. The seashells I'd picked up on the beach at the Gulf of Mexico at the start of the trip had to be planted in the sand at the Pacific Ocean.

The California beach which runs along the Pacific at the end of the border is called Border Field State Park. Once a private practice field for racehorses and before that a Navy training camp, the park is now visited annually by 200,000 people who enjoy swimming, fishing, horseback riding, and bird-watching. Pelicans and terns are common; marsh hawks and prairie falcons have also been spotted. A nature trail introduces cactus, sea dahlias, and poppies. Jackrabbits and ground squirrels live in the marshland. Now and then a roadrunner prances by.

On the Mexico side of the border is Playas de Tijuana, a beachfront area with hotels and restaurants. On Sundays the neighborhood fills with bullfight fans who flock to the Bullring-By-The-Sea just south of the fence.

Twenty-five yards east of where the tide laps up upon the West Coast, the fence stops. The very western tip of the border is unmarked. Americans can stroll into Playas de Tijuana and back again without going through customs or immigration. For Mexicans the beach is an equally pleasant way to enter the United States—no uniformed guards, no fence, no turnstile, no questions. It was a friendly way to end the border.

Many Mexicans take advantage of this friendship. Invariably more people leave the Border Field parking lot in the afternoon than arrive in the morning. On occasion Border Patrolmen perched on a bluff above the beach come down and shoo Mexicans back to their own beach. Once, participants in a Mexican baptism in the Pacific Ocean drifted north to the U.S. side. While the godparents and the rest of the party were celebrating, border guards herded them back to the Mexican side.

On a late winter weekday afternoon I found the park empty.

A strong breeze carried the sea mist inland and the wet sand felt good beneath my feet. The only reminder of a political boundary was a Border Patrol plane circling overhead. As I started to bury the seashells from the Gulf of Mexico, two middle-aged men, Felix and Ramón, approached. They were from Mexico City, they said, visiting the north to work for a short while before returning. "By the way," Ramón asked, nodding up the beach, "how far is San Diego? Los Angeles? Is it safe to walk on the beach all that distance?" They were full of questions about the north. Is work hard to find? What happens if *la migra* stops us? Should we carry a small bag of clothing? A jug of water? Will we need food or can we buy some from vendors along the way? And why are you burying those seashells?

I answered their questions as best I could, and explained that I had carried the seashells with me all the way from the eastern end of the border, from beyond Matamoros. As my trip progressed, the seashells had come to represent the singular qualities I had discovered about the border. Now I wanted to lay them to rest here at the western end. A stubborn naïveté allowed me to believe that one day frontiers would no longer exist; that the problems of trade and migration would dissolve; that there would be no more visas or customs; that the border would cease to be a barrier to employment or family unity; that a *campesino* on one side would reap the same rewards as a worker on the other.

I finished burying some of the seashells and tossed the rest into the ocean. Finally, I looked up, expecting that Felix and Ramón would be long gone, not comprehending this monologue of foolish dreams. But they had remained, listening, quiet throughout. *Te entendemos,* they smiled. We understand you. And they walked off along the beach to the north.

BIBLIOGRAPHY

Acuña, Rodolfo. *Occupied America*. San Francisco: Canfield Press, 1972.

Bartlett, John Russell. *Personal Narrative of Explorations and Incidents in Texas, New Mexico, California, Sonora, and Chihuahua Connected With The United States and Mexican Boundary Commission During The Years 1850, '51, '52, and '53*. 2 vols. 1864. Reprint. Chicago: Rio Grande Press, 1965.

Border Traffic [Television Program] by Kenneth Harrison and Kaye Northcott. Director Kenneth Harrison. Producers KERA-TV, Dallas, and Kenneth Harrison Films. 1978. 60 min.

Carson, Gerald. *The Roguish World of Dr. Brinkley*. New York: Rinehart and Co., 1960.

Casey, Clifford B. *Mirages, Mysteries and Reality: Brewster County, Texas, of the Big Bend of the Rio Grande*. Seagraves, Texas: Pioneer Book Publishers, Inc., 1972.

Chulas Fronteras [Motion Picture] by Les Blank. Conceived and produced by Chris Strachwitz. El Cerrito, Calif.: Brazos Films. 1976. 58 min. Color.

Chulas Fronteras [Soundtrack]. Arhoolie Records. 1977. Arhoolie No. 4005, with illus. booklet.

Clendenen, Clarence C. *The United States and Pancho Villa*. Ithaca, N.Y.: Cornell University Press, 1961.

Demaris, Ovid. *Poso del Mundo*. Boston: Little, Brown and Co., 1970.

Douglas, William O. *Farewell to Texas*. New York: McGraw-Hill, 1967.

Emory, William H. *Report of the United States and Mexican Boundary Survey*. 3 vols. Washington, D.C.: U.S. Department of the Interior, 1857–1859.

Ferlinghetti, Lawrence. *The Mexican Night*. New York: New Directions Books, 1970.

Fernández, Raúl A. *The United States–Mexico Border.* Notre Dame, Ind.: University of Notre Dame Press, 1977.

Gunn, Drewey Wayne. *American and British Writers in Mexico, 1556–1973.* Austin: University of Texas Press, 1974.

Heck, Marlene Elizabeth (Project Director). *Proceedings—An Exploration of a Common Legacy: A Conference on Border Architecture.* Austin: Texas Historical Commission, 1979.

Hill, James E., Jr. "El Horcón: A United States–Mexican Boundary Anomaly." *The Rocky Mountain Social Science Journal.* Vol. IV, No. 1. Ft. Collins, Colo. (April 1967): 49–61.

Hine, Robert V. *Bartlett's West.* New Haven, Conn.: Yale University Press, 1968.

"Hit and Run: U.S. Runaway Shops on the Mexican Border." *Latin America and Empire Report.* Vol. IX, No. 5 (July-August 1975). New York: North American Congress on Latin America, 1975.

Horgan, Paul. *Great River.* New York: Holt, Rinehart and Winston, 1954.

Jamail, Milton. "Indians on the Border." *The Indian Historian.* Vol. X, No. 3. San Francisco. (Summer 1977): 34–37.

Jamail, Milton. "The Border Industrial Program." Tucson: Unpublished monograph, 1976.

Kiser, George C., and Martha Woody Kiser, eds. *Mexican Workers in the United States.* Albuquerque: University of New Mexico Press, 1979.

Lumholz, Carl. *New Trails in Mexico.* New York: Charles Scribner's Sons, 1912.

Martínez, Oscar J. *Border Boom Town—Ciudad Juárez Since 1848.* Austin: University of Texas Press, 1975.

McWilliams, Carey. *North From Mexico.* New York: Greenwood Press, 1968.

Nelson, Eugene. *Bracero.* Culver City, Calif.: Peace Press Publishing, 1972.

Paredes, Américo. *"With His Pistol In His Hand."* Austin: University of Texas Press, 1958.

Price, John A. *Tijuana: Urbanization In a Border Culture.* Notre Dame, Ind.: University of Notre Dame Press, 1973.

Ross, Stanley R., ed. *Views Across the Border.* Albuquerque: University of New Mexico Press, 1978.

Russell, Philip. *Mexico in Transition.* Austin: Colorado River Press, 1977.

Samora, Julian. *Los Mojados: The Wetback Story.* Notre Dame, Ind.: University of Notre Dame Press, 1971.

Samora, Julian; Joe Bernal; and Albert Peña. *Gunpowder Justice: A Reassessment of the Texas Rangers.* Notre Dame, Ind.: University of Notre Dame Press, 1979.

Stoddard, Ellwyn R. *Patterns of Poverty Along the U.S.-Mexico Border.* El Paso: Center for Inter-American Studies at the University of Texas at El Paso, 1978.

Tyler, Ronnie C. *The Big Bend, A History of The Last Texas Frontier.* Washington, D.C.: U.S. Department of Interior, 1975.

Young, Arthur and Company. *An Economic and Demographic Study of U.S. Border Cities.* El Paso: Organization of U.S. Border Cities, 1978.

INDEX

217

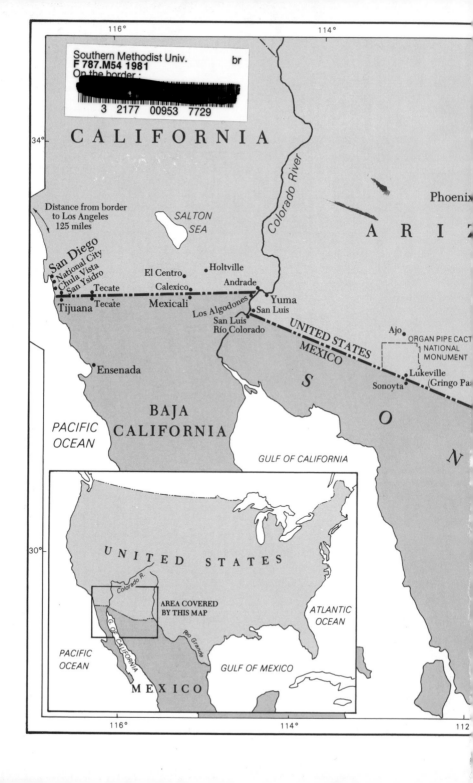

116°

114°

112°

34°

30°

C A L I F O R N I A

Colorado River

Phoenix

A R I Z

SALTON SEA

Distance from border
to Los Angeles
125 miles

San Diego
National City
Chula Vista
San Ysidro
Tecate
Tijuana
Tecate

El Centro
Calexico
Mexicali

Holtville
Andrade

Los Algodones
San Luis
Río Colorado

Yuma
San Luis

UNITED STATES
MEXICO

Ajo
ORGAN PIPE CACT
NATIONAL
MONUMENT

Lukeville
(Gringo Pa

Sonoyta

S

O

N

Ensenada

BAJA
CALIFORNIA

PACIFIC
OCEAN

GULF OF CALIFORNIA

U N I T E D   S T A T E S

Colorado R.

AREA COVERED
BY THIS MAP

ATLANTIC
OCEAN

PACIFIC
OCEAN

G. OF CALIFORNIA

Rio Grande

GULF OF MEXICO

M E X I C O

116°

114°

112°